TREASURE IN THE FIELD

TREASURE IN THE FIELD

The Archbishops' Companion for the Decade of Evangelism

Edited by

David Gillett and Michael Scott-Joynt

Fount
An Imprint of HarperCollins*Publishers*

Fount Paperbacks is an imprint of
HarperCollins*Religious*
Part of HarperCollins*Publishers*
77–85 Fulham Palace Road,
Hammersmith, London W6 8JB

First published in Great Britain
in 1993 by Fount Paperbacks

1 3 5 7 9 10 8 6 4 2

A catalogue record for this book is
available from the British Library

ISBN 0 00 627635 0

Typeset by Whitelaw & Palmer Ltd, Glasgow

Printed and bound in Great Britain by
HarperCollinsManufacturing Glasgow

CONTENTS

EDITORS' INTRODUCTION

This book seeks to stimulate ongoing debate and action at a point well into the Decade of Evangelism. Evangelistic thinking and endeavour could so easily receive the Church's attention (even, in some cases, reluctantly given), and then fade out as the decade proceeds, under the unspoken collusion and corporate sigh of relief, "Thank goodness they've let that drop." This book is committed to raising evangelism above and beyond the decade concept. We hope that it will encourage people to begin the shift from seeing the nineties as a decade for particular projects and become one that changes the attitudes of the whole Church.

Unashamedly, this book is first and foremost a platform for both Archbishops to share with the Church their vision, their concerns, and their convictions. The Archbishop of Canterbury sets the scene with his opening chapter on the challenge presented to the Church by the Decade of Evangelism. Revealing a different, yet complementary approach, the Archbishop of York provides the final chapter as an epilogue to the whole book. Our task as editors has been to provide an environment and context for these two major chapters. We hope that the other contributions together provide evidence of the wide range of thinking and good practice that is present in the Church of England.

Evangelism has often been seen as the preserve of one particular section of the Church. Our conviction is that there are many examples of significant evangelistic approaches over a whole range of churchmanship and theological position. We have attempted to give examples from as wide a range as possible. Because of this we have allowed some repetition to remain in order to allow people to give an indication of the breadth and scope of their own particular approach to evangelism. We have also resisted ironing out inconsistencies of approach, or imposing any editorial judgements as to what views of evangelism are permissible. There are views expressed which neither editor would propound himself, but we believe they form part of the material on which ongoing thinking and endeavour need to be based as we work hard and consistently at becoming a Church, and local churches, who are discovering how to become more effective vehicles for the good news of Jesus Christ. After our dialogue with the authors, which in some cases has been extensive, we have refrained from taking issue with any of the views finally expressed – our comments, which occur in italics throughout, are merely to link the contributions together.

The book does not pretend that the Church of England is an expert in evangelism, and certainly would not want to suggest that it can lead the world in evangelistic outreach to Western society! There are other sections of the Christian community that have often shown greater commitment and enterprise in evangelism. But we are convinced that the Church of England has a unique position and opportunity in this country as far as evangelism is concerned. It is probably going too far, however, to say that there is a distinctive Anglican approach to evangelism – the variety within the Church, and the multiplicity of types of communities and subcultures within the nation as a whole, make any such claim simplistic. But we do believe that clear themes begin to emerge as we consider the most encouraging thinking and endeavours in evangelism within the Church of England. We hope that readers themselves will discover these as they read, and will be encouraged to develop further their own theology of evangelism as well as explore new avenues of working this out in practice.

The book also reveals that we still have much to learn from others, both here and from around the world. We are glad that several of our contributors are from other churches – Dan Beeby, Lavinia Byrne, Anne Forbes, Susan Parsons, Keith Stubbs – and that some represent the perspectives of the Church in other parts of the world – John Sentamu, Michael Nazir-Ali, and Chris Wright. Perhaps the commitment of the Diocese of Southwell (referred to by their Bishop in chapter three) to have a Partners in Mission consultation peopled by the Church from other parts of the world will encourage others to look at this opportunity whose potential has been too little realized within the Church of England.

David Gillett
Principal of Trinity College, Bristol

Michael Scott-Joynt
Bishop of Stafford

CONTRIBUTORS

Kenneth Adams, CVO, CBE
  Industry Fellow, the Comino Foundation
John Allen
  Provost of Wakefield
Peter Barnett
  Team Rector, St Paul's, Bristol
Paul Battersby
  Rector, St Peter's, Darwen, Lancs
Dan Beeby
  Co-ordinator of the Project, The Gospel and our Culture
Brother Bernard
  The Society of St Francis
Angela Berners-Wilson
  Senior Anglican Chaplain, Bristol University
Chris Brain
  Team Leader, Nine o'Clock Service, Sheffield
Lavinia Byrne
  Associate Secretary for the Community of Women and
  Men in the Church – a programme within the Council of
  Churches in Britain and Ireland
George Carey
  The Archbishop of Canterbury
David Chamberlain
  Vicar, All Hallows, Easton, Bristol

Daniel Cozens
  Evangelist and Ely Diocesan Missioner
Peter Crook
  Headmaster, St Peter's Collegiate School,
  Wolverhampton
John Dalby
  Vicar of Clapham-with-Keasden and Austwick, Yorkshire
Graham Dow
  Bishop of Willesden
Irene Durndell
  Parish Deacon, St Paul's, Northumberland Heath, Kent
John Finney
  Bishop of Pontefract
Anne Forbes
  Worker in the Leeds ecumenical project, Faith in Elderly
  People
Patrick Forbes
  Broadcasting Officer, General Synod of the Church of
  England
Carl Garner
  Canon Missioner, Diocese of St Albans
Richard Giles
  Vicar, St Thomas', Huddersfield
Michael Green
  One of the Archbishops' Advisers on Evangelism, with
  the Springboard initiative
Tim Gouldstone
  Vicar, St Keverne, Cornwall
John Habgood
  The Archbishop of York
John Harding
  Vicar, St Martha's, Broxtowe, Nottingham
Richard Harries
  Bishop of Oxford

Contributors

Patrick Harris
  Bishop of Southwell
David Hawkins
  Vicar, St George's, Leeds
Roger Hooker
  Seconded by CMS to work among people of other faiths
  in Birmingham
John Hughes
  Vicar, St John's, Harborne, Birmingham
Don Humphries
  Vicar, Holy Trinity, Cambridge
Nigel McCulloch
  Bishop of Wakefield
Michael Nazir-Ali
  General Secretary, Church Missionary Society
Susan Parsons
  Principal, East Midlands Ministry Training Course
Alan Price, CA
  Development Officer, Anglican Renewal Ministries
Donald Reeves
  Rector, St James's, Piccadilly
Philip Seddon
  Lecturer in the Department of Biblical Studies at the
  Selly Oak Colleges, Birmingham
John Sentamu
  Vicar, Holy Trinity, Tulse Hill, London SW2
David Stoter
  Chaplain, Nottingham University Hospital
Keith Stubbs
  Executive Officer, West Midlands Churches FE Project
Angela Tilby
  Writer and Television Producer
Peter Ward
  Youthworker and Tutor, Oxford Youthworks

John Wesson
   Vicar, St Martin's in the Bull Ring, Birmingham
Michael Wooderson
   Vicar, St Anne's, Chasetown, Staffs
Chris Wright
   Director of Studies, All Nations Christian College, Ware

Chapter One

THE CHALLENGE
FACING THE CHURCHES

The Archbishop of Canterbury

An unbiased observer looking at the situation facing the Christian Churches in England today would probably think it far from encouraging. There has been a massive evacuation from the pews over the past hundred years. In 1851 – the year of the only religious census England has ever had – roughly half the population went to church. That in itself caused a shock. One of the reasons the religious census was not repeated was the sheer riskiness of the enterprise. It was disturbing to discover that in Christian England half the population did *not* go to church. That knowledge, however, did encourage efforts by all the Churches to remedy the situation. The late nineteenth century was one of the great ages of church building. But effective evangelism needed more than the simple provision of church accommodation. Since then, all the Churches have experienced the ebbing away of manpower, resources and support. The reasons for this are complex, but they have their origins in issues facing the Churches a century ago. There are at least three major elements to the problem.

THE WORLD OF IDEAS

The Church emerged from the encounter with Darwin and Freud as the loser because of its mental rigidity. The centre of intellectual life moved away from its long association with religion. And religion responded – at least at first – largely in a negative spirit. It lost an opportunity to absorb new insights, not least because it was too firmly wedded to the science of an earlier age. Worse, the Church failed to grasp the significance of the new intellectual challenges to Christian faith, and when it began to do so at the turn of the last century, much damage had already been done. The conditions had been created for the growth of an implicit agnosticism, which was largly the consequence of the steady erosion of a dynamic and speculative approach to theism. The discoveries of the eighteenth and nineteenth centuries (made by those who were, in the main, practising Christians) were vitiated by the Churches which found new ideas deeply shocking. Matthew Arnold's poem "Dover Beach" illustrates the way in which people were shaken.

> The sea of faith
> was once, too, at the full, and round earth's shore
> lay like the folds of a bright girdle furl'd;
> but now I only hear
> its melancholy, long, withdrawing roar,
> retreating to the breath
> of the night wind down the vast edges drear
> and naked shingles of the world.
>
> Ah, love, let us be true
> to one another! For the world, which seems
> to lie before us like a land of dreams,
> so various, so beautiful, so new,

> hath really neither joy, nor love, nor light
> nor certitude, nor peace, nor help for pain;
> and we are here as on a darkling plane
> swept with confused alarms of struggle and flight,
> where ignorant armies clash by night.

It is clear that Arnold did not think the tide was running in the Church's favour. It seemed impossible any longer to preach with confidence that God loved and cared for a creation in which the development of species so greatly favoured the strong over the weak. What were his purposes for the human family if Darwinism showed humankind to be simply one of nature's very late developments? How secure was the testimony of Scripture if its claims were so deeply at variance with modern science and knowledge? What was to be trusted – the discoveries of science or the written word of God?

At least these questions are now addressed. They will never be answered finally, but science and religion are no longer at war. Theologians and scientists generally recognize that their disciplines complement one another. To discover how the world works is not to answer questions about ultimate meaning, though it may illuminate it. But in the popular mind the questions remain, and have largely been answered in favour of the truth of science and against the veracity of Christian revelation. It is commonly thought that science has superseded religion, and has disproved the truth of the Bible. The impact of the victory for empiricism is not wholly liberating. There is a sense around of the ultimate futility of all things. And whilst it is tempting for Christians to believe that this suggests a search for meaning which may predispose people to respond to the Gospel, the prospects are not altogether bright. For alongside this sense of futility, we need to recognize that for secular men and women today ultimate truth is to be found, if anywhere, in human science and technology, not in religion. The claims of revelation are generally ignored.

Hence, the ground needs to be prepared if the word of God is to be heard. Any initiatives in evangelism which avoid the world of ideas will simply be bypassed in our secular culture. We are not able to prove the existence of God, but Christianity is not an irrational religion. Whilst men and women are rarely, if ever, argued into faith, barriers created by misconceptions, misunderstandings and misapprehensions can be removed. In doing so, it is the popular understanding of what is happening in the world of ideas (not always the same thing as what is truly going on) that claims our attention. We need a fresh Christian apologetic.

THE BREAK-UP OF COMMUNITY

The second reason for our current problems is much more prosaic. The break-up of community has isolated the Church within the associations and groupings of modern society. The contribution of churches to pre-industrial societies is well known. They were at the heart of the community. The parson (the very word emphasized his community persona) was a key person in the education of the young and in social welfare. The church was central to the social and leisure activities of the community. Even today, the role of the parish church in rural areas may still be pivotal to a community's wider life and well-being – but in the cities, towns and big villages of our country, all that has changed. Indeed, though we are still inclined to speak of "communities", the word is largely evacuated of content. Humankind now generally gathers together by association –

at work, at play, or through interest groups. We live in one place and may find our "communities" elswhere. Thus, the Church has been left largely isolated by such a significant drift away from community, and has itself become no more than another association of like-minded people. For many, therefore, the Church is "irrelevant" because it is no longer central to their needs or interests.

This problem was observed a long time ago. In 1828, Charles James Blomfield became Bishop of London. During his 28-year episcopate 200 new churches were built and consecrated in his diocese, chiefly through his own zeal to meet the spiritual needs of the many thousands of people crowding into London. With impressive energy he set about raising vast sums of money to accommodate the influx of new citizens in these churches. He thought that all that was needed for the Church's message to be heard was the creation of new opportunities for worship, and the raising of standards of clerical life and ministry. But people did not come when the churches were built. They did not find that religion connected with their new industrial, urban lives. As we look today at so many large Victorian churches in London, we often assume they had a golden age when they were filled to capacity. Some were. But a very great many were headaches from the beginning – empty symbols of an evangelistic idea that simply did not work.

However, little comfort can be taken from that. There is a lesson to be learned, though, and it is this. Any form of evangelism in our cities which is simply centred on buildings is doomed to scratch only the surface of the problem. The demise of community and its replacement by associations ordered by contract and nourished by individualism is still one of the greatest challenges facing the Church.

THE GOSPEL AND CULTURE

The third element of our current problem lies in our need to *inculturate* the Gospel. By *inculturation* is meant that process by which the faith takes root in our society, so making it possible for Christianity to be understood. For hundreds of years the story and imagery of the Christian religion has had a hold upon the hearts and minds of the majority of people in our land. Through the regular ministry of worship, and faithful catechizing in our parish churches, the steady work of pre-evangelism has gone on. The pioneering work of Sunday schools and the emergence of Church Schools – well ahead of any provision by the State for education – ensured that children grew up with a knowledge of Scripture and an understanding of the framework of Christian faith. The majority would have had some knowledge of the Ten Commandments, the Lord's Prayer and the great Bible stories, which remain so fundamental to Christian education. But we can no longer assume that this is the case. Indeed, we have contrary evidence. Perhaps the majority of children in the United Kingdom do not know the basic story of the Christian faith, or the more familiar stories and parables of the Bible. Generations of children now grow up with but the haziest ideas of the faith which has done so much to form the culture, traditions and morality of our nation.

The reasons for this are complex. It is easy to put the fault on parents who do not teach their children to pray or help them to discover the spiritual side of their nature. It is easy, too, to put the blame on educational policies which have mistakenly assumed that confessional Christianity has no place in religious education. A phenomenological approach to religious studies has its value, but should not exclude the possibility of presenting the truth claims of the Christian religion. But we cannot simply say that home and school are at fault. The churches are also culpable. We have to recognize the many missed opportunities for *inculturating* the faith in the minds and hearts of young people. Too often we have found ourselves unable to include the young in our liturgies, affirm their enthusiasms or find a way of expressing the Gospel in youth culture. It has been less a failure of nerve than a failure of imagination. And imagination is usually lacking where there is fear. Often we are fearful of noise, spontaneity and colour in the controlled environment of our church life. We have often deprived ourselves of the fun to be had in expressing faith. We rob ourselves, as well as the young, of the chance to encounter the richness of liturgy and the wider contacts which faith can make with culture.

Last year I was part of two very different events which taught me something about the breadth of possibilities for *inculturating* the Gospel for young people today. On a wet November Sunday afternoon, I went to a large inner-city church in Leeds. St Aidan's Church is a monument to late Victorian confidence. It was built to serve the terraced houses of its parish a century ago. It has some beautiful mosaics. The smell of incense lingers. On this Sunday afternoon, however, the chairs in the church had been removed and several hundred teenagers were taking part in something called "The Ultimate Christian Rave". Everyone was busy – some painting, others making a video, some creating a dance routine, or preparing a dramatic sketch. There were puppeteers, music makers, young people cooking and others composing. The church was alive. Gradually I discovered that everyone was working on a single theme – the parable of the Prodigal Son. And at the end of the afternoon these young people created an imaginative and contemporary act of worship, based on all they had done in their workshops. The Gospel was expressed in their own culture.

And I saw just how creative young people can be when given the resources, freedom and confidence of the Church.

Earlier in the summer I spent a week in Taizé. I was accompanied by a thousand young Anglicans aged between 17 and 25. Another three or four thousand other young people were staying at Taizé that week. They came from all over the world. At Taizé, the worship was quite unlike the experience at Leeds. Everyone has to keep silence from the moment they enter the community church, where the three daily services take place. And silence forms a significant part of the worship itself.

I had never before prayed in silence with several thousand young people. You could hear a pin drop. Here was the other side of youth culture – a readiness to respond not to a jokey or superficial faith but one rooted in religious seriousness. Young people will respect a serious search for faith, whether in an Ultimate Christian Rave or in silent prayer. Their culture demands authenticity. And to the authentic they will often respond.[1]

My brief analysis so far cannot do justice to the many serious challenges facing the Church today. But I want to stress our need to see evangelism in the light of a culture which is moving away from the Church, not towards it. But despite this, ours is not a culture, I believe, which is fundamentally antagonistic to the Christian faith. I mentioned those two experiences with young people to illustrate the possibilities still before us. There are many people in our society deeply sympathetic to faith and eager to see it flourish. A society without religion lacks the glue which gives it a corporate identity. Religion is to do with "binding

---

1. See Chris Brain's contribution (at the beginning of chapter five) on the approach of the Nine o'Clock Service in Sheffield for a clear attempt at relating to the youth culture of today.

together". Christians believe that people are bound together in love and loyalty to each other when they are bound to God in Jesus Christ. Many people do have a hazy sense of God. Many pray. Many continue to identify with the Church at times of special significance in their lives. Though we are told that we live in a post-modern, post-communist, and even post-Christian world, there are few, if any, voices which talk of this being a post-religious world. The collapse of communism in the Soviet Union and Eastern Europe, followed by the resurgence of Christianity and Islam (even when, as in Bosnia, it assumes the dimension of tragedy) shows the strength and power of religion. Even in our own country the emergence of New Age movements and the growth of fundamentalist groups show that we would be very unwise to predict the demise of organized religion in our land. But we must ensure that it is not religion *per se* that flourishes. We want Christian faith to flourish. Religion can be the seed of division, hatred and conflict. Michael Ramsey was fond of saying that religion itself needs to be redeemed. It needs to be redeemed by Christ.

MACRO- AND MICRO-EVANGELISM

This takes us into the nature of the evangelistic task. How does God redeem the world? How do we co-operate with his mission? I believe we need to distinguish between what I want to call "macro-evangelism" and "micro-evangelism", if we are to avoid simplistic solutions.

Macro-evangelism puts the task firmly in the context of who God is and what he has already done. Evangelism must never be regarded as merely what the Church does, but it must be rooted in the person and work of God as Father, Son and Holy Spirit. Evangelism does not start from us, but from God. He is an evangelizing, outward-looking God. Upon his own character the Church of Jesus Christ is shaped. This is a familiar biblical theme. In the Letter to the Ephesians we read in cosmic language about the work of God in Christ.

But God who is rich in mercy made us alive with Christ . . . It is by grace you have been saved . . . and God raised you up with Christ and seated us with Him in the heavenly realms . . . (Ephesians 2:4–6).

Here we find the root and source of evangelism. What the Church does when it proclaims its message is to declare what God has already disclosed and done in his Son. Grace is already given. We can only repent, turn and seek God's forgiveness because God has already made it possible. Just as television and radio signals are carried on airwaves which have always existed and which make these developments possible, so the task of the Church to make disciples rests upon the fact that God's mission to the world is, and always has been, an evangelizing one.

Christians often feel guilty about their failures in evangelism as if God's saving work depended entirely on them. But the perspective of macro-evangelism is a corrective to this. God in Christ has already saved humankind. He is present and active in the world. He wills the salvation of all people. He has taken the initiative, and done so in Jesus Christ in a way which applies to people everywhere and in every age. God is at work on the *macro*-level. Our task is to work on the *micro*-level, in our local community, amongst our friends and neighbours, assisting people to respond to what God has already done for them.

The diagram that follows makes explicit the difference between macro and micro views of evangelism.

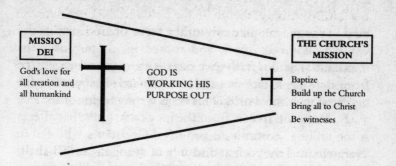

MISSIO DEI	GOD IS WORKING HIS PURPOSE OUT	THE CHURCH'S MISSION
God's love for all creation and all humankind		Baptize Build up the Church Bring all to Christ Be witnesses

As the term suggests, macro-evangelism begins on the largest of scales – at God's end of the work of mission he has entrusted to his Church. It relates to issues concerned with God's work in the world, his providence and his call to human beings. Micro-evangelism, on the other hand, has a more limited agenda. It relates to the work actually done by the Church. It concerns the particular ways in which discipleship is encouraged, in which people are led to baptism, and in which the Church is helped to grow in faith and numbers.

Both these dimensions are essential. But it has been expected that the concentration in this Decade should be upon the "micro" end of the scale. I am constantly asked what the Church is *doing* that is new in the Decade of Evangelism. This book gives many clues to a whole area of particular activities. But I want to direct our attention to what God is doing and has done in this and *every* decade. We need to recover our sense of God's own mission to the world before we can fully participate in it.

The Importance of Macro-evangelism

First, evangelism, like any other form of ministry in the Church, is God's work and rooted in his purposes for mankind. Theologically, we can take great encouragement from the simple fact that God is ultimately responsible for his mission to the world. This takes wrong forms of anxiety away. It should free us from the inevitable guilt that affects some willing, committed and loyal Christians who fail in evangelism. Even when and where we fail – as we shall, again and again – we trust in a God who will not leave himself without witnesses on the earth, and whose only demand from us is that we give ourselves and our best to him. This also takes from the Church any tendency to become Pelagian. Pelagius, a British monk who taught in Rome at the end of the fourth and beginning of the fifth century, believed that human beings were able to save themselves. In some ways, it's a curiously British heresy. As an island people, we pride ourselves on a certain sturdy independence. We admire self-reliance. All this has its virtues. But in Christian life and faith, such assumptions are perilous. The prosperous and flourishing congregation is peculiarly susceptible to Pelagian attitudes, especially when its members work on the assumption that they are doing God a good turn by making the Church so successful.

Thus, I believe that undergirding our evangelism must always be a deep trust in God's way with us. Our task is to keep in step with his faithfulness.

Secondly, it is my hope that we shall listen to our world and its questions. I have already written about the intellectual climate which makes it difficult for people to put their trust in God. Whilst no doubt a great deal of lack of commitment flows from deliberate refusal to follow, we must not assume that this is always the case. There are many who simply do not believe that the Christian way is any longer intellectually credible. Therefore, the thoughtful exploration of questions that so many people ask has to be done in this of all decades. The questions I have in mind are ones like these: "How do you know there is a God? If there is, how does that fact affect me? How do you account for the existence of other faiths? Are they true? Are they blessed by God? Is there such a thing as the human soul? After death, what next? Isn't it simply too naïve to consider that Jesus is unique? Why do you think that the death of Jesus has anything to do with me? Isn't life simply a game of chance?" All these questions, and there are many more which are often asked, are not ones which the Church can dodge. They may be glibly trotted out by some people as an excuse for examining the claims of faith, but my experience suggests that for many people these are questions quarried from hard experience of life, from people whose rejection of the Church's faith is reluctant.

But such listening will also deeply affect the life of the Church itself. It must be taken into our systems of training as well as into the life of our local congregations. I think, for example, of the training of ordinands. Theological training can never be effective if it is divorced from the culture in which contemporary ministry is set. Fresh attempts must be made again and again in our theological faculties and colleges to work *from within* our culture. There must be an attempt to work out a theology from within influential literature, the world of contemporary art or current notions in the philosophy of science. It is not that we simply wish to put a theological construction on such disciplines. Merely to give them a religious gloss would be pointless. But what we have to recognize is that it is in these areas that so many contemporary questions about God are articulated. Thinkers like George Steiner and Peter Fuller have made it clear that the questions being asked by science and art are thoroughly theological. This is the Decade in which we must engage with them, not ignore them. The Christian Church has no monopoly itself on theological questions. Its task is to understand and interpret the questions which society asks of its faith.

In some measure the outworking of macro-evangelism in the life of the Church will be seen in its openness to the society in which it is set. It will be demonstrated in the way the local church welcomes those who do not believe, and whose lifestyles are alien to its own. On the fringe of every healthy church are those who cannot believe and who are perhaps afraid to articulate their half belief or unbelief. A church that is truly open will be so secure in its own faith that it can listen to those who doubt and, indeed, from within its own faith, admit that it does not have all the answers or is unaware of the problems.

A third element is necessary. Evangelism is directed towards the manifestation of God's love by calling people to respond to him. Macro-evangelism possesses a corrective to narrower forms of evangelism by promoting those initiatives and activities which demonstrate so clearly the love and mission of God. I think primarily of the faithful, ongoing ministries of our many local churches up and down the land. The problem with the language of mission and evangelism is that few would be inclined to give our regular ministrations such names. But there is nothing more evangelistic or missionary in its impact as the ministry that is done as part of routine parish work. Sunday-school teaching, the preparation of candidates for baptism and confirmation, the visiting of the sick and dying, the regular preaching and teaching, the celebration of the sacraments, week in and week out. Statistics show that the vast majority of people become Christians through the ordinary, everyday, pastoral and teaching ministry of their local church. This has much more impact overall than the special evangelistic outreach events, even though it might gain much less attention. If the Church were ever to sacrifice the routine ministrations of faithful parish ministry in favour of special events or if it were to allow its ministry to be narrowly focused on "leading people to Christ", I have no doubt that a fundamental mistake would have been made. Thankfully, we don't have to make such choices. We have only to ensure that both go on. Thus, this Decade must include the encouragement of parish ministry. It is done best by men and women who genuinely love others and long to see them embrace Christian faith and be nourished by the Church's sacramental life.

Alongside this, we should recognize that there are many initiatives which have evangelistic impact, even if they are not considered primarily evangelistic enterprises. I think of a report like "Faith in the City", for example, or its sister report, "Faith in the Countryside". Last year, I visited a number of Church Urban Fund projects in Barking and Dagenham, my home area. I was immensely impressed by the scale of the Church's commitment there, by its life and vigour and its contacts on so many different levels with the wider community. In many ways, the picture I got was of a Church more alive in its ministry and with deeper roots in the local community than I remember as a young man. I met many of the leaders of voluntary agencies and charities in the area. What struck me was the Christian commitment of so many of those who gave their time freely to secular charities. Indeed, someone remarked to me that if you took the Christians away, the voluntary services in the area would collapse. Upon this sense of service to the wider community the Church Urban Fund has built. It has been the focus of the Church's renewed attention upon the needs of deprived urban areas. I asked the local archdeacon what impact this had made, and he replied swiftly: "All this has made the Church credible. We can now speak with authority about God and his care, because we have put our money and resources where the problems are."

MICRO-EVANGELISM

I have been talking about the larger context of evangelism, because it gives foundations for what I call micro-evangelism – the individual, targeted and specific activities which help nurture discipleship. On their own, these activities could become narrow – simply the building up of an organization for its own sake. But when seen in the wider context of the mission of God in his world, they are given new meaning.

A good deal of this book is related to forms of micro-evangelism. It includes descriptions of evangelism undertaken in specific contexts – rural, suburban, inner-city. It talks about models of evangelism in faith-sharing teams. It includes a description of initiatives such as the March of a Thousand Men. I do not want to duplicate what will come later in this book. The value of local and specific forms of micro-evangelism is undoubted. And I hope that this book will be a good resource for those who actually want to know what is going on in this Decade. There is simply one matter which I wish to stress now. That concerns the importance of those who have evangelistic gifts. The Church of England does not have a good record of calling and encouraging evangelists. It is a mistake to think that the gift of the Holy Spirit called down upon those who are ordained somehow also includes evangelistic gifts. Some bishops, priests and deacons do possess such gifts. They require nurturing. But there will be others within our churches who are greatly blessed with evangelistic gifts, but who have no call to ordained ministry. We need to give more attention to the task of identifying all those with such skills, and equipping and releasing them for their work.[1]

The Church of England possesses the office of Evangelist. At present, those who are admitted to that office are Church Army officers. I hope there might be ways of extending our use of that office, and heightening its place within the Church at large. I hope, too, that initiatives such as those in the diocese of Rochester to identify people in local parishes with evangelistic gifts, and to equip and train them, will spread elsewhere.

However, the Decade of Evangelism will have to be regarded as a failure if it does not result in local congregations becoming more aware of their individual responsibility to witness to God's love in Christ and encouraging growth at every level. Already many local churches have begun to set up their agendas for the Decade, and are re-assessing how they engage in God's mission to their local area. Again, there is much in this book to inform us and encourage us about the mission of our local parish churches.

But an archbishop has a special responsibility to express the faith of the Church of England as a national and Established Church. To this I now turn.

---

1. Michael Green (in his contribution in chapter three, Local Lay Evangelists) deals with the way in which local churches can identify and encourage those with specific evangelistic gifts.

EVANGELISM AND THE ESTABLISHED CHURCH

The Church of England holds what some regard as a very privileged position in the life of the nation. The privileges are not as numerous as some people imagine. The clergy are not paid by the State (as in some other parts of Europe), nor are cathedrals and church buildings maintained by the Government (again, unlike certain other European nations). But twenty-six bishops sit in the House of Lords and thus the clergy have a part to play in the nation's government. As a consequence, Anglican clergy are barred from election to the House of Commons, so the privileges do have a price. They also bring responsibilities.

Whilst no-one would be likely to maintain the view that being a citizen of this country and being a member of the Church of England were nowadays coterminous, there is still an expectation that the Church of England (and particularly its archbishops and bishops) should articulate what faith the nation still feels able to express corporately. This is exemplified at times both of national disaster and national joy. The Zeebrugge disaster or the loss of the Marchioness – these are times when the Church of England is looked to as a bearer of the nation's grief. It also provides a national focus at times of hope and happiness, and it is the Archbishop of Canterbury who crowns the Monarch. This is the clearest demonstration of the intimate connection between Church and State. That connection is evident in other ways too. The General Synod of the Church of England is the only body (apart from Parliament) which can frame legislation. Once endorsed by the Commons and Lords, that legislation is not simply rules for governing the Church's internal life, but becomes part of the law of the land. Senior church appointments still involve the Monarch and the Prime Minister, and so are not simply regarded as ecclesiastical matters alone.

In many ways, however, the significance of establishment does not simply lie in the details of the specific links between Church and State. There is a wider way in which the Church of England remains the national Church. It is reflected in the way many people still register as "C of E" when asked their religion upon admission to hospital. It is seen in the way in which so many people who form part of no regular worshipping congregation seek baptism for their children, or wish to be married in church. It is evident in the still almost universal custom of providing Church of England funerals for the unchurched, whether in crematoria, cemeteries or private funeral chapels. Church of England clergy spend a great deal of their time ministering to people who do not form part of their regular congregations. But there are some clergy and laity who hope that the Decade of Evangelism will make the boundaries between the Church of England and English society clearer. They are sceptical about the advantages of a Church which allows such nominal adherence.

We must be careful where such an argument will take us. On the one hand, we have to acknowledge the strength of church life when membership is clear and people know to what and to whom they are committed. Churches with clear boundaries are often those which are growing. We must not be churlish or dismissive about this. Following Jesus Christ calls us into an obedience which is distinct and far-reaching. Christian life is not compelling when it is half-hearted. But we need to remind one another that the Church of England has inherited a position which makes it a custodian of faith in our land. It has a special vocation. Our parochial structure is such that those who live in our parishes are welcome to participate in our life to the degree they choose. They are encouraged to look upon their parish church as "their" church. I remember the time when that was important to me when I entered my own parish church in Dagenham for the first time. The church on that council estate was "my" church, even though I had not been part of its regular worshipping life. This is, I believe, an important element that should not be sacrificed for the sake of forms of evangelism which might make us more definite but less able to exercise a national pastoral and parochial ministry. If disestablishment were to lead to the Church of England no longer recognizing its responsibility to serve the wider community, the cost to the spiritual foundations of our country would be very great.

The presence of a diffusive form of Christianity in our land is much to be preferred to millions of people being disenfranchised by churches cutting them off because they are unwilling or incapable of embracing credal forms of Christianity. Those who mock folk religion should pause and consider the damage that could be done to many expressions of faith in God, which are the foundation for so much of the Church's evangelistic activity. In my own parochial experience I always valued the most tentative faith on the part of parishioners whom I would meet at times of crisis. To despise or dismiss such folk religion is often regarded by the people themselves as a dismissal of them as human beings. Loving pastoral care can be an effective midwife for a more thoroughgoing Christian faith. But the erection of barriers and the defining of clear boundaries only leads to the exclusion from our Church's wider life of those who firmly regard themselves as full members of the Church of England. Bishop Hugh Montefiore warned about sectarianism in his contribution to *The Gospel and Contemporary Culture*. He wrote:

There has been a tendency for all mainstream churches to become more sect-like. The characteristic of a sect is to look inwards to itself rather than outwards to the society of which it forms a part, and this tends to make people outside its membership disregard it.

This is well put. Anglicans reject forms of church life which are sectarian. But we mustn't be boxed in to accepting a false premise. It is not necessary to set a firm, intelligent and personal faith over against breadth and diffusiveness. I believe it is precisely within a Church of blurred and ragged edges living fully within the world and open to its influences that true faith is born, and has the depth to grow into a full and vigorous Christianity. Faith born within the so-called "security" of a closed ecclesiological system often does not have the depth to withstand the challenges of secularism when harsh winds blow in personal experience, or when faith is shaken through encounter with others of different faiths or none at all.

EVANGELISM AND ECUMENISM

The Decade of Evangelism is not simply an Anglican enterprise. The Catholic Church some time ago prepared itself for the 1990s to be a Decade of Evangelization. The majority of the mainstream Churches in Great Britain have also declared their commitment to the Decade. Indeed, one of the most impressive characteristics of this initiative is its ecumenical character. It was not planned ecumenically, yet the Churches are so much at one in their life and thinking in the late twentieth century that it has seemed a natural path for each to follow.

All that I have said about the character of the Church of England as a national and Established Church does not imply any exclusiveness in its mission. I believe that the Church of England does have particular responsibilities and opportunities, but it does not pursue them in isolation from its sister Churches. The Church of England has proved disappointingly unable to translate its ecumenical vocation into schemes for national organic unity, yet it has proved capable of working imaginatively in local ecumenical projects with Methodists, Roman Catholics, Baptists and United Reformed Christians. There has been ecumenical progress in mission and evangelism at this "micro" level. In this case, the "macro" level has been slow to catch up.

The ecumenical vocation of the Churches presents us with a big challenge – to share our common life and mission in such a way that we are partners in evangelism, offering our gifts not only to God but to other Christians too. The challenge is deep because our instinct is often to make disciples for the sake simply of our own ecclesial bodies. Such is our sense of self-preservation that we may not really want other denominations to be at work in our area. I well remember an Anglican priest once saying to me, "I am glad to say that we have no need to be ecumenical in my parish. The only other place of worship here is a Kingdom Hall for Jehovah's Witnesses!" But ecumenism transcends the narrow confines of geographical parish boundaries. I doubt if there is any parish in the land which does not have at least a few non-Anglican Christians within it, even though they may have no place of worship of their own in its boundaries. Our self-confessed "jealousy for God and His mission" may have other motives lurking within, principally "jealousy of other Christian Churches". Anglicans are particularly prone to this as it is easy to assume that other denominations have no right to exist within the parishes for which we have care. "Devils" like this can only be exorcized by a true spirit of fellowship at the ministerial level, and by a deep commitment to one another within our respective congregational life.

But another "devil" has to be exorcized too. In all churches, as well as between the denominations, suspicions about theological differences have an effect on our willingness to co-operate or share in evangelism. Evangelicals may find the idea of sharing in evangelistic work with churches in the Catholic tradition impossible to contemplate. Liberals may have difficulties in sharing with either evangelicals or Catholics. Indeed, they may question the whole evangelistic thrust of this Decade. And there are other difficulties just as complicated to sort out – the nature of music in worship, our behaviour and posture when we worship God, types of liturgy, to say nothing of whether we are able to receive the sacrament together. Progress can only be made when we are prepared to acknowledge that though another Church's way of doing things is very different from our own, it is still authentically Christian. This basic understanding then leads the way for further exploration and co-operation.

For if we are blinkered to the truth to be found in other Christian Churches, how can we expect those outside the Christian faith to find God's truth in our own? Evangelistic enterprise should cause us to look outwards, to purge ourselves of self-satisfaction and complacency, not least about our own faith. For we ourselves need to be evangelized over and over again. That is another theme of this Decade. For I believe that evangelism is not something Christians do with or for others. We need to preach to ourselves, to be continually renewed by the call of God heard with fresh and invigorating force in our lives. "We preach not ourselves, but ourselves as Your servants for Jesus' sake." We must not limit the Holy Spirit's capacity to convert even the preacher by his own preaching. Many are the clergy who know the experience of having to preach when at a spiritually low ebb. Many too, thank

God, know the renewing experience of that act of preaching.

EVANGELISM AND OTHER FAITHS

Last September, Bishop Michael Marshall and Canon Michael Green were commissioned as the Archbishops' Advisers in Evangelism. They are both gifted evangelists – one from the Catholic tradition of the Anglican Church, the other from an evangelical background. When I was appointed Archbishop, many people wrote to me and asked that a way might be found for these two gifted men to be brought back to England to "spearhead" the Decade of Evangelism. I am glad that a way has been found to do this, and the two Michaels are already making an impact. What I had not expected, however, was that the initial name for this project, Spearhead, would arouse such hostility. Of course, military images can seem threatening, but we continue to sing hymns such as "Soldiers of Christ, arise, and put your armour on" without reflecting that what is imagery to us may strike those outside the Christian faith as very threatening indeed. And military images have often been used in evangelistic enterprise, as the very existence of the Salvation Army and the Church Army illustrates. What I had not known when choosing Spearhead as the name for this initiative was that this was also the title of the magazine of the British National Party. The politics of the extreme right, especially the anti-Semitic right, had already appropriated it. And so the idea arose that this initiative was targeted upon other faiths, whereas nothing could have been further from our intentions. Indeed, if there was any specific target it was the many millions of nominal Christians, whose allegiance to the Church is so tenuous.

All that is in the past, and the initiative has gone forward under a new name – Springboard. But it is worth recalling, since it illustrates how evangelism in any form can be seen as potentially threatening for other faith communities. For Jews, there are fears associated with images of pogroms, and the continuing reminder of the Holocaust, which is forever seared on their hearts. It is often difficult for a dominant religious group to feel what it is like to be part of a minority who are on the receiving end of evangelistic enterprise. For Muslims, the image of the Crusades is evoked by Christian evangelism. And Western European Muslims who are already alarmed by the impact of secular materialism on their young people are likely to find the activity of Christian Churches promoting a renewed Christianity to be worrying and menacing. However false the fears might be, we must recognize the validity of these emotions.

It cannot be stressed frequently enough that the Decade of Evangelism is not an assault by the Churches on the other faith communities in the United Kingdom. It is a way of enhancing, even recovering in some places, our integrity as Christians. For Christianity, like some other faiths, has not merely a tradition of mission but finds its identity in mission. It is how that identity is expressed in a Britain which is now pluralist in its culture and faith, which provides a new challenge. It is a challenge to our integrity and tolerance.

A Christian's integrity demands that he or she should acknowledge the lordship and sovereignty of Jesus Christ. Christians cannot remain silent about something so deep within them. So, too, for the Churches of which they are part. It is my hope that the integrity of our Churches in expressing our faith in this Decade will lead also to a deepening respect for the integrity of other faiths. Other faith communities are not the victims of the Decade of

Evangelism. It is my hope that the different communities will instead be allies in standing up for the integrity of each other's faith traditions.

Other faith communities do not expect Christians to soft-pedal their beliefs. They expect to hear clearly that *for us* Jesus Christ is the full and definitive revelation of God and that it is our desire for Him to be known by all. Indeed, the Christian faith is incorrigibly missionary in its orientation, and it would be apostasy to falter in our missionary ideals. We are "compelled" to preach Christ. But we are not compelled to preach him with arrogance or insensitivity or by falsely making claims for Christianity which are simply untrue. We need to value other faith traditions for what they are and what they have given to others. It is fully possible to acknowledge that God has made himself known through other faiths while still believing with conviction that in Christ God is fully known to humankind. We simply cannot limit the activity of God by suggesting that his grace cannot be experienced by non-Christian believers. Christians have no monopoly of grace. Integrity works both ways.

Tolerance, as well as integrity, is a mark of a mature faith. True tolerance has little to do with putting up with another faith as if we have no choice but to accept its presence, regarding it as an inevitable nuisance. Baroness Wootton once observed that "people are tolerant only about things they don't care about". I believe true tolerance only begins when people of different and incompatible views recognize the right of others not simply to exist but to have full equality in society. The test of true tolerance is our capacity to tolerate another person's divergent opinion on a matter about which we feel passionately. Where religious faith is concerned, it involves entering into the strangeness of another religious tradition, seeking to understand its life and worship. Central to this is the need to learn about that other faith. It is simply not the case that as we come to know more deeply each other's faith traditions that we discover ever more in common. We may discover how very strange our traditions are to one another. This should be an increasing spur upon Christians to understand what happens in a mosque or a synagogue. Only by so doing shall we be in a position to avert the suspicions and hatreds of inter-faith rivalry, and the ugliness of religious bigotry when it erupts in society, whether displayed in the form of anti-semitism, in the ethnic cleansing policy pursued in Bosnia, or in the conflict between Hindus and Muslims in India.

Tolerance is never a victim when sensitive Christian evangelism flourishes. The sympathetic evangelist recognizes the fact of pluralism, and is earthed in the model of incarnation – the only proper image of evangelism that I know. Only those who care for others and love them are genuine evangelists. All others run the risk of separating word and action, of treating people as things rather than as human beings created in the image and love of God, who at the "macro-level" are already in His care.

CONCLUSION

I find myself coming back full circle to the point at which I started – with decline. Is it possible to reverse the trend in Western European Christianity so that the Church begins to grow again in vigour, life and numbers? There are those who claim the trend of the past century is irreversible, that whatever the Church does we cannot halt the inevitable drift away from institutional religion. But if we begin instead with the God who raises the dead, we have to reckon with One whose continuous activity is one of surprise. It is not for us to lapse into either gloom or complacency. We simply do not know what the future holds. What I am convinced about is that in this Decade the Church must be rooted in its obligation to put God first in all it does and to exercise its ministry with joy and hope. We must take the evangelistic task so deeply into our structures that we become a more outward-looking body. That will restore confidence and, I believe, bring growth.

But my passion in this Decade is not simply for growth in numbers. The primary reason for giving fresh attention to our evangelistic task is in the theology of macro-evangelism, which I have outlined earlier, the basis of which is the love and goodness of God. The Church is called to be a sign of that God in the world – to call even when people do not wish to follow, to point the way even to those who do not want to come, and to be there even with those who resent our presence. In rejection we shall know the true meaning of incarnation, and I pray, glimpse God's resurrection power as well.

Chapter Two

MISSION AND THE PAROCHIAL SYSTEM

A Church in Change

The Archbishop of Canterbury would be the first to admit that Lambeth Palace is not the powerhouse of the Church of England. If there is power in the Church it is to be found in the parishes of our land. This is where the Church of England is at home. If evangelism is to happen, this is where it must take root.

Whatever one may think of the parochial system, and there are some who say it has served its day, this Decade of Evangelism will either have impact through this inherited pattern, or it will die a death in the Church of England. But there are many who still see plenty of flexibility in the parish system — enough elasticity to allow for the developments necessary to be the focus and channel of the Gospel in our secularized and pluralist culture.

The necessary change requires some radical thinking, mixed with imagination, faith and commitment. We have seen plenty of this in those whom we invited to describe their church's approach to mission and evangelism within the parish. In this section we want the descriptions of various parishes to speak for themselves. As editors we have resisted the temptation to judge, evaluate, and promote various approaches to evangelism, on the basis of the parish stories which we have gathered. Our hope is that each one will make its own point, and that, together, they will give stimulus to further thought, discussion and prayer in PCCs and other parish groups.

UPA, Huddersfield

To set the scene, we travel to Huddersfield, in Yorkshire, and take a look at one parish's experience through the eyes of its vicar, Richard Giles:

St Thomas', Huddersfield, is a little oddball UPA parish, a kind of village stuck onto the edge of a town centre, with magnificent views of the Pennines matched by a glorious mixture of races and creeds. Over 60 per cent of the local population are of Asian origin – both Muslims and Sikhs – and a third of our congregation is Afro-Caribbean.

The Christian community has proved tenacious. It has clung to its building (George Gilbert Scott and all that), the natives (first white, then West Indian) travelling back to worship long after the tides of social change had washed them up onto more prosperous shores. It has clung also to its Catholic worship, attracting the politically correct and the articulate, who have helped the church survive all manner of alarms.

"Clinging on" can be exhausting, and in 1987 when I discovered St Thomas', the committed church community was ready for change; to take out the treasures from the vaults, dust them down, decide what was worth keeping and throw away the rest. This we have proceeded to do literally, gutting and completely re-ordering the church by 1990, and spiritually, re-examining and re-expressing "the riches of his glorious inheritance in the saints" (Ephesians 1:18).

Evangelism in this kind of parish, which doesn't quite fit anywhere, is a bit scary. If you've been used to a suburban captive audience sitting at home waiting for your mail drop, then St Thomas' makes you think from scratch. Where on earth is the extra congregation to come from? Thus were we forced back to God in a deliciously crisp do-or-die situation; either he was going to make it grow, or he would close it down. So relax!

In my experience, a clearance sale is inevitably the first step in the process of growth. When a new parish priest arrives it is a good time for members of a congregation to take stock: "Do I want to go where this guy is taking us?" *After this many of his disciples drew back and no longer went about with him* (John 6:66).

Within the first month, an away-day consultation with all the congregation, and some straight talking about the cost of discipleship in a tough missionary situation, helped everyone to read clearly the writing on the wall. Within six months about fifteen of the regulars had decided to look elsewhere. The church had set out its stall and individuals had made their choices. At the time it was distressing, and yet, unavoidable, if the church was to be able to spread its wings.

Having got the taste for away-days, parish weekends have become a crucial part of the process by which we grow. Each year a speaker with a different approach is invited to lead us through 48 hours in which we focus on God's will for us and allow his Spirit to mould us. On these occasions the two-hour Sunday mass with ministry is a time for witnessing changed lives and healed bodies, while the Saturday night cabaret deserves to be featured on Radio 4's *Kaleidoscope*! Costly in time and money, these weekends are, nevertheless, a must.

A plank of Catholic teaching which has come alive for us is the sacramental nature of our buildings and our environment. On the Feast of Christ the King in 1989 we processed with thurible flying to our parish hall to begin a year's sojourn in the wilderness while our church was being knocked about a bit. Here "outside the camp" (Hebrews 13:13) we found Jesus in the adventure of "making do" in a cramped room with what we could carry with us. After a year we had become a different community, warmer and freer, and less reliant on props. Still aware of beauty and excellence, we made sure that, when we returned to our well-ordered "new" church, we offered to God only the very best, and discarded the rest. As a result, we have lots of space in our new worship area where absolutely nothing happens but in which the serenity of God is expressed and in which we exult in our liberation from crocheted cloths, litany desks and Mothers' Union banners.

Flowing from this is our discovery of the power of music to recall us to the living God and to lift our worship. For two years now a small band of musicians has replaced our organ, and although we shall soon have a small pipe organ on our new gallery to complement the band, we have found too much joy in new music ever to go back. By God's grace, our tradition, our sojourn in the hall, our rebuilding and our new music, have combined to allow us to offer to those who seek the living God a very unusual mixture indeed.

Outreach is focused on our Sunday evening "specials", based on a simplified evening office in which the contemporary French Church is a strong influence. This may be coupled equally with silent adoration before the Blessed Sacrament, or ministry in the Spirit to those in need. There is much switching off of lights and lighting of candles. Those who join us from other "noisier" churches speak often of the deep sense of God's peace and nearness.

Through all these things that God had been doing with us, we now feel ready to advertize in the local press and to spread by word of mouth the fact that Jesus is alive and well and living among us.

Mission at the Heart of Every Parish

We asked Nigel McCulloch, the Bishop of Wakefield and Chairman of the Decade Steering Committee, to address the issue of evangelism as it affects every parish and congregation in the land. At the time we asked him, he was still the Bishop of Taunton, in the South West of England – he did not know that one day St Thomas', Huddersfield, would be in his diocese, but, evidently, he believes in similar kinds of things that were being discovered in his northern diocese before they knew he was coming.

The challenge of the Decade of Evangelism is for the Church to move away from its dominant pastoral model. The needs of today's secular world demand that there should be a massive shift to an emphasis on mission. This requires nothing less than a revolution in the way in which the laity are perceived and used in ministry. Every Christian is to become an agent of mission.

The parish church should not need missions; it should be a mission. The Decade of Evangelism is not about extra events and special campaigns; it is about changing attitudes and emphases.

This is the vision which the bishops have put before the Church; but it will take more than a call from a Lambeth Conference to alter the attitudes and customs of the people in the pews. Vision meets reality in the parishes. It is there, at that local level, that in the year 2000 the litmus test for the lasting effectiveness of the Decade will be taken.

The result will depend on how well the local churches adapt their inherited Anglican structure to meet the new challenge of passing on the good news of Jesus Christ to the increasingly materialistic communities within which they are placed. If the commitment to evangelism given by the House of Bishops and the General Synod is to be the commitment of every Christian, local church strategies will have to be altered in a major way. The size of that task should not be underestimated. The Lambeth bishops talked of "a revolution" to enable the laity to become "the forefront missionaries of the Church".

The deliberately dispersed way in which the Decade of Evangelism was launched meant that not only did more than 100,000 lay people commit themselves to the Decade in major services in their cathedrals, but tens of thousands more laity did so in local acts of worship to mark the launch in the parishes.

How Parishes Are Responding

The early reports about what has happened since these launches have been encouraging. By the end of 1991, only ten per cent of all Church of England parishes remained untouched by, and uninterested in, the Decade of Evangelism. Twenty per cent of Anglican parishes had declared themselves publicly to be committed to it. The remaining seventy per cent claimed to be planning a positive response.

However, the fundamental missionary shift envisaged by the bishops will not be achieved simply by adding "The Decade of Evangelism" as an item on the PCC agenda and setting up a committee – nor just by putting on extra parish events, imaginative and valuable though some of them may be. The Decade is about transforming what is already there – by opening the existing structures of ministry and worship to the renewing power of the Holy Spirit. This has yet to be understood by many Anglicans, both ordained and lay.

A Place for the Laity?

The Anglican service of institution, or licensing, focuses in a potentially powerful way the issues of structures and strategy for evangelism in the parish. Each year in the Church of England there are more than 1,000 of these services to welcome clergy to a new ministry in a parish. With most incumbencies now lasting around eight years, this means that during this Decade of Evangelism the vast majority of parishes will have at least one change of incumbent or minister-in-charge.

The service of welcome, in the local church, will almost always be led by the bishop and attended by large numbers of laity of all persuasions and none. This is one of the most natural evangelistic opportunities the church has within the parish. An inspiring and vibrant act of worship can have a considerable impact on the whole community. It is also an ideal moment to give clear signals about the kind of structures and strategy needed locally for the decade. Unfortunately, even though much revised, the Anglican institution services still reaffirm an inherited structure and tired strategy for ministry. They need renewing if they are to be an effective means of evangelism in the parish today. Two years into this decade the significant and far-reaching aim of making the lay members of our congregations not just sharers in the mission, but actually themselves the forefront missionaries, is still being ignored. On most occasions little more than lip service is paid to the role of the laity. Reading lessons, carrying a water ewer to the font, and saying, "Welcome", merely colludes with the all too widely accepted view that the only ministry that really matters is the parish priest's. The bishop and the archdeacon are seen to place upon the new parish priest not only the care of the church people, but also (and this is what places the

Church of England and its parishes in such a potentially powerful evangelistic role) the "cure of souls" of the whole parish. The representatives at the institution service, from the civic community, from education, politics, business and many other walks of life can be forgiven for going away from such a service with the clear impression that the forefront missionary in the parish is indeed, and is meant to be, the "vicar".

This is precisely the kind of inherited structure which blocks effective evangelism. Impossible expectations and burdens are still being placed upon the parish clergy from the very start of their ministry. Such emphasis is diametrically opposed to the key point about the decade – that the laity, not the clergy, should be the main people to spread the Gospel of Jesus.

SEVERAL STRATEGIES NEEDED

There is growing evidence that more Parochial Church Councils are realizing that parishes need more than one single strategy for evangelism. The chief purpose of the church is to worship God; but the relationship between the church and the people within whose community that worship takes place is likely to vary in at least three main ways, requiring at least three different strategies.

THE REGULAR CONGREGATION

First, there is the close relationship of the committed congregation to its local church. These are the faithful and devoted weekly worshippers who are likely to be involved not only on Sunday but also from Monday to Saturday. Among them may be those who are ready to take risks, be open to change and receive new members – the very people whose imaginations might be captured by the vision of this Decade of Evangelism. Their enthusiasm will probably not be shared by all the deeply committed members, and certainly not by those who, though attending church quite regularly, do not want to be too disturbed. Several may well find the whole concept of evangelism threatening and alien.

Increasing numbers of churches now have "parish days" and "parish weekends" specifically on the matter of evangelism – in order to come to a common mind about how the vision of the Decade can become a reality locally. Not only is there evidence that more PCCs have committed themselves to taking seriously the challenge to every member of the congregation to pass on the good news of Jesus, but there are also clear indications that many churches are making a serious effort to become more user-friendly both in their style of worship and in the welcome they give.

There were horror stories, after some of the major campaigns of earlier years, of people becoming converted at a big rally and commended to a local church – only to find themselves being squeezed out by the regular congregation, which, instead of opening its arms in welcome, seemed to have closed ranks. Hopefully those lessons have been learned. Certainly many parishes have adopted a thoughtful and prayerful approach to working out their response to the Decade. The message is at last beginning to get through, that effective evangelism is more likely to be related to the quality of worship to be found week by week in the local church – and the pastoral care given day by day by its members in the community – than to specially contrived mission events.

The recognition by PCCs and congregations that the onus is really on them has led to a widespread recognition that most lay people are not equipped to be effective witnesses to the Christian faith. Church members want to have more teaching about the faith and how it relates to life. There is a genuine fear on the part of many people about not knowing the right thing to say. As a result, stories are coming in of a heightened awareness of the importance of prayer as we move further into the Decade – and an opening up to the Holy Spirit who will tell us what to say when the time comes. There is a collection of moving testimonies of people who did not believe they could speak about their faith to others, but found that the Holy Spirit did indeed give them the words to say.

The strategy must be about motivating and enthusing each member of the regular congregation. In evangelism, motivation is always far more important than training or techniques. There are reports of parishes which decided they had better do a course on evangelism, but it never came to anything. The congregation had not first been led through prayer and the Holy Spirit to be enthused. Where courses have been of enormous value is when the church members, newly motivated, want to learn more about their faith and thus gain in their confidence in it.

THE FRINGERS

Secondly, there are those in the parish who look to the church for baptism, marriage and funerals – those personal milestones and moments that matter and which have traditionally provided the Church of England with open doors through which, with love and sensitivity, many have been brought to faith in Christ. It is an unwise Parochial Church Council which does not see each of these pastoral ministries as evangelistic opportunities. Indeed it is a tragedy when what should be natural bridges between God and his people are turned into barriers. The opportunities for witnessing to the Gospel of God's love at these times are very considerable and invariably appreciated.

It is of little surprise to me as a bishop that so many of those whom I confirm have been led to their commitment to Christ as a result of the way they have been helped by the local church at a time of birth, marriage or death. The fact that this potential is not fully realized in some parishes may be because the lay members are not sufficiently involved either in thinking and praying through the strategy required, or in the pastoral care itself.

Within this group there are also those who look to the church, not so much for personal occasions as for special community celebrations – Remembrance Sunday, Harvest, Christmas, Easter. Increasingly, ordinations and confirmations (like institutions) are services when the church may have significant numbers of people present who are unfamiliar with worship and even the basic tenets of the faith. The Church of England does not have to invent or contrive evangelistic opportunities for those who are on the fringe of church life. In many parishes it already has them several times a year.

THE NON-ATTENDERS

The third group, which is the largest, and significantly on the increase, consists of those who do not seem to look to the church in any way. It is said that nearly half the population has never been inside a place of worship. Most people under the age of 40 have virtually no knowledge of the Christian faith. They are at least two generations away from any family contact with a local church. Only 14 per cent of children have any kind of contact with a Christian church. More PCCs are now praying and thinking earnestly about these issues – not just a brief prayer at the beginning of the meeting and a quick item on the agenda; but there are still many congregations that remain obtusely blind to the fact that we are in a missionary situation. All too often the only strategy is a vague hope that one day, when things go wrong, people will come back to church. They will not "come back". They have never been there in the first place. This group presents Christians with an enormous challenge which must be faced if our local parish churches are to continue as authentic witnesses to the Gospel in the community.

COLLABORATIVE MINISTRY IS ESSENTIAL

It is obvious that no single strategy is any longer appropriate for evangelistic ministry to the diverse groups within our parishes. No ordained minister can undertake alone the pastoral care and missionary thrust now required of the Church of England and our fellow Christians. If there is to be effective evangelism in the parishes, all church members, and especially the PCC, must collaborate with the clergy in ministry. Together they must use the natural opportunities that confront them daily outside the church to witness to the love of Jesus. Sometimes they will witness best by what they say. Often the more powerful act of witness will be by what they are and by what they are seen to do.

MISSION AUDITS

In attempting to evolve these different strategies for the Decade (for the church members, those on the fringe, and those outside) a significantly growing number of parishes have engaged in a "Mission Audit" – to gather information about and understand the community in which the church is placed. Some dioceses provide people to help a parish do this. It helps lay members to see their individual ministry as crucial to the future of God's mission in their parish. It provides the PCC with the opportunity to be open to the Holy Spirit and act as the vibrant and visionary body for strategic thinking which it is supposed to be. Above all, Mission Audits, when done in the context of prayer, can motivate the members of the congregation to be witnesses for Christ within the community.

WORSHIP

The purpose of evangelism is to lead people to acknowledge and worship God. The way in which people worship in the local church is, therefore, of great importance. The ordering of worship is the combined responsibility of the incumbent and the PCC. They may be faced with the widening gap between what regular worshippers and occasional worshippers like and expect in terms of prayer books and hymns. The burgeoning of new hymns, which is always a good litmus test for revival in a church's life, has accentuated this. The clergy and PCC also have to realize, especially in a Decade of Evangelism, that what goes on in our worship is an alien cultural experience for those who have never been before.

The experience of churches which are growing is helpful here. They seem to have some common features. Not only do they have inspiring worship, positive preaching, good teaching for adults as well as children, and effective systems of pastoral care, but also give very high priority to welcoming people. Several surveys, in which new Christians were interviewed about why they had become church members, show that the top reason given was the quality of welcome which they had received from other lay people. They had been made to feel included and cared for. It has often been said that the best instrument for spreading the news of God's love is a congregation which shows it.

There is much that is enormously encouraging about the parishes of the Church of England in this Decade. Lay missionary work is growing, new strategies and collaborative ministries are developing. Rarely in recent times has there been more creative and lively worship. There is no doubt that in the 1990s many local churches are experiencing fresh optimism, rediscovered confidence and new life.

The View from a Suburban Parish

From 1977 to 1991, John Hughes was the Vicar of St Andrew's, High Wycombe – a suburban parish in Buckinghamshire. He describes something of the evangelism and growth which they have experienced and draws out what the people of St Andrew's believe to be some important lessons which need to be learned in order to facilitate evangelism at parish level.

I came to St Andrew's in 1977 and, in effect, inherited two churches. A young vibrant family congregation meeting on Sunday mornings and the older congregation that had brought the new one into being.

The first five years were spent trying to draw both groups to say, "Yes" to a common vision. My aim was to establish many young Christians in the faith, giving them a deeper awareness of Christ's love and the power of the Holy Spirit in their lives. It was also to help older Christians to remain open to what God was doing today and to the possibility of change. We saw many who, in a community of love and acceptance were able to grow, to face fear and brokeness in their lives and discover Christ's healing. This experience gave them the desire to share their testimony with others.

In this time I realized that God's agenda was to change me. I had many attitudes and fears that prevented growth and real openness to others. It was in this period that God broke me and started to reshape me, so that I could be part of the new thing that God wanted to do in and through his church.

In the early 1980s the church grew to over two hundred. This did not come without facing considerable conflict which surfaced in our worship, due to changes in liturgy and in the style of worship we were experiencing through renewal. We lost relatively few members through this process.

A new phase of growth came through building a church extension for £750,000 which effectively tripled our size and gave us a wonderful plant to use. That journey of faith profoundly affected the whole congregation in experiencing God's miraculous provision, in discovering the power of prayer and in sharing what we were discovering with the wider community. Thus evangelism was happening naturally in the workplace. It was not, "*We ought to share our faith with others*" but rather, "*We cannot but speak of the things we have seen and heard.*"

As a result of this faith project we learned to give sacrificially and to release resources of people, finance and talents. Some fifteen people have gone into full-time ministry here and overseas in the last decade. Teams have gone out from St Andrew's to other churches to share what God has taught us about faith, renewal and witness. The income, which was £1000 in 1970, is now £168,000 of which over a third is given to work outside of the parish.

Lastly we joined with the other churches in the area to

become partners in mission. This has led to a three-year mission called Hope for the Future.

Principles We Have Learned About Growth

1. Growth in the church is dependent upon the leader. Leaders are often the block to growth through their own personal fears and insecurities. They crush lay ministry because they feel threatened. God needs to deal with the leaders' limitations and open them to working with others.

2. Finding God's vision for our church and communicating it clearly in achievable goals is important. We learned to listen to God for his direction and timing, to share that vision so that the whole congregation could own it and bring it into being.

3. Facing conflict was vital to growth. The issue of ownership is crucial for a church to face up to. It does not belong to the vicar or the people, it belongs to God. In taking our hands off, we opened the way for growth. Conflict was painful but it helped us to grow up and provide mature leadership.

4. Faith is the courage to change and to risk failure. Nothing worthwhile will ever be gained by playing it safe or trying to keep everybody happy. God is calling us to be a people who grow up by learning through failure.

5. Vulnerability in leadership is a great encouragement to open and honest relationships, which can make a church a safe place for growth.

6. God uses ordinary people. It is important to see people through the eyes of faith – "what they can become".

Many are now involved in Christian service in ways they would never have believed possible.

7. Continuity of leadership is vital for church growth. The church needs to trust its leaders, and that takes time. A church cannot grow significantly without the commitment of a leader to be there for a long period.

Evangelism in Rural Parishes

In many ways rural parishes preserve more of the features of the traditional parish idea as it has been known in England for centuries. There is certainly a different emphasis from the suburban picture we have just seen, in the description of life in rural Yorkshire where John Dalby is the vicar of Clapham-with-Keasden and Austwick. He has been there since 1978. The differences reflect, to some extent, differences of churchmanship, theology and spirituality; but, on the other hand, there are many similarities between John Dalby's approach and that of Tim Gouldstone, an evangelical and vicar of St Keverne in Cornwall since 1985. Some of his remarks on evangelism in rural areas follow this account from Clapham-with Keasden and Austwick.

"Receive this cure of souls which is both mine and yours." And with the 1100 souls come two parish churches, two daughter churches, two church schools, two village hall committees, four churchyards, two Parochial Church Councils – and more!

Any business consultant would know what to do. Close two or three churches, and at least one school, let the committees get on with it, and concentrate on real mission. A crude generalization, maybe, but not far from reality. Synods, dioceses, and even some rural clergy doubt whether they were ordained to keep expensive structures going. If a prime task is to preach the Word, is this helped or hindered by all the superstructure?

The inherited structure of any rural parish is in place, like it or not. It took me at least a year to begin to understand the complex dynamics of the community. I found out that much that matters to parishioners is bound up in the inheritance of buildings and organizations. I have discovered that, within this structure, there is no need to engineer encounters. You are meeting people all the time, in church, at village hall events, at school, and in the shop. You meet them at funerals, when most villagers turn up, at school governors' meetings, or at meetings of the churchyard committee. There you discuss maintenance with people who have far more of their families buried in neat graves than live at home. The same folks help with Meals on Wheels or playgroup, and I know their children or grandchildren at school. As they grow up, I prepare many of them for confirmation, marry them, and baptize their babies. There is little chance of meeting anyone I do not know. Even newcomers arrive at a steady rate, and are accepted and absorbed fairly quickly into the existing pattern of life. These people and their structures are what I inherited, and they must be where I start.

The villages, the farms, and the surrounding countryside make up complex and integrated communities, where one's attitude towards matters of faith is known and established. There are few chance encounters in church. You cannot be anonymous in a small congregation. Evangelism here must be quite unlike anything that might go on in an urban parish. To confront parishioners with an overt evangelistic message is to invite rejection. I would see such rejection as a self-defence against the desire to sharpen up boundaries best left unclear. To draw those boundaries can force people to reject message and messenger, whereas living with the lack of clarity keeps open avenues for God's grace to work. For example, to operate a strict baptism policy may not only deny family links that are important, but will certainly cause a ripple effect through a wide community.

I try to build on the many encounters afforded by the role of vicar, to allow people the space to express the things that matter to them, and to answer the questions they want to ask. The privilege of many meetings flows from our unique position as the Established Church, a precious birthright with deep roots in the countryside. Establishment brings a distinctive role with many opportunities. The inherited structures can be seen as part of our birthright, or as hindrances to the spread of the Gospel. Before dismissing them as hindrances, we should understand their strength and depth. Church matters, even if you only attend rarely. Much rural churchgoing is vicarious. One or two from a family attend, the others are there by proxy. I have heard parishioners who have been to nothing in church except funerals for twelve years, and yet claim to be faithful members of the church. At least such an outlook stresses the communal side of faith which was better understood by previous generations. Establishment means that the church penetrates into most areas of life if the chance is taken. The catalogue of ex-officio jobs that any rural vicar inherits presents a heaven-sent challenge.

At funerals, for instance, it falls to me to say things otherwise not said. I have to speak for the parishioners and for God. For the parishioners, to express for them their deepest and best feelings, their longings and thanksgivings. For God, to keep before the people the eternal truths of the grace and love of God, and the challenge of discipleship. The performance of public worship is the fundamental work of the Established Church. That worship puts life into context, and empowers ordinary Christians to see their lives as having meaning and value. Services need careful preparation, and should be organized so that the liturgy flows. This is just as important for three as for three hundred. Familiarity with all the authorized forms of worship helps the local vicar to celebrate worthily all the great days of the year, both personal and public.

In all our work, the care taken will preach as loud as words of God's care and love for all. Clean, attractive and warm churches will help enormously. What I do is as important as anything I say. Our task of evangelism begins by taking care of what we know, and ends by transforming the familiar into a vehicle for the love and grace of God.

And in the Ancient Kingdom of Cornwall. . .

In the country we need to ask: "What is the most suitable style of worship for our rural church?" Cathedral-style services with ten people in the congregation will fill people with frustration and nostalgia and they will feel a failure before God. If they feel a failure before God then they will sense that their corporate life is irrelevant to their community. All too easily this leads to a remnant theology where "we are just the last few hanging on."

The greater involvement of all in reading, praying and other aspects of worship is of great significance when there are only a small number of worshippers. I believe that the task of encouraging and training lay people to participate and lead in worship in rural areas is one of the best means of getting them to "own" worship for mission and ministry. It is also going to be a necessary process if the Decade of Evangelism is going to realize its full potential in rural areas. The form of the liturgy, which has obsessed the Church of

England for too long, is secondary to the manner of its presentation. I've never heard of anyone converted by one form of liturgy being used in preference to another.

Moving from the church into the rest of the village, it is often said that home groups will not work in country areas, but my experience is that they are a means of growth and an entry point for many into the wider life of the chuch. By participating in them rural clergy are given a means of fellowship and an insight into the priorities of the relationship of the community to the church. Clergy from urban backgrounds can try to run the parish from the study desk, and some still think that they cannot have close friends in the parish. This is a recipe for loneliness and stagnation in clergy life which will be reflected in similar failings in the local church.

As well as home groups, in many villages, events like coffee mornings and the jumble sales are a basic unit of currency! They are social events as much as a means of fund-raising. With creeping sectarianism now affecting the Church of England we must beware that we don't despise such social means of reaching people. Christians serving on local village organizations can be a means of witness to the local community which is more significant than in many large urban eclectic congregations.

The problem for rural evangelism is that individuals find the cost of commitment high as this really does mean standing out from the crowd. However it will come when the church is prepared to show people the human face of God in Jesus Christ, and be prepared to accept people for what they are. The neo-sectarian baptismal rigorism that seems to be affecting some areas of the Church of England would be a disastrous policy to such people; country people do not expect their local parish church to be a sect, and I believe they are right.

Many rural churches have been damaged by petty village politics or taken over by groups who are determined to run things their way; some major spiritual battles need to be fought here. The urban newcomer needs to be aware of the pettiness and family feuds and resulting damaged personalities that deface much of our rural life and can destroy the spiritual life of the local Christian community.

A significant area of ministry is to those who move to the country in retirement and with extra time on their hands participate in the life of the church as part of their community involvement. The church needs to watch out for the urban wiseacres who think they know all the answers. The "locals" will detect these instantly, and they can be a real menace. However, in my experience they form a minority of rural settlers, and in many cases there have been real conversions amongst people who have met with a loving fellowship into which they can grow and be accepted.

There is also a significant minority of people who move to the country in an effort to solve their own personal problems and "make a new start". They too need welcoming, but in most cases such a move makes problems worse rather than better if there is a failure to address the root cause.

People will only grow into Christ, will only see the relevance of the Gospel message when they encounter a loving and accepting community which is being transformed by the power of the risen Christ. This means that rural church agendas cannot be set by either sectarian or charismatic traditionalism. Evangelism in the countryside requires the integration of the loving witness of the Christian community with the wider rural life. It is only in this context that the rural church can meet the challenge of the Decade of Evangelism.

The Church in the City Centre

*At the other end of the scale are the City-centre churches, so often
with little or no resident parochial community – yet even here some
of the themes that have been touched on as we glanced at
evangelism in rural England occur again. There is emphasis on
buildings and traditional religious feelings in the approach to
evangelism adopted at St Martin's in the Bull Ring in
Birmingham where John Wesson has been the rector since 1986.*

St Martin's in the Bull Ring, in the centre of Birmingham, is
surrounded by retail markets, hotels and shopping arcades.
The boundaries with adjacent parishes are blurred and to
some extent arbitrary. But this is not the same as saying the
parochial *system* is unimportant for its outreach. St
Martin's is the "established" church in more than one sense.
As the ancient parish church of the city, it has occupied the
same site for centuries, and has become a place of genuine
affection for many "Brummies" ("St Martin's is our
church"). Requests for baptisms and weddings will come
largely from those outside the parish by claiming some
family link ("my father was a choirboy") or simply a
preference ("it's a nice church and easy for guests to find").

There are few parish residents but those who work in the
retail and leisure industries nearby generally recognize and
welcome the church's right to be involved in the lives of
both workers and customers. So a great deal of the mission
of the city-centre church is to a *transient* community –
shoppers, people passing through, those waiting to catch
the connecting coach or train, those emptied out of the
nearby hostels for the daylight hours. It represents a vast
opportunity to reach many people who have no contact
with the Church in the more conventional suburban
setting.

In our city-centre ministry in Birmingham two particular features are worth noting. First, there is *the opportunity of the building itself as a significant platform for evangelism*. For security reasons, most suburban churches are locked up on weekdays. Christians at Sunday worship will be encouraged to see their work context and their next-door neighbour as the natural focus for their faith-sharing during the week. But our church is open seven days a week and its dominating and attractive profile draw people into some form of contact with the church's life.

Some will step inside simply as tourists to enjoy a beautiful piece of architecture and view the oldest tomb in the city. Then through the personal welcome of the pastoral team, the friendly word of the bookstall helpers, or the impact of some leaflet picked up out of the display stands, we aim to communicate the reality of God's love, incarnate in this place. Others come in to meet their personal need of counsel and prayer. A tearful woman comes from a nearby hospital after a serious diagnosis and turns to the church for comfort and inner strength. A man wants to talk about the fractured relationships in the family. Two teenagers have been disturbed by apparent psychic forces and seek explanation and prayer. The list is endless, and day by day, the ministry of the lay and clergy team is one of great privilege and responsibility. Here are people with some inarticulate sense of God at their point of personal need. We constantly marvel at the straightforward faith of those who write a brief sentence prayer and "post" it on our prayer tree. As part of intercession our Sunday congregation reads and offers these prayers to God, and a sense of significance and loving concern is established.

It is easy to see the church building as no more than a neutral "shell" for Christian activity. But it is much more. It is a place hallowed by generations at prayer. It is a place that speaks of the transcendent and we shall miss opportunities if we ignore this dimension of our situation.

The second feature of city-centre ministry ties in closely with the impact of the building. It is *the opportunity of engaging positively with the "folk religion" of unchurched people*. The Archbishop of York defines folk religion in the Church of England context as "the unexpressed, inarticulate, but often deeply felt, religion of ordinary folk, who would not describe themselves as churchgoing Christians, yet feel themselves to have some sort of Christian allegiance."[1] It is easy for committed churchpeople to get irritated and impatient with those who express themselves in vague and muddled ways. But if we are to follow the sound principle of starting where people are, we cannot assume that the *motives* of such people are superficial, however shallow we judge their understanding to be. In St Martin's we have identified a major task of evangelism as finding ways of *working with* the hesitant and half-formed ideas of God and faith we encounter day by day. A lot of resource material for evangelism, however valuable in other contexts, is of little help here. The approach assumes too much, begins in the wrong place, and is altogether too cosy. A lot more attention needs to be paid to the area of *implicit religion* and its characteristics as identified, for example, by Edward Bailey.[2] We are, as Lord Runcie observed, "the Church of the smoking flax," and ways of fanning the flames of faith require much more study and effort.

1. *Church and Nation in a Secular Age*, London, Darton, Longman and Todd, 1983, p.78
2. Edward Bailey, "The Folk Religion of English People" in *Religion State and Society in Modern Britain* ed. P. Badham, Lampeter, Edwin Mellen Press, 1989, p.145 ff.

The Kingdom of God at the Heart of the City

For the past decade much of the thinking at another city-centre church has been to see evangelism as the task of seeking to establish signs of the Kingdom of God at the heart of the life of the city. Graham Dow, Vicar of Holy Trinity, Coventry, from 1981 to 1992 (and now Bishop of Willesden) writes of their approach.

The church has the responsibility to make clear at the heart of the city that the Kingdom of God is a present reality with which everyone must reckon. Jesus showed us an incarnational pattern: he went to the people preaching and teaching about the Heavenly Father; he demonstrated the power of the Kingdom in a ministry of healing and wholeness, of acceptance of the marginalized, of forgiveness, deliverance and practical care and, when appropriate, he criticized the ruling leaders.

At Holy Trinity, Coventry, starting in 1986, we began a programme of open-air outreach in the city centre for approximately 4 weeks in June. It lasted from 10 a.m. until 1 p.m., six days a week, and took the form of singing, drama, preaching, healing and testimonies, either on the church steps or in parts of the pedestrian precinct allocated to us. Refreshments were available in the church. The programme concluded with a communion service on the church steps; people were invited to take part straight off the streets. The first theme was "Happiness is a Friend Called God." Clown costumes gave the presentation a light and unthreatening style. So positive was the city's reaction that the Holy Trinity clowns were invited to be among its representatives at the Stoke Garden Festival.

Over the years a few people have come to faith through this presentation. More significant, however, is the fact that the profile of Christian evangelism in the city has been heightened. Christianity is again seen to be a faith with a message, shared with the world by ordinary people. Its drawback was that we tended to reach mostly the weak – those with time to loiter in the city centre. We also experienced some distancing from Christians who disliked our style. The leaders of some of the other city-centre churches in Coventry were originally cautious, but, interestingly enough, have now adopted a similar model for a united Holy Week presentation.

MIDWEEK CONGREGATIONS

The proclamation of the Kingdom of God continues, of course, all the year round, in the church, through the services provided. Over 150 people attend services midweek who do not attend Holy Trinity on Sundays. While many belong to other churches, quite a number do not, and there is an emerging pattern whereby a considerable number of people choose to find their place of belonging, Christian-wise, at a midweek "church". Holy Trinity offers a lunchtime eucharist with preaching and laying on of hands for healing on Tuesdays. It offers a mid-morning eucharist with preaching on Wednesdays. This is the high point of the week for many elderly folk; coffee is served afterwards, birthdays are celebrated, friendships are made. The eucharist is a powerful proclamation of the Kingdom of God. At Thursday lunchtime the service is non-eucharistic consisting of songs, consecutive teaching from the Bible, and some practical follow-up to the message, e.g. sharing in pairs, prayer ministry or testimonies. This is the largest of the midweek congregations, but all three described have their own identity, and their own staff. There is constant opportunity to reach new people through these congregations and there is a steady stream of people growing into faith.

Signs of the Kingdom

It has been important at Holy Trinity to restore to a central place the ministry of healing following the pattern of Jesus' ministry. There are many indications that this ministry, at the present time in our society, is particularly effective in drawing people to make contact with the Church. Inner healing associated with counselling meets needs in a society which may be advanced in medical care for physical conditions, but which is also opening up great emotional needs in areas such as stress, breakdown of relationships, loneliness and unemployment.

Out of the open-air outreach in 1986 there developed a community for the lonely and disadvantaged. "Meeting Place", as it is called, started in November '86, twice a week in the daytime and similarly in the evenings – now restricted to evenings because of practical considerations. Members of Meeting Place are a familiar sight at most Holy Trinity services. They are welcomed, even with their unconventional ways. Making good Anglicans of them is quite another matter!

Another sign of the Kingdom has been the unity in which the churches have sought to work. Since 1989 eight city-centre churches have been covenanted together. Holy Trinity and the Cathedral, which stand next to each other, now have regular joint staff meetings so as to work together co-operatively wherever possible.

Prayer at the Heart of the City

We found it helpful and strategic, from time to time, to hold at Holy Trinity united gatherings for prayer. In a bold and definite way we prayed for the Kingdom to come, focusing on areas of the city and their problems, and confessing the sins of our own and past generations. It became the growing conviction of the leaders of several churches, with our people, that much spiritual life and human well-being would grow in response to prayer. Interestingly enough, my first prayer request, from the moment of my appointment to Holy Trinity, was always for the well-being of the city, in and through the name of Jesus.

INTERPRETATION OF POLITICAL AND SOCIAL ISSUES

There is plenty of support in the Bible for a prophetic role for the People of God, although this frequently brought opposition, as it does today. As chaplain to the Freemen's Guild I had an annual opportunity to preach in the presence of leading Coventry citizens. It was an opportunity to speak to the circumstances of the city in the light of Christian truth, but needed considerable care. Such comment will always be better received if it is supported by well developed friendships between the vicar and the people addressed. This serves to highlight the great dilemma in choosing priorities in a city-centre ministry. Time spent in building relationships around the city is worthwhile, but it means less time in teaching and equipping the Christians. I made the choice that it was more strategic to be equipping several hundred Christians than to be developing personal links with those in key positions. Others working in the city centre have chosen differently.

St James's, Piccadilly

Before we leave the somewhat unique but thought-provoking ministry of city-centre churches, some extracts from the ten-year vision for the 90s, produced by Donald Reeves, the Rector of

St James's, Piccadilly, offer further insights into the approach to evangelism in the modern city.

COHERENCE OR CHAOS?

What has caught public attention over the years about St James's, Piccadilly, is the wide range of activities the church houses. Is St James's an adult education centre, a day hospital, an advice centre, an art gallery, a concert hall, a forum for the great national and international issues of our day, a social club, a retreat centre as well as a church? Do the events advertised in our monthly programme, in all their diversity, add up to a coherent whole? Is there a fundamental unity in our projects and ministries?

The answer to the first question is "Yes it is all these, but is it wholly coherent, essentially united?" To the other two questions the answer is "No". Yet questions about our unity do not go away. There is a sense, especially in a church setting, that we should all face the same way. This challenge persists despite the clear fact that Christians have rarely agreed about anything, and that the history of religion is littered with the memories of cruelty and oppression perpetrated in the name of God.

Today, near-anarchy prevails in the churches. The language and the symbols of Christianity have become so fragmented, that we are only left with the appeal to personal experience. And this at a time when we are starved of our inheritance. We barely know how to be in touch with the tradition (the teaching and experience of Judaeo-Christianity) so that faith tends to become trivialized, privatized and one-dimensional.

TRUTH

We are not concerned with Mickey Mouse religion. This is the sort of Christianity that thrives on "sound bites", removes all the difficult questions to "All for Jesus" and ignores both the agony, complexity and also the ecstasy of human experience. In an uncertain world, Mickey Mouse religion is thriving – drawing more and more people, especially the young, into a make-believe Disney World of vacuous optimism and gross simplification. St James's, Piccadilly, rejects this perception of religion.

Truth is always before us: the truth of God is bigger and smaller than all our formulations, however precious they may be. The search for God's truth is not merely an exercise of the intellect: the Beatitude "Blessed are the pure in heart, for they shall see God" is a strict reminder that explorations have to be lived out and embodied.

EMBRACING THE CHAOS

Vision, and the energy which helps each one to take a step forward to realizing it, is given when there is the willingness to face up to all the difficulties and disturbances, to embrace the confusion, muddles, hurts and pain. To distance ourselves from chaos by denying its existence is to sink into apathy, and comfortable helplessness, and a complacent passivity so that it seems nothing can be done. That way there is no energy, no vitality, no hope. And without hope, there is no Christianity, no church worth bothering about.

COMMUNITY

When we say we want "community", we want the opposite of fragmentation, competition, depersonalization. We see comfort – not conflict; intimacy and warmth between persons – not distance; affirmation, goodwill and collaboration instead of criticism. The Christian tradition affirms that the human being is necessarily social; the Kingdom of God is a social reality in which all can participate; and much teaching of the Church as the Body of Christ in the last fifty years has reinforced the understanding of the Church as a community.

The community should draw its members not away from the world but deeper into it – into the social, economic, political and public realms where the struggles for the alternative "new" values of God's truth and God's Kingdom take place. No one is barred from membership of the community. There can be no outsiders, for no one is beyond the inclusive, generous love of God. In other words, St James's Church, Piccadilly, should become known as a community of hospitality – where those who are not "like me", "like us", are particularly welcome. A natural part of our hospitality is providing time and space for those troubled in mind, body or spirit. The Centre for Health & Healing allows those who come opportunity to regain their health, and to discover a glimpse of what they could become. New forms of "being the church" are called for if such a community is to emerge – in which the nourishing, challenging and truth-seeking can take place.

CONTROVERSY

The "new" is not popular. We shall continue to be the target of abuse from the fearful and prejudiced. Controversy for its own sake is futile. But controversy can be enlivening; it is a necessary agent through which change can happen.

Today in Britain, the notion of the "public" has almost disappeared except as a threat. A major task of a city-centre church is to appropriate the notion that public occasions – meetings, conversations, discussions – particularly of different and contentious issues, are essential to the health of our democracy and the quality of both public policy and the common life. And because such discussions always contain grave matters of personal and public morality, it is absolutely right that the church offers its hospitality and its wisdom.

Placed in the midst of a city where many voices struggle to be heard, St James's, Piccadilly, stands as a church for gatherings of every sort where questions of truth are kept open, for all truth comes from God and is open to God. Never has there been such a need for public discussion and argument about long-term goals for our own society and for the wider world. We need to become a more high-profile community which tries at once bravely and sensitively to explore the various possible "futures" between which Britain and the wider world are inevitably choosing, scenarios which governments will be forced to take seriously. The media are too preoccupied by reacting to events; the universities by the demands of respectable scholarship. Who are now left? Only the churches – potentially places of lively, creative and necessary speculation and controversy – may have the persistence and commitment to see the world's horrendous and interconnected problems as a whole.

EVANGELISM

There is no doubt that both Church and Society need to be challenged by the Gospel – greed and self-interest for starters.

Evangelism will happen simply and naturally when faith moves from the realms of feelings and ideas to being embodied and lived out – usually in the most uncomfortable and disturbing places, when this embodiment is a corporate matter – lived out together: and when there is honesty, realism and knowledge of God's commitment and grace – which enables time and space for levity and laughter. I remember Mother Teresa's visit to St James's, Piccadilly; Ed de la Toree, from the Philippines, Jon Sobrino, from El Salvador, liberation theologians caught up in the struggle for justice in their countries, and Emma Maschini from Soweto – every one of these people who embodied the Gospel, were part of communities of the sort I have tried to describe – they were honest, clear, realistic, passionate women and men – full of grace – embodying the alternative values of the Kingdom.

Evangelism can thus take care of itself – faced with such human, holy and sometimes difficult people. And NONE of us is too insignificant to stand on the shoulders of those who inspire us.

Evangelism in Urban Priority Areas

We began this look at parishes and evangelism with a UPA parish in Huddersfield; to conclude we journey south via Nottingham to Bristol. John Harding introduces us to the parish on the Broxtowe Estate in Nottingham where he has been vicar since 1987.

The Broxtowe Estate was begun in the 1930s and completed just after the war in order to cope with the overcrowding of inner-city Nottingham. In its design the estate is unimaginative, monotonous and basic. All amenities are scant. There is a small church, St Martha's.

Within the estate live nearly 7000 people packed into 2000 red-brick buildings. Although many houses and gardens are lovingly cared for, there is an overall feeling of tattiness and isolation. It is a typical urban priority area, seen by many as synonymous with poverty and deprivation. Yet if the residents were asked whether they were poor or deprived, they would be most offended. "We definitely have our problems, but I'm certainly happy to live here." Beneath the impression of subsistence living there are great resources. Yet, every now and then, the community reels from a viciousness that seems to erupt for no apparent reason.

The people of Broxtowe have been teaching the people at St Martha's how to share the message of Jesus. "Don't assume anything, vicar – we know more than you think." There is a perception of the reality of God. At a funeral visit I was amazed when the son commented, "I agree that the Gospel is about repentance, a complete change of heart and mind. The trouble is I don't see it in church – so I don't go." On the other hand there is the ignorance as we deal with the third and fourth generation that knows nothing of Jesus. "Jesus died about 200 years ago." "Wasn't he about 80?" "No, more like 18 when he started doing all those miracles." God was here before the church and has been working full-time within every heart on the estate. The Christian's job is to identify what the Lord is doing and saying, and then simply share that insight with those concerned.

The church's purpose, its joy and vocation, is to worship

God. It has been important for St Martha's to express its worship in a way that is indigenous and understandable. Rite A Holy Communion gives structure and pulse to the worship and into this we weave old and new worship material, using a variety of instruments and people. Everyone, including children, are given a significant place within the worship of the church. Dialogue sermons, liberally illustrated, prayer requests and testimony of the Lord's working from among the congregation, all have a place. It is a Gospel from the heart rather than from the head, a Gospel that is understood only when it is done. A strong and relevant worship leads naturally to evangelism by a church family who love God and each other, and who are willing to welcome others into the church.

Following Jesus also means serving the community. Instead of setting up schemes and structures within the church to cope with local issues, church members have become involved with the local councils and many estate initiatives and groups. This draws on other skills that the church does not have on its own, and keeps open the opportunity for the non-church person to hear the values and concerns raised by the church. This also keeps the church's feet placed firmly on the ground within the world.

For five years or so St Martha's has joined together with two other UPA parishes in Nottingham and two churches in different types of area. This has been a great resource for all the churches involved. For two years nearly 300 went on a week's holiday to Kinmel Hall in North Wales. Over 50 per cent were non-church folk. Many have come to faith through this holiday project, and others have been strengthened in their ability to share their story of faith with others.

The work of the church must never become just a cosmetic exercise. A modernized house may not make a home, another worker on the estate may not make a friend. The life-changing power of the Gospel must be demonstrated by those who worship the Lord. The hope is that the Broxtowe community will begin to trust and respect God's people as they continue to affirm the hopes, purposes and dignity of all who live on the estate.

The church and community together give a sense to birth and to love, to suffering and to death. It is a sign about poverty and also a sign about wealth, a sign of hope within anguish, wholeness within brokenness. It may be then that the rumour of God being alive will become a reality for many.

The Kingdom, the Parish and Evangelism

Finally, from Peter Barnett, since 1983 the parish priest in the St Paul's area of Bristol, comes a challenge in strong words, but one that recalls us to the vital relationship, which several contributors have highlighted – that between the Kingdom, the parish and evangelism:

I believe that UPA parishes are most able to be authentic in the proclamation of the Gospel in England. They can genuinely live out the commission of the Church in John 20:10–23: Jesus showed the disciples his hands and his side – the marks of his Passion – and then he said, "As the Father has sent me, so send I you . . . receive the Holy Spirit."

We fulfil Christ's commission when the scars of his Passion are recognizable in the body of Christ. This proclaiming Church is much closer to the biblical context and priorities in geographical areas that are poor, oppressed, multi-racial and multi-faith. In the global context this would be found in the poor areas of the so-called Third World; in

England this is found in our UPAs, especially in the inner city. With St Paul, we are "always carrying in the body the death of Jesus, so that the life of Jesus may also be visible in our bodies" (2 Corinthians 4:10). I am not saying that these circumstances cannot be found in suburbia or the country; what I am saying is that most UPA parishes cannot avoid having the scars of the Passion in their body, whereas other areas can, and often do, avoid this dimension of mission and so conform to the values of the materially successful world. This is why the Archbishops' "Faith in the City" report affirmed the necessity for UPA congregations to be "local, participatory and outward-looking." A severe threat to this authentic characteristic of parochial mission in this Decade of Evangelism is the rise and growth of eclectic congregations that bear little relation to their local community and gather like-minded people from all over the city.

The mission of the Church is to be a sign, instrument and foretaste of God's Kingdom in a local place, in the parish. Jim Wallis put it well: "With no clear proclamation of the Kingdom of God . . . the disastrous result is 'saved' individuals who comfortably fit into the old order while the new order goes unannounced. The social meaning of conversion is lost, and a privatized Gospel serves well the interests of wealth and power" ("The Call to Conversion"). When the majority of parishes in a city or diocese are relatively wealthy and have enjoyed taking advantage of the many policies of privatization in England during the past twelve years, then you can see how easy and comfortable it is to avoid proclaiming action for God's Kingdom as a strategy for mission – it will not necessarily fill the church!

The local church must develop a sensitivity to perceptions of the Church and the Gospel that are often very different from those with which it is familiar. For example, our theological stance is very often from a white, male, middle-class point of view. We need to get into the shoes and see through the glasses of the poor, the immigrant or refugee, the socialist, the single parent, the unemployed, the widow, the homosexual. It must follow that if a parish church is not being controversial it is not being evangelistic. We must explain the controversy in the name of the Gospel of Christ and by the standards of the Kingdom – justice, option for the poor, compassion: the same evangelistic methods that Jesus used as we see him portrayed in the gospels.

Chapter Three

PATTERNS OF MINISTRY

Developing Patterns

In looking at evangelism in the parishes it is clear that some of the differences stem from the styles of ministry which govern the approach of both laity and clergy. This chapter seeks to explore the models of ministry which lead in different people, and in diverse situations, to effective evangelism. First of all, John Finney, one of the Archbishops' Officers for the Decade of Evangelism, reflects on recent developments in patterns of ministry within the Church of England.

Models of Ministry and Mission

1997 sees the anniversary of the coming of St Augustine and the death of St Columba. While it is a gross over-simplification of what they achieved, they stand for two different styles of evangelism. Augustine required order and hierarchy on the Roman model. The structural aim of his evangelization was to establish bishops in their dioceses and under them their parish priests in every village and town. The Celtic method of Columba was very different. It was the evangelistic method of the community – the bishop and his team, both priest and laypeople, going into unevangelized territory. They would form a community base, usually in a town of some importance, and from there they would evangelize into the surrounding countryside. This Celtic method was more corporate and freeflowing than the Roman.

The Archbishop of the Indian Ocean told of the missionary endeavour in the mid-nineteenth century in his area. The Anglicans were first in the field and they sent a solitary missionary (usually with a wife) to Madagascar, to the Seychelles and to Mauritius. Some years later the Roman Catholics sent a team of a dozen priests, nuns and laypeople into the area, who formed a strong base, and from there went out evangelizing. At present there are some eight Catholics for every Anglican. In that area the Celtic evangelistic method was more effective. Current interest in "Celtic" methods such as church planting, culturally relevant worship for the young, team and group ministries and the designation of mission areas within dioceses are all indications that the "Roman" parochial system is groaning at the seams. It is arguable that it has great strengths in a predominantly pastoral situation but it is less than adequate in one where the main need is for evangelization.

As we have seen in the previous chapter, there is life left in the parochial system. Nevertheless it is likely that Celtic-type insights will be grafted onto it. Already many dioceses are seeing themselves in terms of a team of people acting in accord with a "diocesan strategy" – often one which they have collectively compiled after much consultation. The initiative of the Decade of Evangelism has brought out a rash of such strategies – guidelines which apply to the life of the Church in that diocese. The diocese is being seen as a corporate whole to a far greater extent than was the case only ten years ago. Often it is seen sceptically as the bringing of modern techniques into the life of the Church. In fact it is a reversion to an older methodology of mission and one which may be more appropriate to a post-Christendom situation.

If this corporate view of mission is becoming the norm, then there will need to be priests and laypeople who can work within it. No longer will every parish be able to wander off on its eccentric course. There will be the need for mutual accountability – both of priest and parish to the diocese and the diocese to the parishes. The Celtic method is both more supportive and more demanding. On the one hand it does not leave individuals or churches to sink or swim without the possibility of help. On the other hand, each has a part to play in the wider whole. It is not a structure which looks for the one-man-band approach to ministry, or for laypeople who cry "hands off our parish".

The question marks cluster around the demands of such a missionary structure when it is superimposed on the parochial system. The Celtic pattern presupposes the bishop with a team around him whom he energizes and leads: the present organization requires a bishop with too many priests and parishes for such a personal ministry. The Celtic pattern requires a sense of forward momentum and the reinforcing of success: the present structure regards as essential the equal distribution of resources to every parish. The Celtic pattern requires priests and laypeople to be ready to move to exploit promising new areas of work: the present pattern prefers stability to mobility.

And these Celtic methods are not something which might one day take place. As we have seen they are already happening and being rather clumsily bolted onto the existing structures, and at considerable cost in terms of tension between the two patterns of working.

STYLES OF MINISTRY

Rapidly changing situations require confident and appropriate leadership. The difficulty is that the Church of England is trapped in a style of leadership which has served it very well in the past but may no longer be appropriate and from which it is struggling to be free.

When I was ordained in the late 50s the main leadership style required was pastoral. I was meant to visit the sick, prepare sermons to teach those inside the Church, keep the organizational machine in motion. At clergy chapters there were desultory discussions about changing the liturgy and about new social patterns but it was not expected to produce any action. The style of ministry within the Church had not altered for many, many years and there were few expectations that it would.

It was a Church dominated by the clergy. They provided the pastoral care, and the laity received it or rejected it. The great majority of people still came to church at least when they were children and so the clergy were well known figures. The ordination service still portrays in most dramatic form the cleavage between lay and clergy, for there we watch people enter a separate caste. The cathedral is full, those to be ordained come in, white-faced yet excited for this is the culmination of a long process of calling and selection, of training and preparation. Their families look on with pride and apprehension for they are changing before their eyes. No longer will they be part of normal human society – they will be "The Rev", wear curious clothes and be treated differently from those around. They are acquiring an aura. No lay ministry – reader, evangelist, churchwarden – is treated with anything like the same seriousness, except for someone entering a quasi-clerical religious order. Further, they enter a caste which has certain privileges and curiosities. The priest may well be presented to an incumbency by patrons who are not in line management; it is as though managers in Marks and Spencers were appointed without their senior management having the final say. Once appointed they have the freehold which means that the diocese has to house and pay them until they retire, whatever their ability to care for people and the church.

It may have made sense when parishes required a pastor who protected them from marauding, politically appointed bishops but in the 1990s a different style of ministry is required. In a largely static situation the amount of leadership required is limited. When the scene is changing there is need for a different style – more dynamic, more obvious, more quickfooted.

PASTORS, EVANGELISTS OR LEADERS

When choosing people for the ordained ministry we are looking for the person whom God has already chosen rather than trying to pick someone for a particular job: indeed that would often be seen as vulgar as well as impossible. But it is not so simple. The selector will have an often unacknowledged image of the sort of person who would make an "excellent deacon," a "good priest", or a "faithful reader". Usually the picture is that of a "pastor". It is seldom that of someone who fits the description "evangelist". We can highlight this by setting out two personal descriptions: the first for an evangelist and the second for a pastor. It could look like this:

EVANGELIST	PASTOR
Centre of interest is outside church	Centre of interest inside church
Creative innovator	Adaptor of other's ideas
Interested in the stranger	Interested in ongoing relationships
Routine is irksome	Routine is a necessary framework for life
Probably extrovert	Probably introvert
Not frightened of conflict	Abhors conflict
Mercurial, unpredicable	Steady, reliable
Ambitious for Christ	Limited ambition
Impatient of structures	Happy to live within structures
Individualistic	Works well in a team

In selecting candidates for ordination training we have tended to choose the pastor. They are more predictable, fit into the existing system more easily; they are the sort of person the parishes expect and the bishops like!

But we cannot expect churches to be led in mission by

people who have been chosen primarily because of their pastoral gifts. On the other hand, the answer is not simply to replace all our pastors with evangelists. It is not necessary to be an evangelist to have a heart for mission – an amalgam of a care for people outside the Church, a deep love of God and a desire to introduce the one to the other. And we need this in anyone chosen for positions of leadership in the Church – as clergy, readers, churchwardens or house group leaders, etc.

What we want are *leaders*. And the personal description for a leader could look like this:

Analytical and strategic thinker who can convey vision
Administrator
Team builder who gets the best out of others
Deep personal spirituality
Able to face conflict and enable change
Warm personality with a heart for mission.

A modern congregation will probably respond best to someone with the qualities listed last. A pastor will give them a sense of well-being and of being cared for. A pastor's church is like a warm bath, but it can be enervating for there is little opportunity for the personal growth of the members of the congregation. It feels as though it is not going anywhere and those who see the church as serving the community feel frustrated. Indeed they also feel guilty because their longing for something to happen is balanced by a wish not to hurt the nice person who cares for them so deeply. An evangelist's church will be so orientated towards the outside that those inside feel unloved. The fish are being brought in but then left to flap on the deck until they expire.

On the other hand, a church run by a leader will have a

sense of vision and cohesion. It will be truly "collaborative" for the gifts of everyone will be being honoured and developed. It will balance the need to move outwards in mission with the need to care for the personal needs of the congregation.

Team Leader

During the 1970s the clergy were searching for a role. Conference after conference tried to discover it. Many priests found that the parochial ministry was unsatisfying and there was a rush into sector ministries or into work other than the stipendiary ministry.

During the 1980s the parochial ministry appeared to become more attractive. There was no longer a queue of people trying to escape. Although many clergy are still unsure, the role which seemed to be so elusive seems to have become more definable. Perhaps it matters less to be able to set out a tight job description. The survey carried out in 1985 in preparation for "Faith in the City" found "that clergy reported a level of job satisfaction that was very high compared with those found in other 'white collar' occupations . . . and clergy in the UPAs were more satisfied than those in non–UPA ministry" (ACUPA 2.40). It is doubtful if the same could have been said in 1965 or 1975.

In part this change is because of a shift in perception. To help people with their "spiritual" needs no longer seems so clearly inferior to serving their material and emotional needs. "Religion" and the spiritual dimension in life has become more interesting rather than less as the increasing amount of space given to the subject in the media testifies.

Perhaps also bishops and synods are now more clearly prepared to engage more realistically with the new challenges and the frustration level is therefore lower.

Indeed there are many in the clergy who find the pace of change unsettling. For every one who cries "Forward" there is another who cries, "Backward".

Above all the 1980s showed that a ministry based upon a leadership style which both has a vital role for the leader and also brings out the full potential of others is enormously satisfying. In the 1960s and 1970s many clergy discarded the inherited hierarchical model and stood back to become "enablers" – like the Duke of Plaza Torro, they preferred to lead their troops from behind. The deficiencies of this sort of ministry became obvious – it devalued the priesthood, it marginalized the clergy and, above all, it failed to provide the leadership that people need. Nevertheless it contained an important truth – that the ordained ministry was intended to serve the congregation so that they could do their work of mission in the world.

During the 1970s some clergy, most of whom were involved to some extent with the charismatic movement, were developing a more robust ministry and both experimenting and making mistakes with a new/old style of ministry. They went back to the biblical model of the spiritual gifts and saw leadership as essentially plural and so experimented with a group of "elders" in the church. It was spelt out most clearly in the Tiller Report of 1983 in which the minister was seen as having his or her own leadership role as *primus inter pares* with a group of others who were also gifted as leaders.

The clergy who had revolted against the hierarchical model of the past, and had then embraced a democratic schema which failed to work in practice, were now directed to a more biblical model which emphasized the charism of leadership as one among many. In spiritual status all charisms are equal although some are more "honourable" than others and more in the public eye (1 Corinthians 12).

Alongside this the 1980s brought a more "managerial" style. Clergy realized that for better or worse they were running an organization, and that inefficiency in this field could crowd out their priestly ministry. Hence at the end of the 1980s there was a spate of books and conferences on the management of change, the use of time, restructuring for mission and so on. Indeed in some circles it seemed as though organizational skills were all that were required and the church could be run like any other organization.

In short, all these developments together have led to a greater job satisfaction. Finding the appropriate structure for the congregation, discovering their multifarious gifts, and making full use of them is seen to be a fascinating, important and worthwhile task for any man or woman. But it is a process that is only just beginning in the Church of England. The challenge of the Decade of Evangelism is for all bishops, clergy and congregations to work out appropriate styles of ministry and leadership for our missionary situation.

The Diocesan Bishop and Mission

If the changes that John Finney suggests are to happen, or if other ways of developing appropriate models for evangelistic ministry prevail in different contexts, the place of the bishop as the chief model of ministry in a diocese is obviously crucial.

As there is no clear training programme to help bishops handle their task as pastors, leaders in mission, etc., etc., the approaches taken vary enormously. The bishop's individuality also influences greatly how he fulfils his episcopate, and it would be foolhardy of anyone to prescribe too closely what model of ministry would be most appropriate for today's bishop. However, for the vast majority of the Church (who are not bishops!) it is important to

*have some insight into the way a bishop approaches his task – at the
very least, it helps people to understand where he is coming from
and what he expects.*

*We are grateful to Patrick Harris, the Bishop of Southwell, for
agreeing to be our "Bishop in the spotlight" and for describing his
approach to the Decade of Evangelism, and the principles that
have moulded his thinking.*

As a mission partner with SAMS in Argentina for seventeen
years, and now as a diocesan bishop in the East Midlands, I
continue to see myself above all as a missionary. Rural
Nottinghamshire, with its industrial centres and energetic
people, may be a culture and a continent apart from
Northern Argentina with its Spanish and tribal Indian
cultures, but the strategies for mission and ministry are
surprisingly similar. There are also lessons to be learned
and adapted from my time abroad about planting new
churches, and the identification, training and authorization
of indigenous leaders (Theological Training by Extension),
and the priority of prayer.

CREATING A VISION

I came to Southwell in 1988, straight from the Lambeth
Conference, which had set out a clear agenda with its
Resolution on the Decade of Evangelism. I found the
diocese in good heart, but needing a sense of direction and a
strategy for moving forward. My task was to help the
diocese under the guidance of the Holy Spirit, to "catch a
vision". It was important for me that everyone in the
diocese should own the vision rather than it be another
statement from on high. During my first year I spent time
listening and learning. Then in 1989 I presented to the
Clergy Conference a discussion paper, purposely sketched

in general terms, called "Looking Forward and Outward".
In this I identified areas that needed consideration.
I summarized my own vision for the diocese in these
words:

> Each of us is called by God to be concerned for the world
> around us, to seek within the one Holy, Catholic and
> Apostolic Church to care for the world with openness of
> heart and deep prayer. We shall do this by sensitive
> service and energetic evangelism: but each of these
> demands careful thought, an awareness of the cultural
> and social context in which we serve as well as the
> personal needs of the people to whom we go. In short, we
> are called to love the world with the love of God.

My strategy was simple. I needed (1) to hear what God was
saying to us, (2) to allow an open discussion in the parishes
as to the way forward for the diocese as a whole, (3) to
inform my own understanding of my role as bishop. Above
all else, I wanted the laity and clergy to collaborate with
me in setting goals for mission, through a process of
consultation.

CONSULTATION PROCESS

All the parishes were encouraged to find the most suitable
forum for them to discuss the paper, published in the
Diocesan newspaper *SEE* as a centre-page spread. Parishes
and deaneries wrote to me with their comments, suggestions
and criticisms. On the basis of these, I wrote an Action Plan
which I presented to the Bishop's Council and then to
Diocesan Synod. Essentially, it was a distillation of the
responses I received from nearly two-thirds of the parishes
of the diocese; I added a set of Motions and Resolutions to

each section, which identified who would do what and when, and how much it would cost. From this, I drew up our Policy Statement for the Nineties. The whole process took sixteen months.

The Policy Statement spells out my role as both Father in God and Bishop-in-Synod, and as the leader of the People of God in mission to the diocese. It then identifies the so-called "Primary Tasks" as Holiness, Mission and Christian Nurture. Primary Tasks are specific areas which need to be developed in order to translate vision into reality. For clarification, I listed a set of objectives for the diocese to aim for within each Primary Task. I did the same for the "Supporting Tasks" – those essential functions needed for carrying forward the work of the diocese – namely Ministry, Communications, Resources, Property, Finance, Administration, and Staffing.

The success or otherwise of translating vision into a strategy and action plan, hinges on the diocesan structures facilitating the whole process. The way in which resources to support ministry are allocated and financed, how the committees and groups are structured and the work organized, should enable – not hinder – the People of God to exercise their call to discipleship and take responsibility for mission in the service of the Kingdom of God.

In order to maintain momentum during the Decade of Evangelism, we plan each year to focus on a different theme concerned with outreach, to be launched annually at the bishops' Swanwick conference. These themes will then be an integral part of a rolling programme of activities and events. There was an Episcopal Visitation of the Cathedral in 1991; and there is to be a Visitation of the Diocese in 1994, ending with a major celebration. In 1997, we plan to hold a Partners in Mission Consultation. The overseas partners will be asked to concentrate on the diocese as a vehicle for mission, evangelism and service, and not on its internal structures or leadership.

ENCOURAGING LEADERSHIP

Whilst many in the diocese look for strong and dynamic leadership from the bishop, he can also encourage other Christian leaders in the community in the exercise and development of their leadership skills. The bishop can promote collaboration and partnership in ministry by the whole People of God – whether it is the enabling of the rich variety of lay ministries, teams and groups, or the sharing of his episcopate with a suffragan, or the "cure of souls" with a parish priest. For instance, when I chaired a meeting organized by the UN Association in Nottingham, convened as part of the preparation for the Earth Summit in Brazil, it was interesting to note how those Christians who were present felt encouraged and affirmed in their own witness and service.

PUBLIC MINISTRY

As bishop I find myself frequently looked to as the Church's representative and spokesperson on matters of personal faith and public morality. Although time-consuming, I consider it important to respond to invitations from a variety of sources to participate in civic functions, educational events, industrial and commercial gatherings and similar activities. I see these as evangelistic opportunities in the wider community.

Unlike in Argentina, where I had to battle constantly with authorities of all kinds, here I have easy access to people from all walks of life. In the space of a few years, I have established a network of relationships with people of influence in public life throughout the county, offering and receiving friendship and ministering to them in their personal and professional capacities. I regularly meet with the county's leading businessmen, industrialists, local and national politicians, civic leaders for discussions about matters which affect the lives of many.

THE BISHOP AND THE PARISHES

Part of my role as diocesan bishop is to inspire people to tell their story of faith in Christ with a humble confidence, and also to be his unashamed disciples in the world. This is fulfilled especially in my preaching ministry on ordinary parish occasions.

An important tool for assisting parishes plan strategically is "mission audit". On parochial visits I am able frequently to stimulate PCCs to consider having such an audit (with guidance from diocesan trained auditors), to help them set their goals for outreach and ministry in the parish.

Through shifts in population and other developments, there are parishes where the church and its amenities have become remote from the community. There are also other churches where the congregation is now so large that there are problems over accommodation. In both these cases, it is important that as bishop I take the initiative in encouraging and facilitating "church planting".

THE BISHOP AS EVANGELIST

Confirmation services are an obvious and regular opportunity for evangelism. This is not only an occasion when the candidates make a public profession of faith, but also for the bishop to challenge friends and family present, many of whom will not necessarily be committed Christians, with the basic message of the Gospel. On a number of occasions I have confirmed people who began their own journey of faith when they attended a confirmation service a year or so earlier.

I also greatly value invitations to spend longer periods of time in a parish, when I can take on the role of evangelist and lead a mission or faith-sharing weekend. This is of course set in the wider context of my ministry as teacher and defender of the faith, and my pastoral care of the People of God.

Lay Models of Evangelism

From bishops we turn to the Church's main body of evangelists, the laity in every parish! Here there have been a number of developments that have sought appropriate models of ministry to encourage general evangelistic mobilization within the parish context. Michael Wooderson has devoted considerable energy to encouraging one model of this in the parishes where he has served as an incumbent, and also in helping others to try something similar for themselves in their setting. He describes some of the discoveries he has made.

FAITH-SHARING TEAMS

William Temple once said, "We must turn our congregations into teams of evangelists". His vision involved teams of witness going from one parish to another "just as they go to play cricket or football" (quoted in *Towards the Conversion of England* p. 56). He envisaged harnessing the energies of young and old in bold evangelistic missions. He saw it as a co-operative venture in which one parish helped another with its evangelistic task. Sadly his vision was never implemented on a large enough scale to prevent the steady decline of church membership which has been a feature of the past forty years.

But his words did not fall on totally deaf ears. The Church Army, for example, has always drawn extensively on ordinary church members for its evangelistic teams. The Lee Abbey Community draws not only on its own community but also on the Friends of Lee Abbey and on members of the local parish when it conducts evangelistic missions. And in the diocese of Bath and Wells in the 1980s the late Jack Mardon used faith-sharing teams in diocesan-wide parish missions, training some 500 lay people in the process. University and College missions involve large numbers of lay people, both on the mission team and among the students themselves. These represent a few examples of lay people being involved in faith-sharing opportunities as a team. Such teams have proved to be a wonderful training ground in evangelism. But all such initiatives together only account for a small percentage of the million or so adult Anglicans who worship each Sunday. There is enormous scope for the Church to benefit from the growth of the practice of faith-sharing teams made up of ordinary church members – and in two particular ways.

In Other Parishes

Faith-sharing across parish boundaries has much to commend it.

1. The receiving parish benefits from having to decide the aims and objectives of the mission and work out an effective strategy; from mobilizing its own members to host meetings, to provide hospitality for the visiting

team, to cultivate contact with non-church members etc., so that everyone has a part to play. It benefits from the impact of the visiting team on its own members. The example of ordinary church members engaged in evangelism can act as a spur, a challenge or an encouragement to the receiving parish. They can be a catalyst for change.

2. The visiting team benefits from the prayer, preparation and training that are required; from the experience of working in a team (when so often they have to bear witness to their faith as an isolated Christian); from the opportunity of talking about the faith to people whom they do not know. Because they are engaged in an important and challenging spiritual task their faith will be deepened and the confidence they gain will equip them for further service in their own parish and beyond. Their experience of another parish will broaden their understanding of the Church and, if the mission has an ecumenical dimension, their experience will be that much richer.

Clearly, such inter-parish missions have great potential, but they do require considerable planning and organization. They can, therefore, easily become the preserve of larger and stronger parishes, while the smaller and weaker parishes which most need them are least likely ever to take such an initiative. Strong parishes can readily field such teams from among their members. But what about those people languishing with evangelistic gifts unused in parishes large and small across the land? There is great need for initiatives like those taken by Jack Mardon to organize teams that function across a wide area. On a smaller scale it ought to be possible for Councils of Churches or Anglican

Deaneries to draw together and use such teams. If each deanery had a pool of people willing to take part in faith-sharing missions a lot could be done to help smaller parishes with their evangelistic task. A visiting faith-sharing team drawn from across a deanery and incorporating members of the inviting church could provide the momentum needed to kick-start a parish that had got stuck, or to encourage one that was losing heart. Of course, the ongoing evangelistic task has to remain firmly in the hands of the local Christian community, although some parishes may need support and encouragement over a number of years. If this is to happen, the cherished independence of parishes will need to give place to a greater sense of interdependence and a willingness to share human resources. It is so easy for strong and "successful" parishes to spend all their energies internally and to function in splendid isolation from struggling neighbours; but it is not always easy for struggling parishes to ask for help. As in most things, so much will depend on the attitude of the incumbent or the PCC who can effectively block any evangelistic enterprise.

IN YOUR PARISH

During my eight years as Minister at St Thomas', Aldridge, in the Lichfield Diocese, we pioneered a method of using faith-sharing teams which later became known as "Good News down the Street". It has been widely used in churches of all denominations both in this country and abroad. How does it work?

The congregation is mobilized in teams of three, available to go on invitation to any home willing to receive them. On offer is the opportunity for people to have a series of six informal discussions about the Christian faith without any prior commitment to the church, and on the clear understanding that they can opt out at any stage. The team members use a simple outline based on the life of Jesus as a framework for each week's discussion, but there is plenty of space for free-ranging questions and the sharing of views. No pressure is put on people to agree with the views of the team, but the course is designed to lead people to a clearer understanding of the good news of Jesus Christ as they read the Gospels, and to give them an opportunity to make a personal response of faith if they are ready for it. The informal setting of a home and the simple structure make it possible for ordinary members of the congregation to take part without any formal training. They learn "on the job", dealing with difficult questions as best they can, not afraid to confess their ignorance or admit their inadequacies, but eager to find out and share what they can on the next visit. This is a far more natural process than going in with a carefully worked out set of arguments, or a neatly packaged presentation. It enables people to meet as people in a relaxed environment where they can talk quite naturally about their faith.

Four important principles underlie this approach:

1. As the task of evangelism belongs to the whole congregation we must find ways of involving as many as possible and excluding as few as possible.

2. As training will exclude some people (perhaps because they have reading difficulties, etc.) we need to set up situations in which everyone learns "on the job" and training is not required.

3. We should be willing to go to people on their own ground and on their own terms.

4. We should have a strategy of continuous evangelism in the local church and not rely solely on periodic missions. Our aim should be to make evangelism the normal activity of the whole congregation.

Central to the outworking of this strategy are the teams of three lay people. The selection of each team is crucial. It is important to get a well-balanced team and a team that will relate well with people who will be receiving them. A team leader who can handle the situation is needed and it helps to have someone who can support him or her. The third member of the team can be anyone. This makes it possible to involve people who would otherwise be excluded. If a different combination of church members is used in each home you can move towards the goal of mobilizing the whole congregation for evangelism.

This strategy is clearly set out in the Grove Booklet *Good News down the Street* and the results of its use in two sociologically different parishes over a period of fifteen years is fully documented in *The Church down Our Street* (Monarch 1989). Suffice it to say that when such faith-sharing teams are established as a normal part of church life they have a considerable impact on the congregation, both in terms of new adult converts being added to the church and in the deepening of faith and fellowship among existing members. As people are involved on teams their faith is stimulated and stretched and in the process some are "re-evangelized". This is a strategy that puts evangelism within the reach of any congregation, however small. It does not require organization or human resources because it can begin with one team of three and expand from a simple base.

William Temple's vision still remains to be implemented seriously. The potential in such teams is enormous. They are a way of mobilizing ordinary church members for evangelism that could revolutionize the life of all our churches.

Local Lay Evangelists

However successful a parish may be in seeking to mobilize all of us in evangelism, there will always be some who show very obvious gifts in this area which seem to leave the rest of us standing. These are the kind of people that Michael Green, one of the leaders of Springboard, is particularly concerned to motivate and train further.

In every congregation there are budding evangelists! They are the ones with the talent to explain the way to faith convincingly and clearly, the talent to precipitate decision for Christ. This is one of the gifts of the ascended Christ (Ephesians 4:11f). It is not given to everyone; but it is given to some. It is the task of leaders in the church to teach the existence of such gifts, and to look out for those who may be gifted in this way without knowing it.

Discovering Who They Are

The budding evangelist will often be bringing people to church. He or she will feel very much at home in the company of non-Christians and not in the least embarrassed about being known as a believer – laughing off the jeers and cheerfully accepting the taunts while remaining friends with the mockers! There is your natural evangelist. Generally it is someone who really likes people and is never happier than when in their company. But God is never dull and monolithic. No single personality type can be labelled "evangelistic". Some Christians live quiet lives, but there is something about them which prompts others to ask them questions, to which they can respond effectively. Sometimes people do ask leading questions such as, "What is it you've got which I haven't?" or "How can you be so cheerful on a Monday morning?"

SPECIFIC TRAINING

Having discovered some who seem to have evangelistic gifts, training is important, and they will normally look to the leadership in the local church to provide this. There are various ways in which it can be done. There can be a course on how one individual can help another to begin a friendship with Jesus Christ. The minister can either devise a course, or derive one from books and experience. Subjects handled include the mindset of modern people who are indifferent to God; the need of people for the Gospel; the person of Jesus and what he has done for mankind through his incarnation, death and resurrection; the way to personal encounter with Christ through repentance, faith and baptism; the common objections that are met with; the grounds for Christian assurance; and the first steps in Christian growth. Part of the programme should be a deliberate attempt by each member to nudge one of his or her friends towards Christ during the course or in the weeks immediately following.

Another much more demanding way of going about it is to apprentice people and go out onto the streets! They could go out in pairs, armed with a questionnaire, and graciously approach passers-by to ask them a few questions. One might be, "Are you a regular worshipper at any church?" This might lead to, "Who do you believe Jesus Christ to have been?" which in turn could give way to some such question as, "If it were possible to meet him, would you want to?" Questions like these, if asked with due sensitivity, can lead to good conversations with complete strangers. The couples then retire to the church, pray, discuss how they got on, and learn from their experience.

A third way of training is to make use of a video. There are one or two videos specially designed to help people in sharing their faith. The video, only part of a weekly session, is complemented by role play, discussion and practical experience. An excellent training video called *Person to Person* is available from the Bible Society, and another, *Saints in Evangelism*, has recently been produced by J. John.

MODELLING

It is a fairly basic principle of leadership that you cannot lead anyone further than you have gone yourself. Evangelism does not happen in a great many churches for the simple reason that the ministers do not stress it and, worse still, they are not seen doing it. If we expect to see a congregation come alive in sharing the good news, then it stands to reason that the leaders must be deeply committed to it. They do not need to be very good at it. But they do need to have a go at it.

The congregation will particularly notice the minister's approach to evangelistic preaching. Leaders must be prepared to do it, even if they are not particularly talented at it. They must, like Timothy in the New Testament, "do the work of an evangelist" (2 Timothy 4:5). They must also be prepared for others to do it instead of them. And this takes a good deal of courage and humility – courage, because once a minister starts preaching for decision in church, noses get put out of joint – and humility to stand aside for a layperson who is a more talented evangelist. But it is unquestionably the way to grow evangelists in the local church, evangelists who will be able to affect the neighbourhood.

SHARING

From modelling we have already strayed into sharing. It is hard to keep the two apart. So strongly do I believe in this principle of sharing that I rarely accept invitations to engage in evangelism on my own. I try to take a team with me, large or small. It may be over 100 or it may be two or three. The principle is the same in either case – once reconciled with God we are reconciled into one body. And in evangelism we need not only to proclaim that reconciliation, but to exhibit it by partnership and the quality of our mutual relationships in the team. In this way the unspoken message that comes across from the team reinforces the thrust of the words they speak. Each member of the team grows from being part of a shared enterprise like this.

SENDING OUT

As the church becomes more at ease in the realm of evangelism, opportunities will grow. The ministers will be asked elsewhere to speak about the subject or to conduct some mission or outreach. They need to take care not to run themselves ragged by responding positively to every invitation, but provide occasion for others in their congregation to go instead. There can be delicate moments in taking this step. If the minister declines, but instead recommends a group from the congregation, they may not take up the suggestion! But, after a while, trust will be built, the team will go out on its own, and both clergy and congregation will have passed an important milestone in the understanding and practice of mission in the local church.

I can recall in a previous parish a delightful, cautious, gentle doctor. He was a very good doctor, and he was very dubious indeed about evangelism. I managed to persuade him to come on some team I was taking out. He came, and came again, and again. Now he not only takes teams all over the country as opportunity offers and as his time allows, but he organizes the whole outreach ministry of the church. He was given the opportunity to take part, then to lead, and now he takes others. And so the good infection grows.

But it is not necessary to wait for invitations to come in. Once a few of the congregation have some experience on their own ground it should be possible to suggest a team visit to a nearby church. I always feel this is a "no-lose" situation. If the team does well, they return home thrilled, and the receiving congregation is glad to have had some down-to-earth laypeople ministering to them instead of the usual ordained professional. If the team is a bit shaky and hesitant, the result can still be positive. The receiving congregation may say, "Well, we could have done better than that," and they take an opportunity to go and improve on what they have seen.

ENCOURAGING

Evangelism is both demanding and exhausting. Those who engage in it can easily become burnt-out. We all need encouragement, and never more than when we are engaged in the difficult task of seeking lovingly to change the whole direction of a person's life, to bring it back to its proper source and goal in God.

That is why those who are most engaged in evangelism in the neighbourhood should be especially well cared for: with acts of thoughtfulness, the occasional gift, or a "fun" happening where all they are expected to do is to relax and enjoy themselves. If this loving care is exercised, the emerging gifts of new evangelists will have the chance to develop without being lost through over-use.

Budding evangelists can be encouraged in a variety of ways. There are annual get-togethers for those engaged in extensive evangelism. To attend a meeting like this among like-minded peers can be a tremendous encouragement. It is also encouraging to be invited to share in the nurture of new believers in short courses of eight weeks or so which are expressly designed for new converts and those on the edge of commitment.

TAKE COURAGE

Confidence makes all the difference in evangelism. When I began, I was so amazed that God should use human beings in partnership with himself to kindle new life in others, that I was sometimes tentative in laying the issues on the line. I think I was terrified that if I was too clear and decisive nobody would respond, and I might look like a fool or a failure. I guess I am not alone in feeling like that! What is more, Western culture is so pluralistic that we shy from making absolute claims for Jesus. On the surface at least, our culture is so polite that we feel almost discourteous about challenging people to repent and believe. Yet that is what Jesus did. If we are faithful to him, we will want to do the same, and with experience we will find that God honours this holy, loving boldness.

Training Clergy

Bishops and laity – but what of the clergy? So often the effective development of ministry and mission in a parish depends on whether they have discovered the appropriate model of ministry which enables them to lead and encourage mission and evangelism at parish level. We asked Susan Parsons, involved in the initial training of clergy as Principal of the East Midlands Ministry Training Course, to give us some insight into this subject from her particular perspective.

SUCCESS-DOMINATED MISSION

Everyone is producing mission statements these days. In popular usage, the term suggests a person with a goal to achieve by determined effort, who carefully sets priorities and makes decisions which relate to the realization of this vision. Upon hearing of "a man with a mission", we anticipate someone who is single-minded in the pursuit of an important end, and we expect to step aside so that we may not be in the way of its attainment. In business and industry, the term is applied to a corporate vision which seeks thereby both to clarify the aims and objectives of the company, and to ensure the commitment, loyalty, and hard work of employees.

Last year a theological student brought to me the "mission statement" of the Post Office, for which he worked. "The Post Office MISSION is to . . . anticipate and satisfy the requirements of our customers . . . create a positive working environment . . . foster innovative product development . . . deserve national confidence." Employees were expected to share these aims and to focus their behaviour on its values, which are listed as "care" and "pride". The intended effect of such a statement is to draw all who work there into a sense of common purpose and shared effort, so that ultimately the corporate interest is served. Beyond this interest, of course, there is reference to those outside, and some judgement is made about what people really want. In this statement, customers are said to expect "value for money, reliability, courtesy, integrity, security, and prompt and timely service", expectations which are to be met by the "care" of those within the company. It is essential that the company relates its mission to this wider context in which its own purposes are supported and valued, and from which its ultimate rationale for existence may be drawn.

A particular interpretation of the world underpins such mission statements. I read them as fundamentally competitive, assuming a context of scarce resources in which successful companies are rewarded by attracting business, or by consumption of their goods and services. Society is understood as an open market, in which people are expected freely to choose without favour to historical precedent or established groups. Within such a market, each organization must stake out its place and function in order to attract customers, and then must maintain its distinctiveness to ensure their continued adherence. The measure of oranizational success in this process is the control which may then be exercised in future planning and in the manipulation of factors to corporate advantage. "Doing well" gives the company greater power to determine its own future, to shape the attitudes of customers, and to develop new fields of operation. These statements thus revolve around competition, consumption, and control, and they make particular sense within a world of such realities.

THE CHRISTIAN CONCEPT OF MISSION

The uses of the term "mission" in the wider culture suggest to those of us in ministerial training that we need to be thoughtful in our use of the term. In many respects, the churches are reflecting this emphasis on goal-setting and attainment, on corporate identity and loyalty, and on meeting effectively the needs of the world. And there may seem, on the surface, to be no problem with that. Indeed each Anglican theological course and college has been asked to produce a "mission statement" of its aims and objectives which can provide the framework for its educational programme and assessment procedures, and by which its quality can be appraised. In this way it is hoped we may become more clear about exactly what it is we are doing, and for what purposes, and to what effect.

What we may be more cautious about is adopting the world-view upon which this sense of mission is built. A recent article from America entitled "The Quest for Quality", argues that "People expect value and quality from church life; successful churches seek to provide them." The author tells us that competition between churches for people's money, time, and loyalty should be a stimulus to the development of quality church ministry, for "Little of consequence will happen in a church with a lazy, insincere, burned-out or managerially incompetent pastor." Indeed the minister must bear responsibility for the success of a particular church, or it is "doomed to a second-rate ministry", and s/he must be trained to render such quality in order to retain a position of leadership. Since "denominational loyalty and distinctiveness are fading fast", the search for quality must pervade all aspects of the church's life. Only churches which are able to offer this service in "meeting the needs of others in the very best way possible" will fulfil God's will for the Church and be able to "bring participants closer to God."[1]

One could easily imagine substituting any other institution for "church" in this piece to have a perfectly acceptable statement of a company's aims that would pass our attention unquestioned. To train ministers in this cultural milieu highlights issues of "Gospel and Culture" very sharply. For the article quoted above assumes as given facts of our society its competitiveness – which the churches are now experiencing in a world of so many options; its consumerism – which presumes a lot of people are out there ready and waiting to buy what the churches may offer; and its concern for control – which assumes that those with the strongest beliefs and firmest commitment will be furthering God's purposes in the world and will actually be able to bring people to God. What part does the ministry and mission of the Church play in this unwritten language of our culture?

One of the essential aspects of ministerial training is surely that there is an opportunity to startle received assumptions and to examine values theologically. This is especially important in the area of mission and evangelism, an area in which we become so aware of the entanglements of the language of faith with prevailing themes and values of culture, and in which we become more sensitive to potential distortions of

1. Charles N. Waldo: "The Quest for Quality" in *Interpreter*, Volume 37, No. 4, May-June 1992, pp. 17–19. This journal of the United Methodist Church comes complete with its own mission statement. "The MISSION of Interpreter is to help local churches foster the ministry and growth of God's reign in their communities and around the world." (p. 3).

the history of mission. Since we hope for ministers who have the capacity to speak to the Church with courage and with compassion, we have a responsibility to infuse the whole programme of training with a critical awareness of ideologies, to offer serious and practical reflection on differing models of mission, and to consider carefully both historical precedent and biblical text.

PREACHING THE GOSPEL

Evangelism entails "Preaching the Gospel". The use of this phrase to define a Decade in the life of the Church is relevant in a world in which such "preaching" is necessary (for there are many who have not heard), and in which "the Gospel" may be good news (for there are many who long for understanding). In thinking through the implications of preaching the Gospel, another picture of mission may become clear, a picture which is different from the one above and which opens up new dimensions for the training of the Church's ministers.

Firstly, in preaching the Gospel we are speaking with our fellow human beings as friends. So many features of our contemporary life conspire to shrink the dimensions of our humanness: our needs are quantified, we are treated passively as the empty recipients of goods and services, our behaviour is generalized and predicted, and we are presumed to be gullible and easily led. Above all the Gospel addresses us as subjects, by assuming that already we are puzzled, and concerned, and wondering, and caring human beings. These activities are stirred to new life by the Gospel and are stretched beyond the boundaries we had set for them. Our uniqueness and worth are affirmed in the particular details of our lives, and we are drawn beyond ourselves into horizons we had not anticipated. This takes place through conversations in which the faith of one meets the faith of another, and both are transformed in the presence of the God whom they seek. In training, we seek to inspire in ministers the desire and the capacity to be friends, to engage fully in the flawed and ambiguous tussle which such friendship requires, and to enable others to befriend in their own place and context.

Secondly, in preaching the Gospel we are touching the social realities of human life at their most sensitive and awkward points. When faith is understood as something privately given and churches set out to provide individuals with consumable experiences, then the structures of social life are rendered invisible, and whole dimensions of this reality go unnoticed and unchallenged. We cannot be involved in the fullness and ordinariness of people's lives, required by preaching the Gospel, without coming up against these structures that impinge upon us, and acknowledging them in the liturgy and prayer of the Church. And so we must be asking why we are not worshipping with our black sisters and brothers within the Christian community, and why the lives of women continue to be defined by violence and poverty, and why there is always money for war in the world but not for food, and why there are those who live without hope, and so on and so on. In training, we seek to nurture in ministers the desire for justice and for peace, and the courage and confidence to proclaim and to work for that justice and peace in the Church and in the world.

Thirdly, preaching the Gospel asks us to put ourselves at risk. So much language in "mission statements" gives the illusion of human control and accords to those who share in it the privilege of speaking from positions of power. Indeed language about the Kingdom and the reign of God may also carry this cultural baggage, encouraging the notion of a controlling deity who awaits the submission of the world to his will or the bringing of people into his presence by the committed. What a difference if we understand the good news not as God in control, but as God at risk, at risk in the Incarnation, at risk with the apostles, at risk throughout the history of the Church, and at risk now in its mission. To be drawn into this kind of love is to enter the much more fragile community of the beloved, who work and struggle and explore and fail and try again to discover how this love may be made known and embodied in the limited and fallible structures of our world. In training, we seek to encourage ministers in a loving and hopeful commitment to this work of the Church and an understanding of the place of the Church in the establishing and expression of the Kingdom.[1]

Models of Ordained Ministry

In the last analysis, any model of ministry will be intensely personal. The variety is as extensive as those involved. To give some clues about how clergy have looked at their own ministries as they seek to lead in mission and evangelism, we asked four people to reflect on their own personal model of ministry.

1. For a fuller exposition of these three themes in Christian ethics, see Sharon D. Welch: *A Feminist Ethic of Risk*, Augsburg Fortress Press, Minneapolis, 1990.

For an application of these themes to this topic, see Kenneth R. Cracknell: "Protestant Evangelism or Catholic Evangelization?", a paper read to and published by the Methodist Sacramental Fellowship, 1992.

Finally, thanks to my colleague, the Rev. Michael J. Taylor, Vice-Principal of EMMTC, for his work on our Course document "The Capacities Being Sought in Ordination Candidates" from which these aspirations for training have been drawn.

We let each one stand on its own to form the stimulus for further consideration.

1. DAVID CHAMBERLAIN

David Chamberlain, the vicar of All Hallows, Easton, a UPA parish in inner-city Bristol.

When I became incumbent of this parish two things were clear both to my wife and me, namely: a. I was being called to exercise my priestly ministry in close partnership with my wife as prayer companion (not as unpaid curate!); b. we were to live and work under the personal direction of the Lord Jesus Christ whose church it is and whose will and plan for our personal lives and for the corporate life of the church, even in specific details, we were to make it our primary task to discern and fulfil.

Following the pattern of the New Testament and a growing inner conviction, I am in no doubt that, as a priest, my primary task in partnership with my wife is to be wholly centred on God in deepening, joyful submission to his will in all things and to use all the available resources in the church in order to grow in the knowledge and love of God and of his Son and to live more and more in the victorious love of Christ over against the rebel principalities and powers in the Church and in the world. Offering the daily Mass to the glory of God, for the good of his Church and for the salvation of the world is the lynch-pin of our shared priestly ministry. Without that, along with the Daily Offices, a monthly confession, a twice-weekly fast, early morning prayer and meditation and a daily praying of the rosary I doubt whether we should have survived here with our faith and hope in the promises of God intact. Contrary to our expectation and previous experience, and certainly contrary to what the congregation expects of us, we are being led by the Spirit not into an active ministry fuelled by prayer, but into a demanding contemplative lifestyle in which prayer, especially intercession, and spiritual reading claim first place in our lives without it displacing the essential parochial duties. Time and again we find that an insuperable difficulty in a person's life or in a particular situation is mysteriously resolved without any direct human intervention. The timing is always God's, so to him be all the glory.

We all carry a load of negative forces within us inherited from the past which distort our personalities and impair our capacity to give and receive love. It was and is essential in our priestly ministry that in the first place my wife and I receive progressive inner healing, involving as it sometimes does the ministry of deliverance – thanks to God's gifts of the discernment of spirits, the word of knowledge and wisdom and, above all, as a fruit of our Lady's intercessions. We are discovering that by entering into a deeper personal relationship with the blessed Mother of God through praying the rosary and encouraging others to do so, celebrating her feasts, making pilgrimages to Walsingham, Medjugorge and Fatima we are experiencing in ourselves and in God's people progressive release from bondages of the past, reconciliations within the family, protection against the assaults of the evil one, and a growing desire to do only what is pleasing to God.

All this we see as the necessary preparation – in answer to our constant prayer for conversion, healing and a new Pentecost for all of us in the church – for the fulfilment of the risen Lord's intention to send the promise of his Father upon us as upon his first apostles. We are to stay in the city until we are clothed with power from on high because without that power all our efforts of evangelization and service in the community would, as we have proved, be ineffectual and of little worth.

Such a turning point in our individual and corporate lives would, as in the New Testament church, which for us remains the norm and standard, lead to a distribution by the Holy Spirit among the members of the congregation of a rich variety of complementary supernatural charisms for worship, for building up the body in love and for bold, effective witness. The parish priest then graduates from being the minister to becoming the director of ministries who encourages each member of the congregation to discover and exercise his or her particular ministry in collaboration with one another, under the direction of the Lord of the Church.

My priestly ministry in partnership with my wife could be summed up in our aim to betroth each one to Christ, to lose none, and to prepare a people of faith, of loving obedience and of praise – among whom God is pleased to dwell.

2. RICHARD GILES

From St Thomas', Huddersfield, the parish whose story began the previous chapter, Richard Giles offers his reflection on ministry.

Two things stick in my mind about the Vice-Principal of Cuddesdon in my time; if you were to invite him for a sherry before Sunday lunch, he would fix you with a steely eye and demand to know whether the sherry was South African; and when he expounded the St Matthew's gospel, he was astounded that the angel (28:2) should roll away the stone and sit upon it.

Two tiny un-related fragments of memory, and yet they symbolize two aspects of ministry which I have tried to live out; confronting problems immediately and from principle, and a delight in little things.

Just think how many episodes of soap operas are strung out simply waiting for X to tell Y a difficult truth – what agonies of indecision and delay, what enormous opportunities for misunderstandings and falsely raised hopes. In priestly ministry, the consequences of delay and dissembling are (or should be) frightening to think about: all those "harmless" little clergy who, through inaction and avoidance of trouble at all costs wreak havoc in our Church. They belong to what might be called the Public Convenience School of Ministry, their whole concern being to treat their parish like a lavatory – to be left in exactly the same condition in which they found it.

To be human, let alone Christian, one has no choice but to be a sacramentalist, and that was reinforced for me by those sessions uncovering the totally prosaic approach of the Evangelists who couldn't have rigged a story to save their lives. The details within them, like the angel sitting on his stone, are all so extraordinary that they shout out the total authenticity of the New Testament, and lead us to find God likewise in the minutiae of parish life and the ridiculous antics of us all, his holy and crazy people. For good measure, my Vice-Principal also managed to annoy greatly my diocesan bishop when preaching at my ordination. Whilst annoying bishops is not a particularly godly virtue, to be fearless and unrelenting, and sometimes tiresome, in one's pursuit of truth certainly is. This fearless honesty is not that of the common-room or the library, but of the pulpit, the doorstep, and the coffee area after mass. "Radicalism" has a bad name with me because it is nearly always theoretical; the bishops and theologians who shake foundations in television interviews seem to be exactly the types who in a parish setting would balk at suppressing the eight o'clock separatist movement, or toppling the empire of the robed choir. The awkward questions need to be asked in the detail, where God is.

All this may well make the priest a troublesome and restless soul, but so be it. I am just so grateful that someone showed me clearly enough that prophecy is not just a matter of rolling stones around, it is also about coming down to earth and sitting on them.

DON HUMPHRIES

Don Humphries is the vicar of Holy Trinity, Cambridge.

When Jacques Derrida, the French philosopher, travelled to the Sheldonian Theatre in Oxford to discuss his new message of Deconstructionism, he began by saying that he had come without prepared lecture notes in order to be completely vulnerable and unprotected. He was ready to be devoured and mauled by the Oxford dons and the young undergraduates, let alone the highly critical late-night intelligentsia of Channel 4!

Whatever we think of the pros and cons of his message, Derrida himself is engagingly winsome. You had to listen and respond even if in the end you were forced to dismiss his new creed. It took courage to go into the lion's den, willing to be eaten alive, a reminder of the pressure on the early Christians in the gladiatorial arenas of Rome. They were willing to shed blood and tears for the sake of their faith, a very powerful witness to what they believed.

Tears and sacrificial blood were not unknown to Jesus and were an important ingredient of his ministry and mission. The model of ministry he set before us was an incarnational one. By his incarnation, rich as he was, he became poor and met people where they were, identifying with their total humanity, sharing their vulnerability and "by his wounds" they were healed. His salvific message was a healing message and his ministry was a Divine Healing Mission, not on the twentieth-century tele-evangelist model, but one of flesh and blood mingling with flesh and blood.

Likewise, the missionary-minded parish priest will be an incarnational priest, vulnerable, open to criticism, ready to be wounded for the sake of the Gospel. His scars will purposely be plainly visible. His ministry will be that of identification with local humanity, not hiding in ivory towers, walking the corridors of power, ashamed to appear in the market place, or hidden in ecclesiastical fortresses – be it study, synod or sanctuary. Rather he will seek out the community centre, pub, school, town hall, football club, hospital or home. Fired by the vision of "healing evangelism" he will seek out people where they are, not where they are not (in the pews!). He will share his failure, take down his professional guard, be seen to be human and not attempt to divinize himself. His salvation message will be a healing message touching primarily the wounds of sin dividing people from God, but also a message of reconciliation healing the scars within families and communities and in the process will be a message touching the raw nerves of internecine strife raging within each of us.

As Anglican parish priests our worship will reflect this incarnational missionary model. The wounds of Christ will be manifested and communicated through our own wounds, both in word and sacrament. The message preached will be of God's healing ministry in Christ visibly demonstrated on the cross, appropriated by faith and experienced sacramentally in the eucharist. Opportunities for incarnational mission and ministry will also present themselves through the occasional rites of passage as we meet people at times of need. Our counselling ministry also presents ideal opportunities to share in the sufferings of Christ for the world. The visibly scarred priest will more readily be given the world's pain whilst the precision-powered, professionally-polished priest will more likely alienate.

Incarnational ministry is very stressful and needs the resources of team ministries, be it lay or ordained. Constant meeting for prayer with others and sharing Scriptures together will stir up the gift of God within. Our need for personal Holy Spirit ministry increases with the expansion of ministry opportunities. The increasingly common "burn-out" experience needs regular ministry through counselling, spiritual direction, wilderness retreats and planned sabbaticals. Episcopal oversight needs increasingly to be pastorally orientated rather than management directed, but our constant resource continues to be a close walk with the chief Shepherd of the sheep.

4. IRENE DURNDELL

Irene Durndell is Parish Deacon at St Paul's church, Northumberland Heath, and also Assistant Director of Training in the Diocese of Rochester.

Maureen came to church after the funeral of her husband because she was offered love in the shape of comfort and prayer. She knew that we loved her enough to visit her and pray for her and her family in the church service. An older couple took her under their wing, guiding her through the service, and they continued to care for her. Two years later she was confirmed, refusing a year earlier because it was too special a step to take just then. God and Maureen have taken time to get to know one another!

Nigel and Jill were slow starters too. They were encouraged to come to church after booking their wedding. It produced some complications, but they were helped through them and, having heard the Bible read and taught, they were able to understand more about their commitment to one another and God's commitment to them in their marriage. They were married and continued to come to church despite two house moves and one new baby. Having heard them talk about the difference that Jesus made to their life each day, though hesitantly expressed, their decision to be confirmed nearly three years after their initial contact with us was a real joy.

Theresa came to church because her daughter joined the choir with a friend. Unchurched, untaught and unread, she willingly came to confirmation classes with the friend's mother (yet another story!), just to keep her company and to see what went on. It became apparent very quickly that she had come home. She started to devour the Bible and to talk and ask questions about Jesus in an atmosphere of safety; she too was confirmed. Her husband, who has a strong Roman Catholic background, came to her confirmation and is supportive of her Christian activities. She knows that he is accepted and loved by God and we believe that God has started the process of bringing him home too.

Brian and Kim have taken the vows they made at their children's baptism very seriously. They were grateful for the time taken to explain what baptism means. Although they had probably made the decision to have their children baptized before my visit, it made them think about their own position before God and of the commitment they were about to make on behalf of their children. They show no signs of wanting to make any deeper commitment at the moment and part of my loving is to continue to encourage them, and pray that God will do the rest. Like many others their story is as yet apparently incomplete.

Without doubt the Church of England, through its occasional offices, has opportunities for evangelism that would not otherwise occur. Three of the people in these stories came to faith as a direct result of that contact. I believe that we have a duty to ensure that all contacts made through these offices are treated with loving integrity.

The only *role model* I can offer for a parish deacon in the area of mission/evangelism (and perhaps in any area of work) is the model of loving. I do not find this easy to do, but I do know that, when I remember how special a person is to Jesus, then such a love is released – and God works. Our prime task is to love people into the Kingdom of God and all the strategies, meetings, teaching and testimonies in the world will have little effect without this overflowing of our hearts. Love has to be the hallmark of our ministry and our churches.

Chapter Four

EVANGELISM AND
THE GROWING GENERATIONS

The Church of England faces a difficult task during the Decade when it comes to the evangelization of young people. Many churches feel sorely pressed just to keep the children of church people within the fold. Looking beyond the church youth group to those outside the church, adult Christians can be confronted with a divide which we often feel ill equipped to cross. Despite its omnipresence on the television, youth culture is a strange world; young people in their tastes in clothes, music and language make us feel out of touch and dated; and for their part, they may have similar feelings about us as they look in on the church. We stand on two sides of a cultural divide; and the challenge to us is to find ways of bridging the gap, and of sharing the faith with young people who are currently outside the cultural and social frameworks of the Church of England.

Youth Culture

Pete Ward questions the perceptions of many who view youth culture from the outside; and he shows how the church may itself be enriched if its members set out to understand the values of young people and to recognize that Christ is already active among them.

127

A TIME OF TRANSITION

Modern industrial society has created a period of limbo between childhood and adult life. The need for more complex education and the lack of a defined economic role has left young people in an "in between" stage, which is characterized by ambiguity in both status and responsibility. Sixteen-year-olds have two years to wait before they can be legally served in a pub, one year to wait before they can start to drive; but they are considered to be ready for heterosexual sex. Drinking beer, driving a car and sex are all significant rites of passage in our society and for the young person they are highly aspirational. The current passion for joy-riding can only really be understood in this context. Driving a car is an "adult" activity. Young people in launching themselves prematurely onto the roads are in part seeking to establish their places in life. But the manner in which joy-riding takes place, in its very irresponsibility, is a spectacular demonstration of how far these young people are from real adulthood. To be adult is to be deemed responsible enough to drive a car; the joy-rider steals this symbol of adult life and defiantly bucks the system.

The point is that young people not only have to become adult but to do so in the right way. The local response in Oxford to the joy-riding craze has been the motor project TRAX. Here young people are encouraged to work on cars and participate in legitimate motor sports. Over a period of time it is hoped that the young people will learn to act more responsibly around cars. If being adult is to be responsible then what holds true for the motor car will also be true for alcohol, sex, shopping, employment and indeed spirituality.

The adolescent's task in life is to grow up: to become adult. The problem is that it is far from easy to pass from being a child to being an adult in our society. A further complicating factor is that adolescence is getting longer. At the one end young people are reaching puberty much earlier (boys 12, girls 11).[1] At the other end the growth in higher education and the prevalence of unemployment mean that adolescent restraints extend, for some, into their mid-twenties.

MEDIA MADNESS

Some would see youth culture as the creation of the modern media. The authors of *Dancing in the Dark* argue that youth culture is fed by the needs of multi-million dollar industries which exploit young people to sell their products. The fashion industry, the film industry, and of course the pop industry all rely heavily on young people to survive. Through the powerful media of radio, video, TV, and film, young people, the authors say, are encouraged to consume prepackaged youth products. Youth culture is sold to young people, with the help of the moral and physical vacuum that young people find in their homes. The absent father and the working mother have abdicated their responsibilities for the nurture of their children and left them to learn about life from the TV screen.

> Teen films are heavily geared toward providing visions of identity and intimate relationships, visions that often function like panaceas. As long as families, schools, neighbourhoods, churches and the like do not help provide more inviting, healthy, and personal ways of meeting these psycho-relational needs, the media will

1. Buckler, *The Adolescent Years*, Castlemead, 1987.

play an overbearing role in determining what youth deem worthwhile and significant.[1]

Though this warm personal approach to young people is important, it is a mistake to overplay the role of the media in the creation of youth culture. Young people are indeed consumers but they do so creatively and socially. One good example of this is the way that many young working-class girls read teenage magazines. Often groups of five or six girls will share a copy of *Jackie* or *Just Seventeen*. The first page to which they turn will very likely be the problem page where relationships and sexual anxieties are aired and advice is given. In Oxford we have observed how the girls will talk about these issues and offer their own solutions. Together they work as a problem-solving group in relation to their own experience of life. One may draw on a story about her sister, another may recall how her mother reacted in a similar situation. The "Agony Aunt" is seen as an expert but one whose advice can be rejected in the light of the wisdom of the group. In this situation repeated in schools classrooms, playgrounds and private gatherings all over Britain the media are consumed in a context of growth and nurture. Nurture firstly happens within the group. The girls help each other to form moral judgements. They are active not passive consumers. Together they try to help each other form an identity in the complex maze of sexual and social relationships that make up their social world. For these girls the stakes are high, for reaching out in love involves the risk of unwanted pregnancy. Nor does the group seek to resolve these problems in total isolation from their family backgrounds; the girls use the experience of

1. Quentin Schultze et all, *Dancing in the Dark*, Eerdmans, 1991.

their mothers and sisters and friends to forge their own way of life. Much the same could be said for TV soaps or videos which young people also watch in groups and discuss at great length. The media are therefore essential to an understanding of youth culture, but we cannot treat them as an isolated text which we can read and assume we know its meaning. Youth culture lives at the "micro" level. It is in small, relational groups in the local area that we see how the media are consumed by young people. This is particularly true when we come to look at the meaning of teenage style.

YOU'VE GOT THE LOOK

It is inaccurate to talk of youth culture as a single generic whole; in fact there are a great many different youth sub-cultures. The best way to illustrate this is to take a walk down your local high street and try to take a note of the variety of ways that young people dress. On my way to work I pass young people wearing baseball caps and others with woollen hats perched precariously on the tops of their heads. I see a student proudly displaying the mysterious logo *Hall* written large on his back. There are young people who have grown their hair into dreadlocks and others who have shaved ridges in short-cropped scalps to reveal the skin underneath. The denim jean is more or less ubiquitous but there are so many different types on show. Large baggy ones which fan out in the wind as you walk, old Levi's cut off at the thigh to make hot pants, tight jeans worn with a variety of different baseball boots. Some of these sports shoes have become so large now that they look like massive sledgehammers on the feet. There are little suede jackets and puffed up nylon ones and of course the everlasting leather biker's jacket.

The sheer variety and diversity in young people's choice of clothes is a strong indication that what we are seeing is not insignificant. These fashion items are at the heart of the need for young people to create their own sense of identity and intimacy. Style divides the world of young people into readily identifiable and commonly understood groupings. More often than not these groups are defined by social class. Working-class young people create working-class youth subcultures and middle-class young people do the same. One interesting phenomenon which I have stumbled on recently is the fact that young people in our locality who are into Heavy Metal music and dress accordingly, i.e. tight denim jeans, a t-shirt with the name of the metal band on it and a leather jacket, are very often characterized by social mobility from working class to lower middle class within their parents' lifetime. This kind of factor would indicate that the meaning of youth culture lies in a dialogical relationship with the popular media. Young people consume images which they then use to create meaning within their own social world. This social world is not handed down to them by the modern media: the pattern of youth subcultures is created by already existing social and economic divides.

In strongly working-class areas young people who have moved off the estate use a style like heavy metal as a statement of their own identity. There is a great deal of antagonism between the working-class young people who are into dance music and rave culture and those who play in heavy metal bands. The cry of "Metaller" is regularly used whenever the heavy metal young people pass by. Seen from the social and economic standpoint this conflict is understandable. The heavy metal group are proclaiming that they are different and the working-class young people know that this is so. The tensions involved in social mobility are played out in the playground and the high street in the symbolic world of teenage fashion.

Young people marginalized from the mainstream of economic life are constrained by law to be in full-time education until they are 16. Given this situation they have used the freedom that they do have to create a world of meaning and identity of their own. Where young people are free is in their leisure time.

All-consuming Leisure

Youth subcultures are a variety of different ways to construct identity through the use of leisure. In the late 80s the prevailing style amongst working-class groups was called "Casual". Casual in fact meant a variety of things because it tended to be used whatever the changes in fashion. At first it was clothing which was festooned with references to the lifestyle of the rich and famous. Later on sports wear began to be popular. Cycling shorts were worn by the most unlikely of physiques! Baseball caps, expensive walking shoes and jackets hit the scene. Some of this is still with us but the message is pretty clear. Leisure is where young people find meaning.

Paul Willis speaks of the way that young people form what he calls "protocommunities".[1] These groupings are informal and temporary networks which are characterized by similar interests and styles of dress and behaviour. These could focus around the support for a football team or the shared experience of a Rave Party. However they come together, "protocommunities" create shared values and perspectives. In the aftermath of the Hillsborough tragedy

1. Paul Willis, *Common Culture*, Open University Press, 1990.

we saw how deep these bonds can go. In the service of remembrance in the Roman Catholic Cathedral we saw the red and blue colours of Liverpool's two football teams on display. Here the informal world of being a football supporter and the more formal liturgical symbols were seen side by side. Such a meeting is extremely rare but it serves as an example of how the concerns of informal "proto-communities" may find an echo in the ministry of the Church. The groups that young people form are of deep significance and they need to be taken seriously.

Middle-class youth subcultures are generally more outlandish and Bohemian in nature. In the 80s groups of young people began to dress in Dr Marten boots and cut holes in their expensive designer jeans. Hair styles became much more ragged and some imitated the black style of dreadlocks. Bands like The Cure and The Smiths expressed an artistic dissatisfaction with the world. Curiously enough many of these young people who dressed so outlandishly were those who stayed on at school into the sixth form; and nowadays in Oxford young people dressed in these ways are all students at the university. Reading Maths or English does not require the same dress code as starting at Rover or getting on one of the few apprenticeship schemes that still exist. The leisure factor enjoyed by the middle-class young people who go on to university means that they can afford to maintain their rebellious way of dressing for much longer.

As the 90s get underway middle-class youth subculture exhibit a longing for community and spirituality. In many ways reminiscent of the 60s we are seeing the emergence of New Age Travellers who shun the sedentary lifestyle of their parents. The Rave scene characterized by the drug Ecstasy is attractive to many because of the sense of commonality and love it creates. Dancing together has a bonding function but the experience is also a mirror of religious feelings and emotions more common in mystical prayer and the charismatic movement.

The diversity of young people's style is aptly illustrated by half an hour watching *Top of the Pops*. There is a direct correspondence between the style of the artistes on this show and the fashion parade we see on the high street; but it is debatable which comes first. It seems evident that such pop stars do influence the way young people dress, but they also reflect the tastes and choices of their fans; and these "stars" were themselves part of local groups before fortune struck. The style of the British pop star has come from the streets as much as it has been packaged and manufactured by the record industry; and the style on the streets is determined especially by the structural divides in our society.

Young people experience social and economic realities in different ways. The impact of the 90s on middle-class young people heading for higher education and professional jobs will be markedly different than it will be on working-class young people leaving school at sixteen and looking for manual jobs. The trend away from manufacturing and towards high-technology service industries has already meant that many more young people are staying on at school or at colleges of higher education. GCSE retakes and other vocational courses are multiplying. Competition for places at universities is increasing but government loan schemes are at the same time making them even more difficult for the average young person to achieve. A £3000 debt is not uncommon amongst students starting out on their working lives.

GROUP IDENTITY

Young people create subcultures in response to the problems of becoming adults within our modern society. The writers of *Resistance Through Rituals*, concentrating on working–class male groups, identified this as the attempt to creat a "cultural space".[1] In their view when young people dressed in a similar way hung around in a shopping precinct or took to skateboarding through the town centre they were in effect creating a symbolic world which not only gave them a sense of belonging but which also was a resistance to the various pressures and problems which they experienced as they tried to grow up. The same could also be said of the Oxford student's strident display of having made it to Trinity, or the black teenager's bobble hat; both have meaning as symbols of belonging. Hebdige[2] however points out that some of these symbols are deliberately designed to shock. The Punk's use of bondage clothing or the biker's leather jacket point beyond themselves to much darker meanings of violence and sexuality; Hebdige calls this "semiotic guerilla warfare". But the concentration on resistance and rebellion in youth cultural styles, whilst it does point to structural tensions in our society as they impact upon young people, can lead us to ignore the more constructive aspects of teenage life. David Marsland talks of the "auto socialization"[3] of young people. What he means by this is that in their informal friendship groups young people together work out how they are going to move towards adulthood. The support, friendship and shared

1. Hall and Jefferson, *Resistance Through Rituals,* Hutchinson, 1975.
2. Dick Hebdige, *Subculture the Meaning of Style*, Methuen, 1979.
3. David Marsland, *Sociological Explorations in the Service of Youth*, National Youth Bureau, 1978.

values which are an everyday part of many young people's lives underlie the more sensational aspects of teenage style. The peer group, much maligned by evangelical youth group leaders because they fear its influence, is in many respects the one important factor which helps young people to grow up. Youth subcultures are a survival response to which young people themselves have resorted in the face of the many problems and contradictions[1] which characterize modern life.

EVANGELIZATION AND PLURALITY

In the past the Church has tended to be fairly monochrome in its outreach to young people. In one way or another we have said that young people must come to us if they want to be Christian. We lay on youth groups, youth missions, youth clubs and youth services but underlying the "youth" in all of these is a preset cultural package. In the 70s the influential work of John Bennington[2] recorded the experience of a group of working-class young people who responded to the outreach of an evangelical church in their local town. In poignant and very moving terms they described how with their Christianity came a set of cultural ideas and values which over a period of time left them estranged from their mates at work and even from their own families. Eventually they were faced with a stark choice between their working-class roots and their new-found faith. Most chose the former. The message of this book for the Church of England during this Decade is very

1. See Michael Brake, *Comparative Youth Culture*, Routledge Kegan Paul, 1985.
2. John Bennington, *Culture Class and Christian Beliefs*, Scripture Union, 1973.

clear: have we the theological and social courage to imagine the faith incarnated within anything other than a middle-class culture?

Tony Campolo writing of the American scene puts it this way:

> . . . we should be prepared to relate to a variety of subcultural types as we endeavour to communicate the Gospel. Teenagers of one subcultural group will require a linguistic approach, a program style, and a psychological understanding that will be different and distinct from that required to reach another subcultural group.[1]

The plurality which characterizes our society in terms of class, race and gender demands that we adopt a plurality of missionary styles. I use the word missionary deliberately. For what we need is an approach at a local level which involves committed adults reaching out to groups of young people. We may well learn a good deal by analysing the latest trends in video-making or the values portrayed in teenage magazines. But the key to evangelization will only be found if we are there with the groups of young people as they unpack these products of the media. The incarnation of the Gospel will involve us in thousands of such discussions. Our presence in these places will mean that we are able to work within the cultural frameworks and friendship groups which the young people create. To speak Christianly in these places will mean not simply that we take a pre-packaged Gospel as the panacea for all ills. It will mean that

---

1.   Anthony Campolo, "Youth Culture in a Sociological Perspective" in Benson and Senter, *The Complete Book of Youth Ministry,* Moody Press, 1987.

we have to work at seeing the relevance of the life, death and resurrection of Christ to particular issues.

FRIENDSHIP ACROSS CULTURES

The incarnation of the faith within youth culture will need to start at the level of small groups. Friendship between concerned Christian adults and groups of local young people will first need to be established. The ways that this friendship will be established will be many and varied, however from first to last it will need to be characterized by a concern to understand the concerns, joys, and values of the young people themselves. Mutual respect needs to be established before effective communication can take place. This cannot be got by cultural analysis of the media alone; being with young people is the only way to get street-wise. But "being with" is the first part of an incarnational approach to mission. As Jesus became a human being and lived amongst us the Church needs to stop inviting young people in and start to go out. Our youth services and youth groups are very often an attempt to hide in a safe and controlled environment. Incarnation on the other hand involves a risk. In the first place this means going to where young people hang out and making friends.

Friendship, however, will also involve us in starting to understand the world through another person's eyes; the ability to enter into the cultural world of a group of young people is essential. We need to be able to recognize where Jesus is already at work in that world. This may be in the strength of the friendship within the group, or maybe in some of the attitudes expressed by the group. Spirituality, as opposed to church attendance, is far from dead amongst young people. This is reflected for instance in Rave culture where spiritual ideas are constantly expressed in song lyrics. Young people will often have prayed or have had an experience of God in wonder or fear; so incarnational evangelization in the post modern 90s will need to start with the spirituality which young people themselves have already experienced. In the past in our concern to proclaim a unique revealed Christ we have failed to appreciate the work of the Spirit outside the Church amongst young people. We need to be able to discern these workings of the Spirit and affirm them and build on them.

Incarnational evangelization will readily deal with social issues as well as "spiritual" ones. The culture which young people create is defined by larger macrostructures and problems. To be in touch with young people at the local level is to see the effect that government economic policies have. During the Decade we will need to bring into dialogue those in the Church committed to issues of social justice with those on the ground floor who have befriended young people. This kind of linkage needs to be geared not only to prophetic statements and interventions in the name of young people but also to programmes which enable young people to express their own concerns and anxieties. These initiatives need to be driven from the grass roots up. Many attempts in the past have only served to reinforce the patriarchal nature of the Church by showing its dislocation from relationships with local groups of young people.

WORSHIP AND YOUTH CULTURE

Grass-roots involvement and friendship need to result in a genuinely indigenous expression of the faith. At present there is a remarkable movement towards the creation of new styles of youth worship within the Anglican Church. Not least amongst these is the Nine o'Clock Service in

Sheffield.[1] Incarnational evangelization will reject the temptation to imitate these services in the hope that more young people will be attracted into church. The life which we see in Sheffield and other places is not created by liturgical innovation alone. The heart of such services is to be found in genuine incarnational mission. Young people who are beyond the cultural and social boundaries of the Church are finding faith and expressing their convictions in worship. Such groups move freely within the world of youth culture. However their faith, which is taking root in that culture, is revealing itself in new and creative forms.

The use of visual images in worship is just one example of the way that youth culture through these services is enriching the liturgical life of our Church. In the past the Church's use of imagery was very static; but the idea that a service flows at a visual as well as at a verbal level is extremely important; suddenly another sense is stimulated in worship. Through the use of video and slide projectors and drawing on visuals in pop videos, these services are creating a new language for worship. Here pictures move and change as the worship progresses interacting with the service and moving people at a non-rational level to respond to God.

In these new kinds of services we are starting to see the fruition of evangelization which is concerned to incarnate the Gospel within the cultural world of young people. They point the way forward during the Decade but they also serve as warning. We may choose to simply replicate the results of such worship in our churches but we do so at our peril. These services point the way forward because they have arisen from years of relational outreach within the

1. The first part of the next chapter develops in detail the themes mentioned here in relation to the Nine o'Clock Service in Sheffield.

cultural frameworks of young people. They are an encouragement that the evangelization of young people during this Decade can renew the Church of England. However if we want the fruits without the relationships and friendships then we will soon lose touch with the emerging young generation. Youth culture rapidly changes and to be in touch with local young people is essential to the creation of alternative worship. But is the Church prepared for the costs of the evangelization which results in this kind of worship?

Students in Further Education

Pete Ward notes that an ever-increasing number of the young people about whom he writes are now students, whether in the FE or Sixth Form sector or in Universities or Colleges. Keith Stubbs has worked in FE Colleges, and writes here as the Executive Officer of the West Midlands Churches FE Project.

There can be few more stimulating, challenging and varied opportunities for evangelism among the growing generations, than amongst students. The Further Education sector, in particular, draws together a wealth and diversity of experience and social background. The rate and scope of change occurring in this sector, subject to central government planning and reactive to local needs, encompasses, on 1992 figures, some three million students. The sector is crucial to the churches' agenda for mission. Many Christian staff and students are currently living out their lives of discipleship in this pluralist and secular environment, which mirrors the tensions and frustrations, the hopes and expectations, of wider society. And yet, in a formal or structural sense, the churches have made little attempt to relate to and work alongside this vital sector in education.

In itself, this may not be bad, for the Christian Gospel is concerned primarily and essentially with people. But the good news has a social and community dimension which is concerned with structures and institutions: the reign of God breaks into the social and structural reality of our present age. The Further Education sector is a vibrant organism in which there is living interaction between education, vocational training, industry, enterprise and commerce: each an essential element of society. For many students within this sector, full and part time alike, Further Education represents a second chance to build up qualifications and experience, following earlier experiences of failure. In this lies something of the seed of the Gospel, and the imperative for the Church to understand and relate to the dominant culture and values expressed by students within the sector. This is not to misunderstand *inculturation*, (a term we should become accustomed to using), as *acculturation*, but as a dynamic process by which the Christian message comes to be affirmed and accepted, by the grace of God.

Acculturation is a sociological term describing a synthesis that adapts symbols, values and qualities from another group or society. Thus the missionary movements often imposed western cultural norms alongside their missionary activity. In contrast, *inculturation* is a theological term, describing a process of reliving the incarnation, which inserts the Gospel at the very heart of a culture. *Inculturation* is a real exchange and interaction, and a process of discernment to discover what is at the heart of the Gospel, and what belongs to the churches' culture of the time. *Inculturation*, thus understood, is synonymous with evangelization.

ASPECTS OF MISSION IN COLLEGES

It is important to acknowledge and support the ongoing witness to students by Christians in college. In a real sense, the Church visible is dispersed throughout the week, in witness and service. The People of God are called to be salt and light in their college context. Discipleship, vocation and the work-life ministry are the avenues through which the good news is proclaimed in college. Christian perspectives on issues arising from the curriculum, care and respect for students, good communication skills, management decisions informed by Christian values, and professional competence and integrity are examples of Christian presence and ministry to students in college.

There is little opportunity for overt evangelism, but imaginative and spiritually discerning staff will recognize openings and respond sensitively. Christian staff will develop different "ministries" in college as their discipleship and faith connect with the responsibilities of work. Such Christians are working at the edge, at the interface of secular and Christian visions and values. They need prayerful support and clear affirmation from their churches.

In partnership with local churches, and sensitive to the college context, events should be promoted that proclaim the reality of the Kingdom of God. For example, music, celebration or the action/support of agencies like Christian Aid and CAFOD should be considered as opportunities to "touch base" with students.

A church worker, seeking to work with college students, has no automatic right of entry into a college, and is granted access on the college's terms. This vulnerability is a gift that needs to be acknowledged. Something of the nature of the incarnation is re-enacted in the twin aspects of willingness both to relinquish power and to be exposed. The prologue to the fourth gospel lays the foundation for all we are discussing, "the Word became flesh, and lived among us" (John 1:14).

In seeking to work effectively amongst students, church workers will need to disengage and let go of those trappings and styles of working and thinking encrusted within Christian tradition. Many barriers are raised unwittingly by class, language, and predetermined expectations. Working in a college, and seeking to understand its complex dynamics and ethos, requires patience, interpersonal skills, analytical tools and the ability to reflect before God upon the day's discoveries.

In seeking to negotiate access to the student common room, or to promote events of an evangelistic nature in the college, it is essential that the church worker learns to listen to the rhythm of the college. It is vital to develop a strategy that meets students "where they are". Issues of relationships, study, employment, stress, finance, politics, justice, racism, access, success and competing values and beliefs are serious, everyday encounters for many students. "Loitering with intent", the familiar but overworked phrase to describe traditional chaplaincy work, is unlikely to be either effective or impressive as a style of work when outlined to college management teams. Supportive and genuine relationships are fundamental, but difficult to achieve without a structured vision.

An alternative strategy, and one requiring careful consideration of the local churches' available resources, centres on a curriculum input within the tutorial system. It might be argued that the level of resources made available by the churches is an indication of their commitment: the Further Education sector receives little from the churches. However, a small number of projects involving clergy or lay people from local churches are running in Further Education colleges nationally. These are concerned with an exploration of personal and social beliefs and values. Driving these projects is the desire to create dialogue, and to foster continuing enquiries into the realities of life around the students involved, on personal, community, national and international levels. Dialogue and mutual acceptance are crucial, within which the Holy Spirit is perceived as active. Within the curriculum framework, the teasing out of issues and concerns is the aim. But, connections between Christian faith and everyday living need to be made, and the application of Gospel insights to life is one step further.

Three million plus students present a remarkable challenge and opportunity to the churches. To seize the opportunity requires a reorientation of the churches' concerns, and a grasping of a Gospel vulnerability to move out into God's world.

University Students and Evangelism

In the universities (which now include the former polytechnics) and colleges the churches have a much longer experience of co-operating with the institutions themselves in the provision both of chaplaincy and of chaplaincy "plant". Angela Berners-Wilson, Senior Anglican Chaplain to the University of Bristol, describes some of the opportunities and questions that face the churches amid the varied expectations of students, of the institutions and of the churches themselves.

It is a fact of life in the 1990s that by far the majority of students in Higher Education in both universities and the (former) polytechnics have had little or no exposure to any of the Churches; they do not come from church-going families and they often have only the haziest idea about many of the Christian traditions. Of those who do come from a Christian background, some are keen to drop these ties the moment they arrive at college, as they are eager to experiment with new ideas, views and philosophies. They are also vulnerable to the pressures of the New Religious Movements. For others it is natural that they should seek out a Christian fellowship or denominational group within the college scene, for support, continuity and friendship. Others still will find their way to the Chaplaincy for friendship or hospitality; and some even see Chaplains *in loco parentis*.

Depending upon their previous experience of church and Christians, students will be either hostile to, hopeful about, or totally apathetic towards any evangelistic endeavour. For many, a negative attitude to "the Church", or anyone seen to represent it, is the norm. Students from agnostic or other faith backgrounds find it hard to believe that chaplains really want to help them without an ulterior motive. There is therefore some particular suspicion of Anglican chaplains who mainly see their role as "being there" for the whole institution, not solely for Anglicans; while other denominational chaplains tend to see their role as "being there" primarily for their own students – Catholic, Methodist, etc.

Some students have had bad experiences with school Christian Unions, which can close their minds to all types of Christian influence, however diverse. For students who find coming away to university a big culture shock, those who yearn for definite answers in a grey and perplexing world, and those comfortable with authority structures, the Christian Union approach can be very helpful, affirming and safe. For students of a more questioning nature, those who come from less evangelical backgrounds or more liberal Christian traditions, and those who have experimented with various beliefs, lifestyles and ethical values, the Christian Union approach is unhelpful. They will be more likely to get involved with chaplaincy activities, if they seek Christian answers at all.

Then there is another quite distinctive group who seek out chaplains because of a specific problem or need – relationship difficulties, loneliness, or because they have heard via friends or the grapevine that the chaplaincy is a good place to go for cheap meals, free coffee or a compassionate listening ear. They may be attracted to the activities organized by the chaplaincy, even if they have no particular religious or theological beliefs. One experienced chaplain has even described those who attach themselves to chaplaincies as "the Five Ls: the lost, the lazy, the lonely, the loopy and the lecherous"!

The strength of the Christian Union approach is that it does seem to attract greater numbers, and a sense of commitment, at least while the student is still at college. Its greatest weakness seems to be the very straight-down-the-line views of many of its members which is often a big "turn-off" to many secular students today. The strength of the more open chaplaincy approach is that it appeals to a wider group of students; and while requiring less commitment, it can, at the same time, help students to deepen and grow in their faith, and to feel free to question things in a caring environment where they will not be judged, but rather encouraged to learn about and live the Christian life. Its weakness is that it can be too woolly!

Within the chaplaincy itself there is a great divergence of views. Generally I believe it would be fair to say that Catholic and Free Church chaplaincy is based on a Benedictine viewpoint of offering hospitality and a place for people to gather, whereas Anglican chaplaincy is more Franciscan in its ideals – based on the chaplain getting known throughout the college, helping where needed, and trying to permeate the secular institution with a Christian presence, as well as identifying with other Christians already within the system.

There are of course many overlaps between all these approaches, and it has been a notable feature in recent years that the divide between Christian Unions and chaplaincies is, in many institutions, far less sharp than it used to be. Increasing co-operation between all Christian bodies must be the way forward in today's increasingly secular society, at a time when there is a very deep thirst in many young people for help and guidance about fundamental questions of life, the environment, green issues and justice and peace issues – in other words concerns very close to Jesus' message in the gospels. But they are completely "turned off" by any sort of religious or "churchy" jargon. The very word Christianity is sadly seen in negative terms, although their hearts are, very often, in the right place completely, and their agenda are often more pertinent to the Gospel message than some of the concerns of our churches.

Church Schools

The Church of England is in contact with many thousands of children and young people through its Aided and Controlled Schools. In them, too, thousands of its members, whether as teachers or as Governors, are engaged in working out the opportunities that this historic position affords the Church, as the education reforms of the last decade take effect. Schools are at least as varied as their contexts, and their head teachers as both; we invited one head of an Aided Secondary School, Peter Crook, to describe his own and his school's approach.

Growing up has been a fashionable idea in the mind of adolescents for some little time now! Notions of "what I want to be" pervade human instincts with an energy and an imperative which distorts values all too easily. Newspapers espouse certainties where healthy doubts ought to exist, and television provides role models of self-confident teenage super-heroes who make our own fumbling attempts at a philosophy of life look totally inadequate. Small wonder then, that youngsters are superficially armed with a self-dependence which has little room for a humble acceptance of God.

An openness towards dependence as a virtue is not amongst the listed attributes of those whose formative years were those of a Thatcherite 1980s either. For so many of our teenage children or young parents this has translated into a concentration of vision upon the material-istic and the vocational, and upon immediacy of function or reward.

How do we react to this in leading Church Schools within the state system, especially as this Decade of Evangelism follows such a time? As we may reflect upon the last decade in world politics as marking the beginning of a new era, so we may conclude that all is different and that the old answers will therefore not do any longer. Given the profound changes in the educational world over the same period, some may look at the Church's partnership with the state and dismiss a future for Church Schools as being based on an old order, and no longer relevant. This I cannot accept.

The education of young people is integral to the mission of the Church. Society, for the time being at least, has decreed that young people are brought together in schools. There-fore, *there* must the Church be also, for *there* would Christ himself have been, educating and influencing the masses.

Church Schools are critically accused of seeking to maintain a structural status quo at a time of great change, a dinosaur from an age long past, like black and white television or leaded petrol! However, just as nothing has an undeniable right to survive, so too must the Church School adjust to a new order whilst not compromising the integrity of its distinctive mission.

THE SCHOOL COMMUNITY

Returning to the notion of dependence, as a distinctive of mission, the Church School must assert the value and inherent goodness of a dependency relationship with God which encompasses all within that school, whether care-taker, head teacher, pupil or parent. Recognition of our dependence on God is a key to those qualities which hopefully we may still share with those of a more secular disposition; generosity of spirit, a compassionate outlook and a capacity for warmth in our relationships. We must always seek to create a climate in our schools where these are not seen as childish things, to be put away with the cycling proficiency badge or swimming certificate.

In an age where the media construct role models with alarming and almost instant alacrity, it is vital that youngsters have opportunity for exposure to credible alternatives who can illustrate and exemplify the strength of being a young Christian. It is for this reason that I am even more convinced of the value of 11–18 Church Schools than I would be for those establishments which cater for only the compulsory years of formal education. The value of the peer group as a role model seen daily in the flesh by the young adolescent is a key element of Christian witness in a Church School.

The culture of Christian warmth and love which can arise

from staff-pupil relationships is important, but if a sense of evangelism can be generated within the vertical structures of the pupil population then that sense of evangelistic mission must be strengthened. This may manifest itself in worship. Indeed, the nature of a dependency relationship with God must be based in worship. Visual and experiential opportunities for school worship across the year-groups is therefore vital in asserting the acceptability of mature dependency.

The Sixth Form ethos, which is the flagship of this Christian characteristic, must therefore never be compromised; and to this extent Anglican schools are faced with a dilemma, so familiar to our Catholic colleagues, in terms of admissions: that of the "character of the school". If we attempt a distinctive evangelistic approach to the mission of a Church School, we must show our enduring values even, perhaps especially, in the face of pressures of local financial management, curricular opportunities or direct competition with other providers.

Establishing or maintaining such opportunities for Christian witness is a delicate balance, depending upon one's range of missionary aims. For some, the spreading of the Gospel may be seen as pure evangelism, leading to the conversion of non-Christians. For others, it may be based upon building on the foundations of faith, nurturing a child through a time of powerful and conflicting pressures; illustrating that it is "all right" to be a Christian, and that the Gospel message is relevant in today's world.

THE SCHOOL AND SOCIETY

The implications for admissions policies are obvious yet complex. One issue is that of the religious or cultural affiliation of the intake; the other, in these days of

competitive survival, the socio-economic or even intellectual composition of those admitted.

It is my belief that, just as declaring a building to be of
architectural interest does not preserve it in such a
condition, neither does declaring a child to be born into a
Christian family guarantee an enduring faith. The conflicts
and inconsistencies which a child has to face in coming to
terms with the Gospel in a materialistic world are so
profound that it is vital that Christian families receive
support both from the parish structures and the Church
School. Where a child has individual special needs then this
may be especially necessary. The delicate child or the
individual with a physical abnormality must be supported
within the entire experience of that child – in the classroom,
playground, bus queue and sports field. That child must be
accepted and valued regardless of performance or background. To do this requires an atmosphere of tolerance and
empathy in a school, which is an essentially Christian
attribute and is an atmosphere sought by many of the
Church's schools.

Similarly, in a multi-ethnic and multi-cultural society,
the Anglican Church is forever broadening, and this too
should be welcomed and nurtured within our schools. The
often generation-based struggles of the Asian Christian
family or the tensions of fundamental beliefs within some of
the predominantly black community churches must be
acknowledged for the child by an education where there is a
secure and educative focus on the Gospel message. In this
manner the way to faith may be offered within the focus of
the Church School culture, in the belief that confusing
conflicts of message may be reconciled.

To that extent, I believe that we must open our Church
Schools to other denominations and house churches with
which a relationship can be established, inviting church and

faith leaders into a school communication system as openly as those with whom we have a more direct affiliation. Financial considerations may be raised in terms of the support or foundation of the school, but I believe that the challenge for our future as Christian schools is to be more embracing rather than exclusive in this respect.

This is a part of our evangelistic role, offering a unity of partnership with all Christian homes, parishes and groups for the benefit of a wider spectrum of families than may currently be the case. The accusation often levelled at Church Schools as a middle-class white ghetto should be offset by a more outward approach to those who follow Christ by other paths, to the enrichment of all.

I realize that I may have disappointed those who seek a role for Church Schools which is all-embracing in its intake of students in terms of religious affiliation. Although, in circumstances of plentiful provision of Aided School places, it may be possible to combine the roles of a Church School with those of a Community School, where such circumstances do not exist I cannot reconcile such a notion with my belief in the primary distinctive nature of the Church School, its ethos and holistic view of education of students for this world and preparation for the world to come. However, in contrast, neither do I promote the establishment of new, more tightly protected Christian Schools in which no alternatives to the Christian faith, or even a particular denominational view of it, are known, discussed or accepted as being of worth.

A Breadth of Vision

Because of space restraints I have had to omit a detailed analysis of the curriculum or schemes of work. However, I do believe in spiritual literacy and the promotion of service to God across the spectrum of education. The inspiration of the human spirit in pointing towards the sense of awe is fundamental to a dependency relationship with God. In extending our minds through science as a means of understanding this world we glory in God's bounty to us. Similarly, by exposing children to the wonders of art, music or literature we acknowledge a beauty of form and being rather than mere utility.

The whole curriculum must be delivered in a way which offers respect to the student, based on a relationship of a common journey of learning and a search for truth. As head teacher, I neither want my staff to indoctrinate nor to train, but to educate youngsters in values; for that is the evangelism which will foster equality of opportunity, social harmony and Christian love which we all seek.

Evangelism and Young Children

As long ago as Towards the Conversion of England *(1948), it was said that "Children are told they must wait and prepare themselves before they can fulfil life's big responsibilities. But Jesus needs them now, and they need him, and they can be as real and true Christians as grown-up people". But Alan Price, C.A., whom we asked to write about Evangelism and Young Children, still sees "is it right?" as the first question to be addressed.*

Many adults (understandably) have some anxiety about the evangelism of children with visions of emotional pressure applied to vulnerable children. Much child evangelism has consisted (and still consists) of presenting a condensed summary of the Gospel, with a challenge to respond with some kind of "decision" for Christ. Often the theology is an adult theology simply applied to children as "little adults". But we must not dismiss the numerous times when children's lives have been changed as a result.

Children's evangelists are united in saying that children need to know the Christian story – the basic story of God's love revealed in Christ. Children are able to understand and respond to God's love. They also need to be enabled to respond in a way that is appropriate to the child – but response is important. Each of us makes many responses to God – as adults as well as children, with each response acting like a milestone in the pilgrimage of faith.

HOW AND WHERE?

Evangelism often means setting up attractive special events in which the local church can advertise itself and present the Christian message. Bright, colourful publicity is used – for no one comes to events they don't know about! Some children (like their parents) feel distinctly uncomfortable in church premises. This means that the special "Holiday Week" or "Adventure Club" is therefore held on neutral territory – a community hall or school, etc. This kind of venue is much more easily decorated, especially if an adventurous "Jungle" or "Space" theme is adopted for the week. It also avoids the problem of fixed rows of pews which can dampen enthusiasm and hinder flexibility.

In our climate, open-air events are always vulnerable, but summer Beach Missions, etc., have been an important part of children's evangelism. Whatever the venue, all-age family events as part of a "Holiday Club" can be very productive, but in some areas, parents are simply not interested!

There are also opportunities for spontaneous evangelism with children. The local church could have a group of people, young and old, able to take advantage of a sunny day to go down to the local park or wherever children gather. Using music (live or recorded) and a short story-time (with bright, visual aids), possibly with some games, followed by a written invitation for children to take home, will often result in a number of children who want to know more.

Local schools give a good opportunity for pre-evangelism, establishing contacts between those involved in the children's work and the children as yet outside the church family. This may mean encouraging/enabling a leader in ordinary full-time employment to take an occasional day off to go into the school(s), to lead or speak at an assembly, or help in a lesson – or simply to be around to become known by the children. Establishing some kind of friendship makes the evangelistic process much easier. Some churches have taken the idea further, setting up a team able to visit a number of local schools for assemblies – often welcomed by hard-pressed teaching staff.

The writers of *All God's Children?* have said, "children seemed to gather around Jesus because he was an attractive character . . . His attractiveness lay not in glitter and hype, but in his love for all whom he met and his willingness to listen. He created a space in which they could find God for themselves" (8.25). This suggests that the scale and excellence of an evangelistic event are not as important as the people involved in that and the on-going children's ministry. People need training as well as enthusing. More than ever before, it seems, there is an abundance of advisers willing and able to help, including Christian teachers of day schools and organizations like Scripture Union, the Church Army, the Church Pastoral Aid Society, etc., as well as the diocesan children's advisers.

EVANGELISM MEANS CHANGE

Evangelism always means change – never a comfortable thing, and frequently resisted. In much of the children's evangelism that has taken place over recent years, the follow-up and integration into the life of the local church has often been the "weak link". Children have felt quite frankly unwanted! With poor facilities, few resources and untrained (and often unsuitable) Sunday School teachers, there is much evidence of an attitude that says that as long as children are "looked after", the real work can take place with the adults. Attracting children is easier than keeping their interest. Many churches have wonderful events that attract children in (comparatively) large numbers, but very few come into regular contact with the church. From a child's point of view, what is special and normal to a congregation may be totally alien and meaningless – even frightening. Things may need to change – even things we treasure. Is our evangelism of children just to pass on tradition? Are we expecting the new children to be "just like us", or are they to be allowed to be the new generation of Anglicans? These are the hard questions which will cause much anguish and find no easy answers as we seek to be faithful to God's calling.

Part of the necessary change may be in the theological colleges and courses. Most clergy have little or no training in children's and youth work; yet as curates some are still given that responsibility in their first parish. The colleges and courses must surely make such work more of a priority in training, recognizing the equal priority of children in the energy and efforts of parish staff, whilst realizing that not all ordinands have the necessary gifting for children's ministry.

The final recommendation of *All God's Children?* is as follows: Everyone concerned with children should ask what sort of Church and society they would like to see in thirty years' time – and what needs to be done now in order to enable that vision to be realized (p. 89).

Taizé and Young People.

Many young people have found Christian faith come alive for them for the first time as they have gone away, generally in a group and sometimes wondering why, to an event like Greenbelt, or to a place like Iona or Medjugorge, Corrymeela or Taizé. Last year, as he mentions in his opening chapter of this book, the Archbishop of Canterbury accompanied 1000 young people to Taizé; and in writing about this one particular place, Paul Battersby suggests why this experience of "going away", and of "holy places", can be so powerfully affecting.

In this Decade of Evangelism, and beyond it, Taizé stands as a unique beacon of hope, enrichment, spiritual growth and youthful exuberance. The Taizé community was founded by the young Protestant Roger Schutz at the end of the Second World War. As a direct result of his wartime experience, helping Jewish refugees to escape Nazi persecution by crossing into neutral Switzerland, Schutz began praying for reconciliation and unity with a small group of friends.

They were fired with a vision – a new Christian community dedicated to the ideal of Christian unity, a bridge between long-separated traditions, particularly Roman Catholics and Protestants.

Re-establishing monastic community life within the Protestant tradition is unusual. Brother Roger's community, based by the small village of Taizé in mid-eastern France towards the Swiss border, became widely respected, in ecclesiastical circles at least, in the fifties and early sixties.

He was a good friend of Pope John XXIII and worked behind the scenes at the second Vatican Council where his ecumenical wisdom was much valued. It wasn't however until the late sixties that what Taizé has become internationally famous for began to take root – the vision of a Council of Youth.

It would be fair to say that the student "revolutionary" movements in Paris and elsewhere in the late sixties, particularly 1968, were indicative of the same searching, radical culture of youth for which Taizé became another focus.

At Easter 1970, 2500 people, mostly teenagers, came to Taizé from all over Europe to prepare for the Council, 16,000 in 1972 and 40,000 in 1974 for its launch. By this time, the Community had worldwide links, small "cells" of brothers establishing themselves in the developing world's towns and cities amongst the poor, the homeless and the destitute. Their letters would be read out during worship at Taizé and discussed in groups.

Apparently the original vision in the seventies was that the Council of Youth would draw young people together from all over the world, for ecumenical dialogue, common worship and inspiration to radical action and then cease, having fulfilled its function. Now in 1993 the Council of Youth is still continuing!

The community itself has expanded around the world. There are lay "Taizé" groups in Britain and elsewhere meeting ecumenically for regular prayer, worship and reflection in the Taizé style, but the magnetic draw is still the pilgrimage to Taizé itself.

Much, but not all, that can be said about Taizé can be said about any sizeable residential experience with young people. Whenever young people gather away from home, making new friends, experiencing new and different forms of liturgical design, there is a richness and excitement generated that can inspire and edify.

This can be as true of a parish weekend away at a diocesan youth centre as at Greenbelt, Iona, Spring Harvest, Walsingham or Lourdes. The very experience of a creatively led and well-planned and well-resourced residential event is often seminal in the lives of adolescents and young adults.

There are, however, extra dimensions to the Taizé experience. One of the glories of Taizé is that a group of young people can return from a week's pilgrimage each with a different experience to value and from which to grow, whether they are regular churchgoers or "fringe" people largely attracted by camping in France with friends. For some it will have been the Bible-studies led by Taizé brothers, for others it will have been the experience of the rich Taizé liturgy or the very experience of worshipping alongside 10,000 other young people in the aircraft-hangar of a chapel. For some it will have been the first (and then often lifelong) contact with young Christians from Rome or Rio or Madras; others will have had a unique time of personal renewal in the extended contemplative periods of silence.

There are cautionary tales too. All accommodation is under canvas; meals and ablution facilities are basic. The "on-site" rules can appear unnecessarily harsh to the newcomer on the first day. Sometimes this is due simply to the translated English not containing the niceties of everyday speech – no alcohol on site, no visiting the village, permission needed from a brother to leave the site, segregation of the leaders from their young people, segregation of the sexes, apparently compulsory Bible-studies and the subtleties of sexism in the manifestation of an all-male community brother-hood.

However, for by far the majority of pilgrims, the Taizé experience rises above these early exigencies as new human relationships are forged, Christian fellowship is enabled and the God of peace, justice, reconciliation and love is worshipped and encountered.

Chapter Five

PARTICULAR PERSPECTIVES

For many Christians the Decade of Evangelism brings a very specific and sharply focused challenge. Often, because of their sphere of service, they see a particular need very strongly. They are seeking to interpret the task of evangelism among one particular section or area of our nation's life.

In this chapter we include some examples of these special vocations. By their very commitment and belief in their own vocation, each of our contributors here would want to devote much more space to their theme. We would love to oblige each of them! It is because there are so many areas of concern and priority that we have had to wield our editorial power to confine all but the first of them to a very small section. In a sense we have asked them to set out a particular case in brief; it is for the reader to take it further and integrate it into the total vision of our individual vocations and that of our particular local church.

The Nine o'Clock Service

We open these special perspectives with a challenge from the Rev. Chris Brain. He speaks from his experience as Team Leader of the Nine o'Clock Service in Sheffield, where they have pioneered ways of relating to many aspects of the culture of our day which, on first reading, may seem strange to many clergy and congregations *within the Church of England. We have included this contribution, the longest in this chapter, because we feel it merits reading and rereading to ensure that we explore some of the more radical challenges to our understanding of mission and evangelism.*

The Church in the 1990s is in a completely new missionary situation. Through the power of modern technology and contemporary economic and political realities, a new global worldview is emerging. Our postmodern era has been united by current technologies into an instantaneous 24-hour information world. In the West there is a growing insistence that we must live in the present, with a plural and heterogeneous range of lifestyles and viewpoints. In this multifaith, multicultural, chaotic, white noise society, the Church's language and dogma aren't heard, because the old ways of presenting them just do not work – 97 per cent of the English population is, broadly speaking, outside the Church. Western culture is struggling to come to terms with the new realities; environmental catastrophe looms on the horizon – at the present rate of deforestation, the rainforest will be destroyed in just 50 years, taking with it ecosystems which contain 90 per cent of all the earth's wildlife species, which it has taken 18 billion years of creative process to produce. In the midst of ecological disaster and the decline of Western culture, whose addictive, destructive nature is being increasingly recognized, humanity is in pain. Millions are starving and dying for the lack of basic necessities in the Third World, and people in the West, in relative material affluence, are often in spiritual and psychological agony. The Church seems irrelevant and indeed, to a growing percentage of young people, even part of the cause. The Gospel is not heard.

The enormity and urgency of all this shapes our thinking, and was behind the Nine o'Clock Service's national worship event. "Passion in Global Chaos", described by the Church of England Newspaper as "the largest alternative service ever staged in this country". An explosion of stroboscopic lighting and high-powered computer simulations bombarded the 15,000-strong congregation; performance art and energetic rave dancers led people in worship; loud house music and rap pulsated across the field; and the leaders of the service exhorted everyone to participate in global and planetary salvation, to "make God happen now" and "use their lifeforce". This was the response of one of the congregation: "I went feeling apathetic and powerless about life. By the end, something had woken up. The picture had changed from black and white to colour, and I was kick-started into a new awareness. There was no manipulation – it was a response that came from something primal and aching within me. It was a response to an expression of worship that exploded with life, passion, pain, chaos and beauty." Others, including some of the press, described it as "phenomenal" and "astounding". In stark contrast, a queue of people demanded that the plug be pulled on the service, claiming it was New Age and blasphemous, pagan, overtly sexual and grotesque. This kind of conflict has become normal for the Nine o'Clock Service.

So What is the Nine o'Clock Service?

It is a nascent church, a community of people seeking to develop in practice an authentically Anglican church model, which has been given the freedom to experiment, by David Lunn, the Bishop of Sheffield, on behalf of the whole Church within the boundaries that hold the Anglican Communion together. The Nine o'Clock Service has grown uncomfortably out of St Thomas, Crookes, Sheffield to become a parish church in its own right. It is called the Nine o'Clock Service partly because nine o'clock was the only time available for the congregation to meet in the church building, and partly because it seemed the natural time for people from the club culture to get together to celebrate. Started in 1986, it has grown rapidly. For example, numerically, it has grown from a congregation of only 60 people, to one of over 500, whose average age is in the late twenties; in 1989 100 people were confirmed in a single service. The service has inspired many other groups, and been copied in dozens of places around the country. This growth has been centred around a group of artists and musicians who were on the fringes of the Church, or outside the Christian faith. They were at the heart of house music and multi-media experimentation in the early 1980s, and activists in social, political and environmental concern. This group formed a base community whose initial focus was a discovery of the practical implications of committed discipleship and the development of a just and sustainable lifestyle, which is now at the heart of the Nine o'Clock Service.

The church now attracts two main groups of people – those whose search for God has already been taking place in the world, in their work in environmental and justice issues, which they are then able to redefine through Jesus Christ – they are often looking for a spirituality that their political activities lack. The second group are those who come to find healing – a personal wholeness that happens through social and spiritual healing in the community. Another smaller group are the rebellious returnees – Christians who, because of cultural alienation reacted against the Church, and have now been given a way back in. It's a mixture of people looking to continue their search for, and find practical evidence of, a vision that includes hope, community, healing for the planet, sexual justice and food for the starving, in an open, non-dogmatic atmosphere.

A REDISCOVERY OF THE GOSPEL

Identifying with, and a growing awareness of, the pain of the Third and First World peoples and of the planet itself has led to a discovery of the Gospel imperatives for our time and a new understanding of what salvation means today. Salvation has often only been seen in personal, corporate or political terms, but now the Gospel cries out to us to see salvation in total terms. The context today into which the good news is proclaimed is one of ecological disaster, of planetary death and of human disintegration. The eschatological vision of recovering a good and "perfect" creation from the past is no longer credible, because of what we have learned about the history of the universe from science. The relegation of the Kingdom entirely into the future has equally lost credibility, due to the collapse of modernism and the great utopian philosophies. The "God now" of realized eschatology, in the light of the possible extinction of the human race in the next few centuries, could be seen as the only practical theology.

For the Nine o'Clock Service, co-operating in Christ's saving work now means taking full responsibility for our planet. Denial of that responsibility means denial of the saving work of Christ and collusion with the growth of pollution, oppression and biocide. Salvation will mean putting humanity back together with itself and with creation; choosing life instead of death.

We are reeling under the size of that task. The bludgeoning of media de-sensitization, producing complacency in a culture of low esteem, and the scope and vision of this enormous mission becoming clearer, meant that our need to find a source of energy and motivation to overcome this deadly inertia became paramount.

LIFEFORCE – FUEL FOR RECONSTRUCTION

The Church is discovering this motivation at the very heart of the nature of God. We found that "the Father" was not an emotionally unavailable white male in a lab coat, but that his passion is written large in the Scriptures, in the Passion of Jesus and in the lives of many of the saints. Passion means choosing to live, not merely choosing not to die. It covers a spectrum from the rediscovery of our senses to the refusal to get used to injustice. It means greater play and savouring of life, but also a greater hatred of anything that devalues life, whether it's people's pain and loss, the state of the planet, or destructive immoral relationships. God's passion, his lifeforce, is his "ruach" or "dabhar" (Hebrew words for *wind/spirit* and *creative word*) – the creative energy that brings life into being and sustains it. God's Spirit gives us that same creative energy to drive and motivate us, but its power is weakened by our fear of our bodies and the dualistic dislocation of the spiritual and the material. We try to control and restrain them, but they are a tremendous source of untapped power that can be used in Christ-like affirmation of life. The compassionate power that made Jesus' "guts turn over" and raised Lazarus from the dead is an example of this passion.

The Nine o'Clock Service endeavours to offer a non-dogmatic, free choice, where guilt and repression are lesser motivators, and vision, life, freedom, justice, passion and excitement are real currency. Christian community, in that context, is a place where complacency is turned into compassion. We believe that with the escape from a reductionist, scientifically rationalized worldview, and from the claustrophobic Enlightenment dogmas, religion – a celebration of Life and of what a religious life of faith offers humanity – is critical in finding a new way forward. Surely this is the real charismatic movement. The Nine o'Clock Service is open for anyone, including people of other faiths, to join us in celebration of lifeforce, the ultimate source of which we, as Christians, see as Jesus. We see the Spirit of God at work in the world as people fight for justice, seek out truth, and create beauty, but also at work in the universal Church. The only way, for us, of drawing these together and bridging the gap has been through a dynamic of oscillating between the two. The Spirit of God has again and again drawn us to where he is at work in the world, so that we can define that work in terms of Christ.

A UNIVERSAL LANGUAGE

Because the formation of language and the communication of truth within culture – we now know – are directly linked (*so – Michel Foucault*), the participation of Christians at the forefront of the creation of culture and language is essential today if we are to have the tools to communicate the Gospel. There needs to be a rediscovery, in a secular sense, of many things in common language that in a more openly religious society would describe the reality of God. The Nine o'Clock Service is seeking to use a language that anyone can understand, whether they're inside or outside the Church, so that there's no split between "sacred" and "secular" language. The work of creating this language has been called for over many years. We are trying to parallel in practice the work of theologians such as Jurgen Moltmann (*See his books, God in Creation; The Spirit of Life*) and Hans Küng (*see Global Responsibility*), to use a universal language that connects with the experience of people throughout the world and provides a common framework or communication system between the major world faiths. For example, talk of the "Holy Spirit" is meaningless to many people, but terms like "the spirit of life" or "passion for living" will strike a chord in most people's experience. Hans Küng's work towards a language for the creation of a global ethic centres around defining and agreeing a common understanding of "humanity". The Nine o'Clock Service is working in a world where there is an increasingly open market of religions and beliefs, where Christianity will need to show up favourably in these "God" or "life" terms. However, in this apparently competitive environment, we believe that all faiths, including Christianity, need to be judged in the light of Christ. The discovery of how Christ is "a light to the Gentiles" in our modern world is a central part of the Church's mission.

THE UNFREEZING OF THE UNIVERSE

Many are saying that we are on the brink of a new Renaissance, as significant as the Reformation. Recent scientific discoveries show a universe which is not as hostile to a spiritual perspective as Newtonian science once thought. Previous mechanistic models of nature and consciousness showed a "steady state" universe, where natural laws controlled a clockwork cosmos. This reductionist view of humanity and nature froze time, froze space and eventually froze God. But even quantum physics and chaos theory have shown that these models are incomplete (*see Ilya Prigogine, From Being to Becoming. Time and Complexity in the Physical Sciences*). Creation (including humanity) is more than the sum of its parts. A holistic approach is crucial; relationship and interaction are basic to the way the world works. We can no longer see ourselves as separate from nature – we are all given a chance to participate in the story of the universe. We are all in it together – people, particles and God. This creates a future open to all possibilities, where God's active creativity is happening now. There is a continuing creating process built into the design of the cosmos – God shares in the development of our evolving universe and is "in process", just as the universe is. In this openness to the future, God becomes one who is intimately involved in his universe, who evokes a personal response from her creatures. Through Christ, hope is built into the very fabric of space, time and matter. Now is hope, now contains the possibility of the resurrection.

THE NEW ART

God has made us "co-creators" – creativity is a fundamental law of the human psyche, just as it is for the universe. This is part of the creative process happening. To recover this sense that we are a special part of the living dynamic whole, we will need to release the locked up creativity that is in every human soul, to revalue creativity as a moral virtue. The mechanistic worldview of the past era emphasized the virtue of obedience; the new cosmology releases the virtue of creativity for a "new modern" era. By creativity I do not mean the modern concept of art as an objective consumer product – "art on the wall", but rather the totality of creative humanity seen in the person of Jesus. This is not only expressed in compassion-led justice, but also in worship-making. Through poiesis, through visual spectacle, through the erotic realm of myth, symbol, poetry, song, dance and ritual (*see Mircea Eliade, The Myth of the Eternal Return*), through using the totality of human experience and emotion – body, mind and soul – we encounter the living God and express his nature in the world.

To do this we have drawn heavily on the deep resources found in our own Christian tradition and increasingly on the riches of other world faiths. Some of these allow us to reparticipate with the body of nature, and encourage intimate communion with the natural world. The natural seasons and festivals were at one time integral to church life, which was woven with the cyclical rhythms of the natural order. The significance of these festivals has largely been lost, but in regaining their meaning we can provide the community with a concrete way of understanding God that is not removed from nature, and works out in ritual ways of addressing the cataclysmic problems facing our species. This is where the churches can help to move people towards the dramatic metanoia, the change of consciousness that is necessary within the entire human order. Only this kind of deep repentance will lead our world into feeding the starving and healing the planet, and into the new biospheric politics which the crises of our time demand.

A RECOVERING COMMUNITY AROUND THE ALTAR OF THE NEW CREATION

Walking into one of the weekly services at Ponds Forge in Sheffield city centre, you are confronted by an ever-expanding series of concentric circles – a circular table, which appears at first to be a sun and the crescent moon, but is in fact a picture of an eclipse, the new creation emerging out of the old. The table is in the centre of a ring of pillars, and hundreds of people gather in the circular underground chamber to hear and experience the word of God. All of this is a visual analogy of the planet we inhabit, and of the curved nature of the universe, designed to join with the powerful re-emergence of awe, mysticism and natural theology which is starting to take place. In this picture, the sacraments are at the epicentre of a "New Big Bang", with ripples of lifeforce spreading out like shockwaves. Massive video screens continually feed images of nature, the universe and humanity. It is a sea of paradox – hi tech, but with the ambience of an ancient crypt. It is designed to be a place where beat, meditation, dance and light can reconnect people with God, transforming their vision of the world. This is the Nine o'Clock Service's "Planetary Mass", and the central core of our existence as a eucharistic community.

The service is an interpretative symbol for the reality of the worship already happening in creation. The whole universe is invited to an intimate event – the feasting on the cosmic Christ. In a sense, the church has no walls – we worship with and on behalf of plants, planets, animals and angels, celebrating Christ as the origin, the Alpha, the source of all creation – the local community in the context of the great cosmic community. Creation, aware of its limitations, straining towards its fulfilment in Christ, sees in him the hope of wholeness and of freedom from sin and decay. Therefore, at the communion table we celebrate not only what is, and what is to come, but also becoming. As Christ is behind the creative explosion started at the Big Bang, and is the lifeforce of nature's continuing rebirth on its journey to fulfilment, we break the bread of the universe and drink the blood of the cosmos, a microcosm of the vast macrocosm.

Christ, the new creation, draws all things together – religious faiths, peoples, cultures, history, nature – not into a uniform pattern, but into a kaleidoscope of teeming plurality, of ever-changing, ever-growing life. If the beauty of the world now shows us the incredible diversity, creativity, and contradiction of God, what must the fulfilment – "heaven" – be like?

The very elements of the sacraments – bread, wine, water – presuppose the goodness of creation and of the products of human labour. This is their traditional suitability as sacramental symbols, but complacent affluence detaches us from their value. For example, a slice of bread does not have the same inherent symbolic worth as it would for a Third World subsistence community, or even for our own underclass. In a country of relative prosperity, we can recover the core value of these symbols by ensuring that our worship is truly a global event, where all are in some way represented, our extravagance and the poverty of the Third World side by side. Connecting with the universe and with heaven is only possible by welcoming the poor and their power to reveal where the Kingdom of God is hidden. Otherwise we will not be offering real religion – for "true religion feeds the poor".

EXODUS – STATISTICS TO DIVINE LIKENESS

It is at the altar of the new creation that we can clearly see the damaging effects of our disconnectedness from the earth, from each other and even from ourselves. It is here that we are beginning to find hope of planetary salvation and of human reconciliation, and within our local community, recovery and release. Here we come to the cross, where Christ identifies and is present with us in our pain and oppression. In many ways our church is being birthed out of this pain and profound lack of self worth, caused by abuse done to us, often the abuse of power, and by our addictions to the culture's idols – to work, sex, drugs, relationships, religion, shopping, war – the list seems endless. But now we can see that the Bible clearly states what science is rediscovering – we are linked back to God in creation, and God is both behind the universe in Christ and in our basic nature. We can recover the belief that we are of inexpressible value. We are not just a cosmic statistic. We can experience the power and the hope of the resurrection, coming through and after the dark self-emptying of God on the cross. We can learn to face the violation and destruction all around us and within us. The challenge to us is to form de-centred corporate liturgies that enable us to mourn this destruction and to cultivate a compassion that feels in our own flesh the wounds inflicted on others and on the planet, and an intolerance of the numbness which actively colludes with the death system – to cultivate passion for life and for justice.

The Nine o'Clock Service is struggling to work out new ways of living a religious life of faith in an emergency situation, and to reinterpret the neglected riches of the creation traditions with a renewed vision of redemption, not just to preserve the world but to co-create cultures that will take humanity and creation in Christ to eternal salvation. In this setting, the ritual of holy communion is lifeblood for recovery. Today, we hear Christ calling the whole world together to prevent the end of the planet and to uncover again the hope of the Gospel for a new humanity and a new earth. The high street Pentecostal prophets didn't really understand, but their text rings true to us after all – REPENT, THE END IS NIGH!

Men and the Gospel

There are other (perhaps more traditional-sounding) sections of our community who also seem to be bypassed by much of our evangelism. Often the cry in churches is, "Why are there so few men?" And we all know of the experience of the clergyman calling at a house and the door being answered by "Dad" who keeps him hanging on with the words, "Wait a minute while I fetch the wife." At its best this can be saying something very positive about the mother as the guardian of spiritual interest within the home. Sadly, more often, it speaks of the distance between the Church and most men in our society. Recently there has been a growing concern to reach men with the Gospel. Daniel Cozens, an evangelist and the Ely Diocesan Missioner, has been one of the pioneers in this field. He writes with passion that matches his commitment to his vocation as an evangelist amongst men.

With the exception of Northern Ireland, the churches in Britain are largely failing in the task of bringing the Gospel of Christ to men.

The increasing secularization of our country, the insularity of the Church, and Christians who do not know, let alone love their neighbours as themselves – doubtless all contribute to the difficulty. But the real cause of the problem is more fundamental. It has, I suggest, to do with the lack of seriousness on the Church's part concerning the call of Christ on our lives. Christ taught that discipleship was all or nothing: a person must forsake all to follow him and unless we teach the same we will do no "catching of men".

So often Christianity is presented in terms of it "fitting in" with men and their lifestyles. Sometimes every effort is made not to upset or inconvenience! Yet this is quite contrary to the Gospel. In Jesus' own words if a man does not "hate" his family and even his own life, he cannot be a disciple. In Dietrich Bonhoeffer's stark phrase: "when Christ calls a man he bids him come and die."

I well remember being asked to preach at a men's breakfast which was advertised as follows: "A full English Breakfast; start at 8.30 a.m. and we intend to be finished by

10.00 a.m. so that you can get out on the golf course." I was not surprised when only 13 turned up; I wouldn't have gone had I not been the speaker! When due to speak at another church where a men's breakfast was planned I ensured that that experience was not repeated. It was announced that there would be no food and that the speaker wanted to see all the men of the church at 4.00 a.m. The vicar "negotiated", as he put it, 2 hours compromise and the meeting was set for 6.00 a.m. The room was packed with 90 men and when, following a sermon on single-mindedness for Christ, a response was called for, most of them stood to dedicate their lives to the service of Christ. I know of men who consider that meeting to have been a turning point in their lives and are now, years later, fully involved in evangelism.

A crucial issue, therefore, in winning men for God is, in preaching the Gospel, to make Christianity as important as Christ said it was. C. S. Lewis commented: "If Christianity is true, then it is of the greatest importance. If it is not true, then it is of no importance. The one thing it cannot be is of moderate importance." Moderation produces blandness and men are neither fooled nor attracted by it. In my years of evangelism it seems that it is this "all or nothing" aspect of the Gospel which is particularly compelling to men.

It follows that we ought never to apologize for presenting the Gospel for it is "the power of God for the salvation of everyone who believes". The challenge of the Gospel is bound up in the love and holiness of God and the call to live a life of total dedication to Christ. When Christ and his cross are preached without fear or favour then there is often a very great response in the lives of men.

People outside the Church must see that the men in the Church regard serving Christ as their first priority and that in loving and serving him is a person's full realization as a human being. For many men in our churches their sense of value and self-worth are realized through their "secular" employment rather than through their relationship with Christ. A man will often up and leave, with his family, almost automatically to go anywhere his firm asks him. I am not saying this is necessarily wrong, or that a man should not pursue promotion but Christ must have the first call on our life rather than a man's best energies and first devotion being given to his daytime job.

If we are to reach men with the Gospel we must relate to them as Jesus did. In the story of Jesus' encounter with the rich young ruler we read "Jesus looking on him loved him". There was evidently something in the look and in the body language of Christ that made the people who watched him say "look how he loved him". We too must demonstrate genuine love and be with men where they are in their places of work, in pubs and other places of leisure and recreation. This is where Christ would go and where we must go if we are to bring Christ to men and men to Christ.

Men enjoy meeting with other men yet often in the churches there is little, if any, opportunity for them to do this. So the men of our churches must own the responsibility of men's work by sacrificial prayer and the organization of group activities for men. In my experience, church men's groups can have a lot of fun. Such a group with strong leadership and good planning, whose members are dedicated to Christ and his holiness, who are single-minded and prepared to take risks with regard to sharing their faith, and where Christian care is demonstrated in practical ways, will naturally reproduce.

In addition to activities such as men's breakfasts and supper meetings to which guests are invited, a formula that has been of great value is for a room to be hired in a local pub (landlords are generally very amenable to such a request for a Christian meeting), for the men of the church to pray, for guests to be brought and for a Christian to speak plainly about the love and giving of God through his Son – what the cross of Christ means. The natural setting and the directness of the approach has proved most effective in reaching men.

We were able to put all these principles into practice during the "Walk of 1000 Men", a 3-week mission down the Pennines in 1991 and found that the repercussions were successful beyond our imagining. It caused most of the hundreds of men involved to say, "This was the greatest time of our lives." As someone else commented, "We had New Testament results because we went out in New Testament ways."

We live in an age of great opportunity for the Gospel, yet if we are to see men brought into the Kingdom of God they must see that Christianity is of paramount importance, as demonstrated in the lives of the men of the Church. Christian men whose lives are marked by holiness, love, social involvement and care are the key to bringing others to Jesus, the Son of God who gave his all that we might live and bids us follow him.

Feminism and Evangelism

Daniel Cozen's plea "as a man for men" leads necessarily to a call "from a woman for women". There is a clear indictment here as there was in the call to evangelism among men. The Church is beginning to take note of the shoddy way in which it has so often treated women. Here it is the Church's own witness and attitudes which need evangelizing afresh by the Gospel. And in this Decade of Evangelism, this work of addressing the Gospel within, to our

*inherited attitudes and structures, cannot be avoided. But is the
Decade as we know it obscuring this evangelization of the Church
itself? We are grateful to Sister Lavinia Byrne, IBVM
(Associate Secretary for the Community of Women and Men in
the Church – a programme within the Council of Churches for
Britain and Ireland), for facing us with a feminist critique of the
Decade of Evangelism.*

A feminist critique of the Decade of Evangelism notes first
that the Decade has been achieved at a cost. As it moves into
the light and consumes the churches' money, energy and
resources, so the "other decade" gets cast into the dark and
is ignored.

THE OTHER DECADE

What other decade? 1975 was the United Nations International Women's Year and gave rise to an international
decade for women. At its closing conference which was
held in Nairobi, a Methodist bishop declared, "what we
need is a churches' decade for women". The World Council
of Churches launched this in 1988; its British launch came at
Easter with a large service in Westminster Abbey. 1993
marks the middle of the decade and affords us the
opportunity to assess how well it has been implemented in
the British and Irish context. So far the best response seems
to have come from the Free Churches.

From the beginning the aims of the decade have been
quite clear:

1. Empowering women to challenge oppressive structures
   in the global community, their country and their
   church.

2. Affirming – through shared leadership and decision-making, theology and spirituality – the decisive contributions of women in churches and communities.

3. Giving visibility to women's perspectives and actions in the work and struggle for justice, peace and the integrity of creation.

4. Enabling the churches to free themselves from racism, sexism and classism; from teachings and practices which discriminate against women.

5. Encouraging the churches to take actions in solidarity with women.

It puts the following priorities before the Christian community:

1. Women's full participation in church and community life.

2. Women's perspectives and commitments to justice, peace and the integrity of creation.

3. Women doing theology and sharing spirituality.

Of course there are problems. This decade did not originate in Rome or Canterbury. Arguably it comes to us with the blessing of neither. A product of the Third World and of women, it is easily pushed aside. On the one hand it has become a decade of women in solidarity with other women; at its most unredeemed, it remains a decade – as the previous two thousand years – of women in solidarity with the Churches. The Churches meanwhile persist in upholding a social order which is sexist, and echo the worst faults of paternalism in the way they order their own affairs.

How can any news the Churches offer claim to be "good" when it conspires to undermine the liberating message of Jesus and proclaim one set of values to men, another to women?

EVANGELISM AND TRIUMPHALISM

Hence the insight that the Decade of Evangelism celebrates a triumphalistic way of working and inter-relating. Both its content and now its methodology require a feminist critique. It is about truth certainly, and about proclaiming truth, but the mode that is used is becoming increasingly narcissistic. Some become Narcissus, proclaimers of the word; for others meanwhile the only role is that of Echo. Both stances are radically unhealthy, as they set a scene which is already all too familiar to Christian women, even within clergy marriages. Powerful men with overinflated egos are matched by depressed women. At home or privately, these men may own to fatigue, to questions and doubts: but here again the women who surround them are cast in an all-too familiar role, condemned to wash now their men's socks, now their shirts, and now their emotional laundry.

Whose truth is proclaimed by a Decade of Evangelism? The truth of men, the truth of women or that of all humanity? How is this truth to be proclaimed? By muscle and might? Or by renewal and reform? Muscle and might suppress voices of dissent. Muscle and might ultimately withhold the healing hand of Jesus.

Renewal and reform, meanwhile, offer us a different methodology. The requirement now becomes that we put our own house in order before we attempt to address a liberating word – a Gospel word to the world. The Churches' authority is not absolute; it depends upon the extent to which we are able to listen to the voice of God. And God calls all to repent of real sins, not imaginary ones. God calls us to contrition and never to guilt. Our sins are all too apparent to those outside the Churches, so too could our repentance be – if we were prepared to opt for a renewal and reform which demonstrate our readiness to listen to the voiceless and the invisible in our midst, in a word, to the *anawim* (the "poor" in biblical language), to women in our midst.

A HERMENEUTIC OF SUSPICION

A feminist critique of the Decade of Evangelism offers more than condemnation, however. It proposes alternatives. It notes that a solid-state view of God, the universe and human society will no longer do. A solid-state orthodoxy is judged by the God of process, who calls us to the fullness of truth which lies where Christ stands at the end of the age and the Spirit empowers us all.

A feminist critique offers the corrective of a hermeneutic of suspicion, a refined theology and spirituality which take account of the insights of women as well as men. It demands that we listen to an evangelical or Gospel message. It demands that we recognize the role of women as primary evangelizers. Women foster the first steps in faith of children and young people. Women have ready access to the neighbourhood, the sick, the imprisoned, the dying as well as the workplace and, increasingly, the corridors of power. The vocabulary and language of women has not been clericalized. Women readily turn to Jesus in faith and hope and love and invite others to do so too.

A Decade of Evangelism requires that we be seen to turn to the Christ of the *pleroma*, incarnated once in a Jesus who loved and valued women, known now as the one in whom:

"There is no such thing as Jew and Greek, slave and freeman, male and female; for you are all one person in Christ Jesus" (Galatians 3: 27–9)

The Elderly and Evangelism

If the Church has to look hard at its Gospel and its evangelism in the light of women, there is an equal call to look at the Gospel and elderly people. Too often we have been content with bemoaning the sad state of the Church as reaching "only children and old ladies". Ageism is just as rife within the Church as sexism! What a contrast to the biblical view of the value of age, and the relative ignorance and disadvantage of youth. We are all becoming aware of the increasing number of older people in our society. Perhaps we are beginning to realize afresh that one of the true indicators of a church's health is the way in which it involves this age group at the very heart of its life and mission. Anne Forbes writes from her considerable experience with Faith in Elderly People, *an ecumenical project sponsored by the churches in Bradford, Keighley and Leeds.*

A General Practitioner who has worked for 25 years in the suburbs of Leeds stated recently that when he began he had 3 patients in the practice aged over 90; now there are 30. This example highlights one of the most noticeable changes in the UK population in recent years, namely the increase in the number of people of pensionable age, especially the very old, and the proportionately smaller number of young people. This shift in population is very evident to the health and social services, to many voluntary agencies, and of course to the churches. The consequent challenge for the churches is to recognize the considerable importance of this age group, both as bearers of the good news to others and as people whose own search for God is still continuing.

There are now almost 12 million people in the UK aged over 60, accounting for 20 per cent of the total population, compared with about 7 per cent in 1900. Gerontologists (specialists in ageing) find it increasingly helpful when looking at these changes in the lifecycle to talk about the Four Ages. These are:

FIRST AGE: childhood.

SECOND AGE: paid work and family raising.

THIRD AGE: the age of active independent life beyond child-rearing and work. This can be as long as 30 years.

FOURTH AGE: the age of eventual dependence, often very short.

The term "older people" covers both the Third and Fourth Age, although in both categories there are shared characteristics: a preponderance of women, a great majority of people (95 per cent) living in their own homes, almost half of them living alone. What is it that these older people can contribute to evangelization?

THE VOCATION OF OLD AGE

As Christians we believe that God created everyone for a purpose or vocation. Most people have several vocations, both professionally and in their personal lives. Childhood, parenthood, caring for elderly parents, grandparenting, all call forth different talents and responses. The latter years, especially the Fourth Age, characterize a particular form of discipleship during which there are likely to be experiences of loss, of letting go, of physical diminishment, of plenty of available daily time, less long-term future, maybe less emphasis on material security and more importance placed on relationships. However, it is a time when the sense of physical diminishment and loss can be allied to an increasing awareness of the life of the spirit, as expressed in 2 Corinthians 4:16:

> So we do not lose heart. Though our outer nature is wasting away, our inner nature is being renewed every day. For this slight momentary affliction is preparing us for an eternal weight of glory beyond all comparison, because we look not to things that are seen but to the things that are unseen.

Enabling this form of discipleship to develop is the role of the Church, and the evidence shows that this enabling is taking place in a variety of ways, many of which involve local churches making contact with older people living in their neighbourhood, churchgoers and non-churchgoers alike.

Visiting schemes, informal and formal, are essential, and both require more training than is generally accepted. Canon Michael Butler has pointed out that "a worthwhile visit needs as much thought, or perhaps even more, than an office interview or counselling session . . . Each visit needs to be carefully thought out in advance. What is its purpose? What is the most convenient time to visit? How long to stay? What, if anything, to take with you . . .?"[1]

1. From an article in *Plus*, the journal of the Christian Council on Ageing, January 1991.

Clubs and day centres are an important meeting point for people whose mobility is diminishing. Some luncheon clubs are run by a local church whereas others are run in partnership with the Social Services Dept of the Local Authority, or even under an arrangement whereby the Department rents the premises. Many of these ventures offer undoubted support for lonely people. How far they result in increased church attendance varies, and whether a link should even be made between social provision and anticipated rises in church attendance is controversial. Delivery of meals on wheels, together with provision of mini-buses for transport, is another way of contacting local people.

For most older people, especially Fourth Age people, the sadness of bereavement is a central experience, and bereavement counselling, surprisingly absent from many parishes, offers opportunities for exploring faith issues at a time when questions about meaning and a review of life are uppermost. More importantly, such discussions allow the question of one's own death to surface, as appropriate. When asked how the church could best be of service to older people, one Pensioners' Group urged that as a priority more bereavement counselling be made available in the locality.

Special liturgies for older people must be a special concern of the church. These may be communion services in residential homes, remembrance services both for those killed in war and for all who have died recently, home communion for housebound people, Bible study/prayer groups held at some time convenient for older people, such as the early afternoon or even midday. The Dementia Working Group of the Christian Council on Ageing is now exploring the possibility of developing liturgies appropriate for use with at least some dementia sufferers.[1] Obviously it is vitally important that older people feel part of the full worshipping community but this does not preclude special provision for them in the same way that it is made for other groups such as young people.

A GOLDEN AGE

And what of Third Age people? The reality is that it is mainly this younger age group who carry out the activities described above. People experiencing this "Golden Age" (i.e. those aged between 50–75) are the ones with the time and energy to visit their older friends, to organize the outings, to train as bereavement counsellors, and to become lay eucharistic ministers. What is more it is Third Age members who are starting to speak out on the wider social issues affecting many older people: low levels of the state pensions, the poor housing in which some older people live, the discrimination on account of their age ("ageism") which so many experience, within the church as well as without.[2] Facing up to these justice issues, this too is evangelization, making our society more Christlike in its compassion and in its treatment of the weaker members. Often it seems that older people's concerns are overlooked as they lack the emotional appeal of children's issues and the political attraction of causes such as the environment.

As 1993 is the European Community's Year of Older People and of Solidarity Between Generations, churches should stop apologizing that "many of our members are

1. See *Dementia: A Christian Perspective* by Alison Froggatt and Eillen Shamy, available from The Christian Council on Ageing (CCOA), c/o 20 West Way, Rickmansworth, Herts. WD3 2EN.

2. See *Called to be Old*, an ecumenical report produced by the Faith in Elderly People Project, c/o 53 Cardigan Lane, Leeds LS4 2LN

elderly", and discover with Maggie Kuhn, a leader of the Grey Panthers Pressure Group in the United States, that "it might just be one of God's surprises for us that he may use those closest to death, nearer to that other life, to show the Church how to break with self-centred purposes and goals, and look to the good of all and serve God.[1]

Communities and Evangelism

From three particular challenges we turn to two rather special vehicles for evangelism – communities and cathedrals. These represent two specific and inherited models of mission outside of the parochial structure which have often, in the past, played a significant part in the development of the Church's ideas on mission. Can they be a focus for renewal and mission as we approach the third Christian millennium? Brother Bernard of the Society of St Francis introduces us to the contribution which can be made by communities in the Decade of Evangelism.

Traditional Anglican Communities have changed with the Church and society more rapidly in the last forty years than at any other time in their history. The shift is towards greater openness to the world, greater flexibility, and deeper exploration of the relationship between holiness and wholeness.

Evangelism (not that the word was ever favourite among religious communities – nor is it now) expressed itself mainly through sharing the mission of Christ to the poor, the orphaned, the sick, the prisoners (i.e. the works of

1. Quoted in *Christian Theology and Ageing*, ed. William B. Clements, Harper and Row, New York, 1981. Also in *Ageing* – A report from the Board for Social Responsibility, CHP, 1990

mercy in Matthew 25:35) and following the evangelical counsels of poverty, chastity and obedience (foreshadowed in, e.g. Luke 18:22, Matthew 19:12 and Ephesians 5:21). But itinerancy, reflecting the sending out of the Twelve and the Seventy, has also had its part. The mission priests of St John the Evangelist, for instance, founded in 1866 (the first post-Reformation Anglican community for men) had parish missions as the first on their list of active works. Many sisterhoods came into being to work with Catholic-minded clergy in needy parishes, and their dedication and attempt to identify with those around them was rewarded by the love, respect and sometimes commitment to Christ and his Church which resulted.

A blend of evangelical and catholic spirituality gave these communities their ethos. The Community of the Holy Name founded in Vauxhall in 1865 had this very specific description in its aims: "to win souls to Jesus by intercessory prayer and by the active ministry of love, earnestly striving to bring them to personal union with him". Almost all of the communities have wonderful stories of mission, both at home and overseas. Heroic pioneering work in evangelism, educational and medical work was long sustained and eventually handed over. To mention only the Community of the Resurrection's work in South Africa and the name of Trevor Huddleston is to recall also the public and prophetic witness to Kingdom values given by people whose commitment and lifestyle challenged contemporary assumptions.

The prophetic is alive today, especially among younger religious, fired with justice and peace concerns: against racism, sexism, discriminatory trade practices, exploitation of the two-thirds world, oppression of women and the like. Explorations of the Base Ecclesial Communities, new ways of being church, new ways of living the Gospel with others while seeking to change society – these are some examples of the desire to work with God's mission in the world. It is pursued in hostels, hospitals, colleges, schools, prisons, community work, inner-city parishes, housing estates, often with deprived people. Some religious are in paid work, some voluntary.

But two of the other expressions of the evangelical impulse should be recognized. First there is the parish mission. Father Richard Oakley of the Community of the Resurrection is exhorting Church Union congregations to turn outwards in renewal, mission and active evangelism. Communities which lead mission events often receive many more requests than their resources can meet. Again there is great variety and certainly a shift away from doing mission *for* to doing it *with* a congregation. Very often today the event is ecumenical or with a group of congregations. The tendency is also away from the week or fortnight of nightly mission preaching towards learning together in workshops and small groups. For example, a recent programme led by sisters and brothers of the Society of St Francis included the following ingredients:

1. Neighbourhood groups where local Christians, their neighbours and friends, shared life experience and faith.

2. Peer groups, e.g. for over 60s, young people, children, men only, women only, single people only, which focused on Gospel-and-life questions.

3. Evangelistic preaching through demonstrating and explaining what happens at church services like at a wedding, a baptism, a confirmation or a family communion, and what could happen between God and people within them.

4. Quieter opportunities for people to do personal work with God. These included ways of private prayer, experiencing silence, and the opportunity of personal ministry at the foot of the cross.

5. Lively worship services, culminating in the diocesan bishop re-commissioning the congregation for mission.

Most leaders design a programme with a congregation to give impetus to the direction it intends to follow. Programmes range from open-door retreats, schools of prayer, teaching weeks, mission-preaching services and the like. They are also conducted in prisons, colleges and service units.

The other major contribution religious offer is the sharing of their community life with others. This may be through residential care, hospitality, retreats, personal counselling, spiritual direction, silent prayer sessions or the like. Guesthouses are increasingly popular and well-used, and not only by committed Christians. Some communities have recently upgraded their provision for special needs, like the care of the elderly or for women and girls at risk (e.g. All Hallows at Norwich). Helen House, founded by All Saints Sisters for terminally-ill children, was a first. The social needs of our society cry out for provision: so also do the spiritual needs. Many people look for opportunities of deeper commitment and fellowship than their congregation provides. Many link with communities as associates, tertiaries, companions and the like. They, and many others, come to community houses for times of spiritual renewal, nurture, counsel and encouragement: hopefully they return to their ordinary lives more ready for sharing the Gospel by life and witness. And the long experience of communities of what it is to be human, how much energy and patience it takes to live acceptingly, lovingly, forgivingly and challengingly with others and oneself, and how many layers of human personality there are to be brought to the redeeming love of God in Christ, are put to the service of those who come to them. It is easy to idealize communities – this is part of the price they pay for upholding certain values. It is also easy to idealize the Christian life. But to preach idealism without earthing it in human experience may have short-term evangelistic results but certainly needs the kind of earthing which community life provides. Communities stand for ordered worship and prayer and the costly discipleship of self-giving love.

Communities witness to complementarity of functions within the body (1 Corinthians 12). The Decade rightly stresses activity for change so that the Gospel is heard in our times. "Don't just stand there, do something." There is also a complementary truth to which our contemplative communities witness. "Don't just do something, stand there." Standing in our great High Priest with arms held up in prayer (like Moses in Exodus 17:8–13), "struggling with enemies not of flesh and blood but against the rulers, against the authorities, against the cosmic powers of this present darkness, against the spiritual forces of evil in the heavenly places", "withstanding . . . standing firm . . . stand . . ." (Ephesians 6:12–14) is the vocation of all Christians which some, through particular calling, or at particular times or circumstances of life, especially exemplify. Contemplative communities live out this calling in adoration and intercession, not claiming other justification for their existence.

New Forms of Community

Community is not confined to those in Religious Orders. The names Lee Abbey, Scargill, Post Green, Taizé, Iona, Corymeela indicate the attraction of a variety of expressions of community today. "Evangelism through community" has a popular ring. The house-parties, conferences, and camps lead people to a personal relationship with Jesus. "Since I joined the community" someone said recently, "my two nephews were converted and my aunt and my mother have committed themselves more deeply." Such communities also provide training in evangelism, in Christian maturing and opportunities to work on contemporary issues. People coming find attractive Christians living in community. Other projects develop from these home bases. Lee Abbey, for instance, established first a hostel for overseas students, then a cottage community in inner-city Birmingham: it also sends out teams into parish evangelism. Some of the communities mentioned centre around direct evangelism, some more to issues in society, some to prayer and spiritual deepening: those with long-term membership face the demands of dying and rising in Christ which is the only way of Christian growth. All of them have had a great influence in the last forty years, not least among young people.

Perhaps it is the breakdown of extended families, the greater mobility of the population or the deterioration of neighbourhood awareness which lead to the formation of new expressions of community. Certainly the New Testament with Jesus and the Twelve, the Community of Acts 2:14–7 and Paul's concept of fellowship in the Body of Christ witnesses to a deep human need whatever the social circumstances. To attend a Congress of the National Association of Christian Communities and Networks

(NACCAN) shows what diversity of communities there are today. Some have arisen from the upheaval of the 60s, some from the charismatic renewal of the 70s, most are locality-related, some are committed to evangelism or evangelization. If we add to these the traditional communities, 10 for men, 43 for women, the house churches, house groups, retreat houses, homes of healing, community centres and settlements, congregations and (the most fundamental Christian communities) families, we see the significance of community in the plan of God, three-in-one, a community of love.

The renewal of the communities and the development of new ones will both promote evangelism and also provide places where the good news can integrate into contemporary life. Renewal will mean attraction and integration but also challenge.

Cathedral and City

If, as chapter two said, the bishop is to lead the diocese in mission, we should expect to be able to look to the cathedral as a focus of mission within the diocese. This has not been the normal understanding that most parishes have had about cathedrals. There has often been a feeling that they were involved in a different enterprise altogether than the stuff of real mission which happens in the parishes. John Allen outlines some of the ways in which Wakefield Cathedral, where he is the provost, has been seeking to respond to the challenge of the Decade of Evangelism.

Most cathedrals held magnificent services to launch the Decade of Evangelism in their dioceses. Many have followed those up with other specific events under the umbrella of the Decade. They have included lectures,

Christian Basics courses, displays of parish initiatives, playing host to great mission events and so on. Yet probably the most important contributions that cathedrals make to the Decade, or indeed that others make for that matter, do not carry a Decade label at all. For what the Decade has done is to make us put Mission at the top of the agenda of everything that we do. Indeed here at Wakefield hardly a committee meets without Mission, or Evangelism, or The Decade and the cathedral's plans, appearing as an Agenda item. This applies as much to the Fabric Committee and the Finance Committee, as to the Cathedral Chapter and the Parochial Church Council.

Our preparations for the Decade started in 1987. The following year saw the centenary of this diocese and we determined to mark that by making a major thrust into the secular world. We started by carrying out a Mission Audit, designed locally under the title "Bread not Stones". The Audit Programme was written and prepared in the cathedral, for the whole diocese, as part of the cathedral's contribution to the diocesan commitment to Mission. In the cathedral, everyone who came through the doors during the month of August was asked to fill in a simple questionnaire, as were a thousand passers-by outside. In addition all the employees of two major companies trading adjacently, and a sample of local residents as well as the regular worshippers were also questioned. We then had a much clearer idea of how we were failing to make an impact and to whom we should address the Gospel entrusted to us.

Then the council considered what the cathedral's distinctive contribution should be. In secular terms, we tried to agree on our "mission statement"! We came up with the proposition that it was the cathedral's task

To ensure that the claims of Christ are presented in those places and among those communities that cannot easily be reached by the parish churches, and to do so both in the diocese, and in the whole region where the cathedral is set.

We identified ten major areas, which we are addressing as follows.

1. **Passers-by.** We asked how the building itself speaks to passers-by. Does it look like an ancient monument to be revered for its own sake, or does it invite people to come in and meet a living God who cares? As a result, we have done away with all our boundary walls, and replaced them with terraced steps leading to the main entrances, and designed in conjunction with the whole commercial pedestrian precinct. The cathedral is now clearly *IN* the world, part of it and not set apart from it. We replaced the heavy oak doors with glass porches and heat curtains, inviting people to come in as clearly as do our neighbours the multiples. We have also looked at everything that they will find once they come in, to make sure that it is "user friendly", and conducive to prayer, meditation, study, and counsel.

2. **Local Government.** We have established close links, especially with the Planning, Economic Development, Education, Highways and Civic Functions departments of the Local Council. The Precinct redevelopment scheme mentioned above is only one of the fruits of that co-operation. Others include using the cathedral and its programme in promotional material designed to attract new industry to the area; agreement to open a new Cathedral Church of England Controlled High School, and many others.

3. **Commerce.** Adjacent to the cathedral is the Ridings Shopping Centre. Though now overshadowed in size by the Metro Centre in Gateshead, or the Meadowhall Centre in Sheffield, it remains one of the foremost commercial developments in the north, and is visited by up to twenty thousand people a day, or half a million a week in the run up to Christmas. We serve the same catchment area, and try to arrange joint promotions, bringing in bus-loads to spend the morning shopping and the afternoon in the cathedral or vice versa. Signs in the centre point to the cathedral. The choir sings carols there. The Cathedral Deacon acts as chaplain to some of the stores. In these and many other ways we try to be of service to the many people who work or visit there.

4. **Business.** It is harder to work out how to encourage the many offices around to consider the claims of Christ. Approaches are mainly financial, for that is their business. We encourage sponsorship of choir activities. We have recently experimented with encouraging firms to use our facilities for corporate hospitality purposes, since each such use gives an opportunity both to surprise hard-headed businessmen, and to challenge their assumptions about the Church. And of course each time we ask for help, we have to justify to them the value of recognizing the contribution that the Church makes to the environment in which they do business.

5. **Schools.** It is for the diocesan education team to make contact with Church Schools. But the cathedral provides an indispensable resource to all schools, not just for Religious Education, but for History, Design Technology, Music and the Visual Arts as well. In common with many cathedrals, we concentrate on the LEA schools, offering teachers' packs, follow-up visits,

guides, and space for school parties to have lunch. We are considering ways of using educational trust income to subsidize transport for parties coming from further away. In addition to individual school visits, we arrange children's days both in term-time and in holidays, when the whole cathedral is taken over with a range of exciting activities, culminating in an act of worship devised by the children themselves.

6. **The Arts.** Cathedrals are natural patrons of all the Arts. They are works of art themselves; and each spends the largest part of their budget on music and the development of the choral tradition. In Wakefield Cathedral, besides formal acts of worship, we have some fifty or so concerts each year. Each provides an opportunity to make the claims of Christ known to both concert-goers and artists. The opportunities are endless. For example, some ten thousand people attended one or other of the Advent and Christmas-related musical events held in Wakefield Cathedral in December 1991. A survey of audiences and their numbers has led us to reconsider our strategy in the light of the Decade. We have rostered more clerical staff and volunteers to provide a pastoral presence at each concert; and we have taken a fresh look at the management of the bookshop to ensure both that it is open on each such occasion and that suitable material is on display linking the theme of the occasion to the Gospel message.

Artistes are encouraged by being invited to take part in worship. Dancers, more used to the secular than the sacred, are encouraged to interpret in dance the great themes of Christian worship. An active policy of commissioning compositions from composers known as much for their secular as for their sacred work, encourages them to think about the Gospel message; and the same goes for silversmiths, painters and even carpenters.

7. **Local Mission.** The cathedral is inevitably the largest and most dominant place of worship in the area, even if it does not necessarily have the largest resident congregation. It must therefore take a leading part in any locally organized mission of a more traditional style. The difficulty is in finding the right balance between taking a lead and not dominating; and between our responsibility as a local church in the town, and our role as a national, diocesan and regional centre. The latter cannot excuse us from our duty to the place where we are set. We are therefore much involved in plans for renewing Mission in the city of Wakefield along with all the other churches.

8. **The Ecumenical Dimension.** One of the greatest barriers to Evangelism is the scandal of our divisions. The cathedral probably has more opportunities than most for demonstrating that those divisions are more apparent than real, and that however we humans may behave, Christ himself is not divided. We actively seek ways of encouraging others in their mission, and in their use of the cathedral. In 1990, a Roman Catholic congregation was able to use the cathedral whilst their own church was being refurbished. The Salvation Army borrows the cathedral for their Christmas event. The Methodists will celebrate here in 1993, and the Pentecostals use it for their regional events. These speak even more eloquently than united services of the unity of our common faith in Christ. But of course shared vigils of prayer, weekly ecumenical prayers for peace, and many other shared occasions also make their own witness.

9. **The Diocese.** We must never forget that the cathedral is only the cathedral because the bishop has his throne in this church rather than any other. It follows therefore that whatever else we may do, we must see ourselves as partners with him in his own evangelistic enterprise. Our concern for the unity of all Christian people is no greater than our concern for the unity of the diocese.

   For a start, we must give up any idea of becoming closely identified with any one party in the church. So we encourage all parties to use our facilities, whether it is for a great service of prayer and praise for Pentecost, or a carefully orchestrated Spiritual Pilgrimage to Walsingham. We always give diocesan services priority over others, and consider carefully the type of worship appropriate to them, and whether to use the cathedral choir or a music group from one of the parishes, or both. We try to be at the cutting edge of liturgical reform, as well as the guardians of the tradition, so that parishes can look to us for help, training and guidance. Thus we develop our role as a major resource for the diocese in as many ways as possible.

10. **Tourism and conservation.** It is important that we should always be looking for ways of turning visitors into pilgrims, and pilgrims into believers. Cathedrals have never had so many visitors since the great days of medieval pilgrimages to the shrines of the saints. But I put visitors' needs last, because they can so easily overshadow the prime responsibility of the cathedral. Nevertheless, amongst our visitors are some who cannot be reached by any others, and we must look for better and more effective ways of presenting them with the claims of a Christ who is alive NOW, and not simply one who was alive five, or even nine, hundred

years ago when the building was finished. We therefore need to make sure that they catch a glimpse, not just of the magnificence of the architecture, but of what we are doing under the nine headings mentioned above. Equally, we need to make sure that the fabric is in excellent shape, not just because it is a sacred charge entrusted to us, but because it is a primary tool of mission. All tools need to be kept bright and sharp; but they also need to be adapted to today's task and today's methods. They always change, for our Christ is a very contemporary Christ. It follows that any dean or provost who hands on his cathedral to the next generation in exactly the same condition as he found it has betrayed his trust.

Chapter Six

LEISURE, WORK
AND THE GOSPEL

To the question "How does the Lord God spend His time?" a Jewish Teacher once gave this answer: "The Holy One, Blessed be he, who neither slumbers or sleeps, spends eight hours studying the Law, eight hours ruling the world, and eight hours playing with Leviathan." Much Christian practice has given a very different evaluation to leisure, to work and to contemplation. We asked Angela Tilby, writer and television producer, to explore what can fairly today be called "the problem of work and leisure" from the perspective of the Christian Gospel and Christian witness today.

Redeem the Time

We like to think in threes. The Benedictines divided the day into periods of prayer, manual work and study. These tidy divisions were intended to provide a sane and humane structure for monastic life. There is no formal mention in them of the need for leisure.

No doubt there was festivity and personal space in monastic life, but one suspects it was not separated out.

Leisure time as such may have been seen as idle time, a positive encouragement to the noonday demon of boredom. To our ears the Benedictine day sounds like an over-rigorous day, short on spontaneity. So we rejoice in monastic rebels. The jolly monk, the eccentric monk, the monk who likes his glass of wine. History helps us, for was not a famous Benedictine, Dom Perignon, the inventor of champagne? And what invention more eloquently speaks of the problem for Christianity posed by the polarization of work and leisure? In the green bottle the delicious and invigorating bubbles are pressed in, re-pressed by cork and twisted wire. Christianity thrives on delayed gratification. It works, and yet does not work, for not everyone is prepared to wait for ever for the popping of the corks.

A more recent threefold division of human waking time comes from W. H. Auden. He spoke of work, prayer and carnival as the essential components of life. Work and carnival are clearly different. Work is what we have to do, carnival is anarchic space, time off. They represent polarities in our experience which are not easy to hold together. Carnival disrupts work, yet it needs the boundary of work to contain its anarchy. The cork must be popped, but once it is out of the bottle the fizz cannot be kept for long. As for prayer, is it work or play? It is not obvious where it belongs and what it does.

That is by way of an introduction to the problem posed by the polarity of work and leisure. It has nothing obvious to do with problems which preoccupy the Church, like Sunday trading, or helping the unemployed, or with the merits and demerits of sector ministry. These are moral and practical issues, but their roots are theological and spiritual. But the problem of work and leisure is a problem of our being. It goes deep. I want to start from the fact that there is a human need for structure in our working lives which oscillates with a revolt from structure. We live between self-discipline and anarchic relaxation. Work and carnival are what we do in our lives, but they are often at war with each other. It is not clear to most people that prayer could have anything to do with solving the conflict, and this is true whether or not we choose to pray.

A return to first principles suggests a re-reading of the two creation narratives in the early chapters of Genesis. The first stately, poetic account from the priestly writer sets the creation of human beings in the context of God's holy work of creation. God labours in the production of the universe, God labours to create time and differentiation, God labours to invent plants and animals. Then on the sixth day God creates a physical and visible replica of the spiritual and invisible God, God's human image, man and woman. This brings God's work to an end.

Is God tired? God does not sleep, but the seventh day is a rest day, a holy day, on which God enjoys the fruit of his labour. It is a carnival day, a day of blessing.

This narrative suggests that work and leisure show something of both our likeness and unlikeness to God. We work and we rest, and in this we mirror God, who works six days and rests on the seventh. But God's sabbath rest is an unsleeping rest, a feast of pleasure. We, on the other hand, need a daily rhythm of work and sleep. In this we are like the animals, tied to the natural world of times and seasons:

"Man goes to his work and to his labour until the evening" (Psalm 104:23).

The first creation narrative locates us between earth and heaven. We are made and we are also makers, both limited and blessed.

The second creation narrative is a story. The paradise garden is set in a mythical location, "east of Eden", in a mythic time, before the first rain had watered the earth, before any living plant or animal had been formed. A mist hangs over the earth watering the ground as if in breathless anticipation of the one who is to come. The human earthling is fashioned by God in the most intimate manner, moulded by God's hand, breathed into by God so that he becomes the first living creature. The breathing, conscious manikin is pre-eminent in God's creation. Once the man is made, God creates his environment, producing the trees of the paradise garden which are watered by the mighty river that flows from Eden. Adam is created with a task. He is to till the garden and to keep it. He is to eat the fruit of the trees, but to avoid the fruit of the knowledge of good and evil. The earthling is "a little one'" who needs protection, care and prohibition in his introduction to the world.[1].

Adam is not complete. As readers and listeners we know this. The dream time of Eden is not quite real time and Adam cannot stay for ever alone in the perfection of Eden. He is lonely. He aches for companionship. God recognizes the loneliness of the earthling and tenderly creates and brings to Adam the animals and the birds, solemnly acknowledging the earthling's creativity and quest for self-knowledge as he names the creatures. But even when Paradise has become a game-park, Adam does not find the soul-mate that corresponds to his yearning. He learns what he is and what he wants by what he is not, by play and fantasy, and God accepts the names that Adam bestows. Adam dreams of an end to an aloneness which neither the exotic creatures, nor God himself, can assuage. So God creates Eve out of the rib of the man, Eve, whose name means "mother of all the living". Eden is a place where dreams are fulfilled. But lurking in the swaying grass of

1. See Irenaeus, *Proof of Apostolic Preaching*, 11 and 12.

Eden is danger. It cannot be avoided. Along with the other creatures is the subtle serpent, the wise and deceiving snake, who promises a different kind of knowledge.

The rest of the story is all too familiar. Eve listens to the serpent, she recognizes the goodness of the fruit and its desirability, she eats the fruit of the forbidden tree, she gives some to Adam. Their eyes are opened, and as they recognize that they are desirable to each other, they lose the possibility of dreaming intimacy with God. The serpent has promised them divinity, but the promise is a cheat. What they end up knowing is that they are naked, vulnerable both to the natural world and to supernatural wrath. Nature has seduced them and is no longer to be trusted. The way of exile is opened for them. Banished from the garden the world is now a concentration camp in which human work is overshadowed by a divine curse. The Eden story is a stunningly dramatic and painful account, light years away from the hymnic and ordered creation of Genesis 1.

How can we interpret the two accounts in order to make sense of the demands of work and the need for leisure today? The first account might be taken as what God intends for the creation. It is determinative for us, not because it describes how God made the world, but because it shows what his will for the world is. It expresses how things *should* be. We are created for work and leisure in the image of God, and we fulfil our purpose as intelligent creatures when we seek a balance of work and leisure in our lives. Though we participate with all nature in the rhythms of work and sleep, we mirror God more than other creatures by our capacity for waking rest, for the joy of the Sabbath. This is special time, sacred time, time off when we bless and are blessed.

The second account is powerful and moving because of its emotional realism. It tells our experience in terms which we can still recognize and own. Eden is paradise, the perfect beginning, the idyllic childhood, the long summer when the sun always seemed to shine. No matter that it never happened, and that it is often rather wounded adults who had beautiful childhoods, the idea that it *ought* to have happened is deeply rooted in human mythology and psychology. Eden is a mythic time and place which carries with it the hope of re-creation. In Eden, nature is benign and the child is the king of creation.

In the light of that unfailing hope the second account insists that human work takes place under the shadow of a divine curse which has not been lifted. The exile from Eden corresponds to the common experience that a good deal of human work is not particularly fulfilling. It is a struggle to survive in an environment which is trying and sometimes directly hostile. We all live in conditions of alienation in which the ground is cursed. Yet we know, somewhere in our imagination, that it may not always have been like this. It need not always be like this.

People have always half-believed that unspoiled nature could be a paradise, a second Eden, containing the vital secret clue to who we really are and what we might become. In Christianity we half-believe that nature speaks to us of God. The heavens declare the glory and the firmament shows his handiwork. Yet there is a problem. To believe that God is revealed in nature can be the first step on the road to the idolatory of pantheism. Eden is visible, but the God who created Eden is invisible. God has a voice but takes up no space. The primal sin, according to Paul, is to mistake the glory of the creature for the glory of the Creator. The alternative is to accept the tragic conclusion of the garden of Eden story. Nature is alien and hostile. The only way to deal with it is to master and control it, to make it give up its secrets and serve our needs.

The image of the two earthlings setting out from Eden, like the strained commuters toiling into the city every day, is already an image which cries out for redemption, for something more, for the healing space of creative leisure in which the world can be remade. We believe and do not believe that we are made for more than work, and we believe and do not believe that without this *more* our work itself suffers and our whole life is thrown out of balance. We suspect that we have forfeited the satisfaction of rest by some failure and inadequacy in ourselves. Since the development of the monastic office in the West the Venite has called human beings daily to worship God with the grim warning that God forbids his disobedient children to enter into his rest. Yet that is not the last word of Scripture. Eden may not be available, but the Sabbath is. "There remains a Sabbath rest for the people of God."

We search for the paradise of Eden, for the carnival of the Sabbath, as we thumb the holiday brochures, longing for the dream time where our needs are all provided. Longing for the place where we can catch up on ourselves, "naming the creatures" in an exercise of creativity and the quest for fuller self-knowledge. Eden is the place of companionship, where our narcissistic needs are at least adequately met and matched. Many go on holiday hoping that the tired spouse will revive and become what we always wanted them to be, for us, and we for them. Or that, on the beaches of Palma or the Aegean cruise, or even at the Christian holiday centre for singles we shall meet the man or woman of our dreams. Paradise is a dream of contemplative space, a passivity towards the imagination. It is essential for our wellbeing.

Yet, half-consciously we know that even the Eden of the imagination is a dangerous place. The snake still whispers in the grass, enticing us by the spectacular imagery of the fruit luring us to grandiosity and self-sufficiency. Sometimes the hoped-for Eden turns out to be a cheat and a disappointment. The plane was late, the weather was foul, we caught a bug, we had a hangover, a row, a flat tyre. We are glad to be home. The exile that follows into the harsh world is expected and necessary. It describes what it is like to live and work in a world which is not designed around our personal needs, the rude jolt of reality, the weariness of the familiar, the grey boredom of Sunday afternoon, before the return to the slog of Monday morning. We cannot endure the real Eden, yet we still long for the recreation which it represents.

I find the two very different creation stories helpful in thinking about attitudes to work and leisure that permeate society. First, because both stress very clearly that life cannot be and must not be all work. This is particularly important for those of us who live in modern industrial societies which are fuelled by the anxiety and ambition of individuals, and, which, in turn, wind individuals up to greater and greater levels of stress in order to extract more and more from them, while discarding those who are ill-equipped for the struggle to survive. The modern Church, while full of well-meaning platitudes on behalf of the poor and unemployed, absorbs the message of relentless work without reflecting on it very critically, and there is an unstated expectation on both clergy and committed lay people that there are no boundaries round time spent in the service of God.

The first creation account sets boundaries around the Sabbath and insists that it is kept sacred. Not for the service of God, but for the enjoyment of God. It is a holy day, a space in which we know God differently from how we know God in the working week. In Judaism the Sabbath is a space for drinking and eating and companionship. It is a day for the home. Christianity is ambiguous about the Sabbath–

ideal, but we should not be ambiguous about the need for genuine anarchic space, space without pressure, which includes the possibility of hearing the voice of God. Why do we respond to the picture of Adam and Eve hearing the voice of the Lord God walking in the garden in the cool of the day? Perhaps it is because the picture calls us to an intimacy with God which we know is possible yet believe that we are personally excluded from. We have, like Adam and Eve, lost our innocence and we are ashamed.

In the Christian story it is the Sabbath of Easter Eve which restores our innocence. At Easter the voice of the Lord God is heard again in the garden not in the cool evening of Eden, but at the empty tomb at dawn. Evening, dawn; both are vulnerable times when the roles and structures of the working day are set aside, where nature speaks poignantly of God, where we linger between the possibility of delusion and the risk of revelation. This is the place of death and rebirth and if we have not been there our faith remains dry and distant, safe enough from the snake, perhaps, but far from the tree of life.

Sabbath time, carnival time, time without pressure is important, especially for those in ministry, for whom worship and prayer are rightly part of the everyday working world. I think Auden intended prayer to be the force which bound the polarities of work and carnival together. But most of us do not find this easy. We know how to pray as a working activity. The Benedictines, of whom Dom Perignon, the inventor of champagne, was one, taught that to work is to pray. We do not, however, know how to pray as part of the Sabbath–carnival. This is a loss which others do not share. Among some Hasidic Jews, for example, Saturday evening can be a time to rollick about with a bottle of vodka singing mystical songs in the hope of extending the beauty and glory of the Sabbath. A striking contrast to the desolation towards the end of the English Sunday, with only the sad beauty of Evensong to look forward to. In the sober and industrialized world carnival tends to be godless and God is without much joy. Why?

To an extent the problem is inherent to Christianity. Sunday, the resurrection day on which the primitive Church met for worship, was not the Sabbath, but the first day of God's working week. Christianity was from the beginning a mission, a work, a restless force for change. In the world described by the fall nothing is to be accepted as it is. Redemption is a mighty work of God, mightier than the original creation, and in responding to the grace that saves we commit ourselves to work on and in the world to transform it.

The mediaeval Church came to terms with the human need for carnival and leisure time. The high days and holidays and pilgrimages offered real Sabbath space in people's lives. In Spain, Italy and Latin America the feasts of Our Lady and Corpus Christi are still held with a mixture of solemnity and riot. I think of Tepeyac, in Mexico, where the High Mass celebrating the visions of Our Lady to Don Juan is held in a basilica open to the rowdy and ecstatic rhythms of traditional Indian dance.

The impetus to change the world is strengthened at times of religious renewal. The Protestant Reformation played its part in breaking human links with the natural world. The reformers knew about the longing for Eden and distrusted it. Above all else they attacked idolatry. Sacred wells, healing streams, holy mountains, the gateways linking the natural world to the supernatural world, no matter how much these had been brought into popular theology through the cult of Our Lady – these were all seen as evidence of lurking paganism, of an accommodation with the sin of Eden which had blunted the edge of Christian faith. They were evidence of Eve's mistake, the preference for the image and taste of the apple to the word of God. So the reformers waged war on the spirituality of the senses; statues, images, landscapes, ritual, music, costume – the necessities of carnival. Noses were for smelling. Feet for walking. Eyes for reading the word of God. Holy days and pilgrimages, important Christian attempts to guarantee Sabbath space in the lives of the people of God, were replaced by the Calvinist Sunday. The Calvinist Sunday was God's time, but not time without pressure. The pressure was immense, pressure to learn and respond and succeed in the proof of one's salvation. The carnival aspect was spiritualized out of existence.

Protestant theology had an important effect on notions about work. The fact that we are saved by grace and not by works actually winds us into a psychological bind. If grace is free, the only way we can show forth the fruits of our redemption is by the good works that they produce in us. The radical conversion of the human heart and will seeks expression in the radical restructuring of the world. This includes the possibility of freely investigating the natural world and can lead logically to attempts to tame "fallen" nature in the interests of knowledge and control, progress and justice. While the Catholic Church, with its more generous belief in revelation through the natural world, inhibited scientific research, Protestant countries embraced it.

The Reformation thus prepared the ground for the scientific revolutions of the seventeenth century. A few years after the Act of Uniformity with its attempts to enforce the Book of Common Prayer on English congregations, a strange young man sat in an English country garden and, watching an apple fall from a tree, grasped the mechanism which drove the universe. The universal law of gravitation is the law which holds all things together, and it was Isaac Newton who had the imagination to see it, though it took him years of reflection to turn his intuition into a formal theoretical statement. Newton was a devout believer, a member of the Church of England with Puritan sympathies. In secret, he was a Unitarian and an Arian. The picture of the universe which he developed in his laws of motion and gravity was of a world that was never at rest. There is no such thing as rest in nature. Everything is in motion, everything is at work. The *only* rest is God, who was located, by Newton, outside the machine of the world in absolute space and absolute time.

Newton loved and feared God with all his being, and saw his science as a kind of prayer, in which the scientist was a true contemplative, thinking God's thoughts after him. But the consequence of his discoveries was to distance God from the world of nature and from the human world. God's absolute rest lies outside the system that God has created. Newton's successors gradually recognized that if God was wholly outside nature God became redundant to creation. The world could be broken down into its constituent parts and understood without reference to God. The atheistic world view can give no meaning to leisure. The carnivals of atheistic nations are cynical manifestations of the human spirit. Without a notion of the Beyond in the Midst the individual human being becomes disposable.

Newton and his contemporaries laid the foundations for the industrial revolution. Nature was construed as unruly and wild. From now on the aim was to control nature, to work her and make her productive, by following the laws of time and motion. Millions were driven off the land to work on the products of the earth with machines, pumps and mills, steamships and railways. The result was unbelievable prosperity for many, misery for some and spiritual anguish for those like William Blake who saw the triumph of the machine as a demonic assault on human freedom and imagination. Blake recognized that the "dark Satanic mills" of mechanistic description diminished the doctrine that human beings reflected the image of God. For as parts of nature ourselves we could hardly avoid being part of the mechanistic description. Today it is a commonplace to compare the human mind itself to a machine. And if it is a machine then it can be on or off, asleep or awake, but it does not by right deserve or need that Sabbath space, that contemplative God-time-without-pressure which the first creation account insists on and the second fears that we may have lost for ever. The spiritual vision of nature as a gateway to the divine and eternal world has had to fight with the scientific and realist description of nature as a machine.

We inherit this split and it has affected our attitudes to work and leisure. It is hard for us to see the working world and the world of contemplative play as necessary to each other. In our experience, they fight. We fantasize about our holidays but when we have them there is boredom, restlessness and anxiety. We *know* that the real world is Newton's world in which nothing rests and there is no access to God. Yet our desperate need for genuine leisure remains, split off and disregarded. Some take refuge in a relentless hedonism, going out of their minds at weekends in order to make up for the bruising humiliation of being cogs in a machine during the working week. Church people condemn the hedonistic drive to pleasure, but in truth they have little better to offer. It is facile to think that the need for genuine recreative space can be met by preserving the gentle English Sunday with church bells, silent shops and Sunday roasts (her work in the kitchen doesn't count). What would be worth doing is looking at the vulgar pleasures which are both harmless and available and do offer a chance for inner imaginative space and reflection. If these could be identified it might help the churches to understand better the context in which the Christian Gospel is proclaimed.

It may be a shocking suggestion, but I believe that watching television is one of the areas of genuine Sabbath-time and carnival time for most of our contemporaries. It is easy to condemn television as "wasted" time, but most leisure activities meet condemnation when they are judged by a ruthless machine-like view of human productivity. Careful consideration of the way in which people actually watch television should dispel the myth that television is a series of messages beamed from "them" to "us". Recent research suggests that television watching is far from being the mindless passive event that it is sometimes construed to be. In the twelve years that I have spent as a television producer I have come to the sobering conclusion that people rarely see the programmes that the programme makers believe that they have sent them. Between the viewer and the screen a mysterious inner dialogue often goes on, in which the viewer re-values the world by consent and dissent, naming its beasts and re-defining the boundaries, encountering the serpent and perhaps the voice of God. Television watching is the only form of creative regression available to many people, the only guarantee of an inner life, and a chance to hear the echo of the voice of the invisible God who walks in the garden in the cool of the day. The instinct for recreation is a holy instinct, to carnival, to intimacy with God not as beings apart from nature, but as manifestations of consciousness implanted in nature by God himself and unfolded within the fullness of time.

What is wrong with us is the drive to separate the working, controlling self from its animal roots and spiritual aspirations. The first creation account in Genesis should warn us not to do this, the second account shows how hard it is to prevent it. Our threefold nature is grievously fragmented and the injured parts all tend towards autonomy, each "crying their own cry and going their own way and having no pity for one another".[1] The second creation account warns us that the fragmentation has happened, but that all is not lost, a greater integration is promised. The first account insists that God's creation is a rational whole in which animal, human and spiritual are woven together into God's purpose. Neither account tells us whether or not our shops should be open on Sundays or whether there is a future for sector ministry. They are about awesome problems of our nature and only in their painful and problematic solution is the chance of healing from the deep issues which the Church must still address. For our Gospel is a message of liberation, not only from idolatory, but also from atheism, the bite of the apple and the worse bite of the snake.

The Workplace

How in practice do Christians experience and understand their work, their workplace and the relationships and responsibilities that these provide? Kenneth Adams sees these as a vital point, for anyone who works, both of worship and of witness.

Very few Christians see their workplace as somewhere they communicate the Gospel and yet, for most people, their

1. This phrase is taken from a letter of A. E. Russell to Helen Waddell and it refers to the conflict of body, soul and spirit in the characters of her novel *Peter Abelard*.

work and its location play key parts in shaping their lives. We earn our living by our work; in ordinary conversation we are often asked: "What do you do?", meaning what is your work. We make friends at work; we train to develop our skills and seek promotion in our work; we take quiet personal satisfaction in work we think we have done well, and we spend perhaps fifty hours a week at work including our journeying to and from work. In short, our work is a key factor in our lives and that is why we find unemployment so destructive in personal and social terms.

And yet most Christians do not see their work as an important part of their Christian service and therefore do not see their workplace as an opportunity for evangelism. They keep their work and their Christianity in separate boxes! Regretfully the Church has, in some ways, helped them to do this. For example, in the Index of Prayers in the Alternative Services Book not one prayer, in that long list of things we should pray for, concerns our ordinary work. There are prayers for Church Work and for Vocations to sacred ministry or to religious communities but none for that ordinary work which most of us do for about half of our waking time for most of our life.

Some work is seen to be "Christian". This includes the work of nurses and doctors, social workers and teachers and, of course, the clergy; but work in industry and commerce, in the public services and the home is not seen in that way as Christian caring service. This presents a problem for many Christians in their work situation, although they mostly avoid the problem by adopting the "separate box" approach.

While that approach avoids the problem, it does, in fact, undermine the possibility of living an integrated Christian life. If you can't say a deep "Yes" to the work by which you earn your living you cannot say a deep "yes" to your life as a whole because work forms such an important part of life. If you cannot see and experience your work as an important part of the totality of your life as a Christian you are most unlikely to be able to make your workplace a centre for evangelism. You may see it as a place where you meet many people on a regular basis and you may use those meetings to speak about your faith from time to time; but the actual work itself will play no part in that process other than being the reason for bringing those people together.

Therefore, are there broadly two sorts of work and two sorts of workplace? Is there one which we can see as fully compatible with our faith and which we can, therefore, integrate into our lives and use as an instrument and area of evangelism? This sort of work we might call social and caring work, including teaching and much public service. And is the other not capable of being so integrated and used as an instrument and area of evangelism because it is the field of industry, commerce, finance and journalism where the emphasis seems to be, not on caring, but on making a profit?

The acceptance of this idea of two sorts of work would mean, for example, that those Christians who work with Oxfam and all the other caring agencies in getting food and medical supplies to the hungry and the sick will see their work as their Christian service, while those who produce that food and those medical supplies will not! That is, in fact, the strange situation. It is the situation which we have to challenge before we can *all* make our workplace an exciting arena in which to live out and communicate the Gospel.

A way through to a new understanding of our work and its place in our Christian life and witness is to start by giving thanks to God for the ability which our work gives us to contribute directly to the needs of other people. As we reflect on that thanksgiving we will recognize that our work is a very important way, perhaps the most important way, in which we contribute to the needs of others. It is by producing the things and the services which people require that we make our main contribution to the community.

Christians see this truth when they think about farming at seedtime and harvest; but the same is true for those who produce to meet all our other material needs. Furthermore those materials have to be delivered to us so we need transport and all the distributive services of wholesale and retail – the ships, the railways, the road haulage, the shops, the offices, the petrol stations. Our needs are not simply material, we need medical services and education, banks and insurance, police and defence services; and we need delight, entertainment, fun and these needs are met by those who work in journalism, broadcasting, the theatre, catering, tourism and sport.

Seen in that way our work is the main thing we do for other people. Manufacturers will not manufacture goods if no one wants them. Nurses would not be nursing unless there were patients who needed nursing. Our work is our main contribution to the needs of others; we don't work for ourselves, we work to provide for the needs of others and in that process earn our own keep. We are all totally dependent on the work of other people. This interlocking web of human work is the fabric which maintains us, and our work is our main contribution to that fabric.

This view of our work transforms our approach to it. We recognize the goodness of being able to play our part through our work in meeting people's needs everywhere. We see the evil of unemployment because it denies a person the ability to contribute to the needs of others and we see the tragedy when the fabric of our work breaks down and people die of starvation or neglect.

With that view of our work we can make both it and our workplace the means by which we try to live out our faith and communicate it through action and word. The actual design, production and marketing of the product or service becomes important of itself as, of course, does the network of human relationships in which this activity involves us. This is our starting point for being able to offer our work to God and that offering of our work is the means by which we open up the possibility of using our work and our workplace as a means of communicating the Gospel to others.

Our work as Christians *matters* to us as part of our service to God and our fellow human beings – that is what we have to communicate.

Yet at our work and in our workplace we come across practices which deeply conflict with our Christian understanding. We will sometimes see work shoddily done, leading to poor quality goods or services; we will often experience bad personal relationships; we may see cheating, petty theft, lying, greed, sexual harassment and people being sacked because of cutbacks in business and public services. What can Christians say to these, how can we make such situations areas of evangelism?

The sad truth is that sin pervades all areas of our life and our working life is no more protected from this than is our home or social or church life. As we reflect we will recall, with sadness, that we have seen all those sins present in our other situations – at school, in the hospital, in our homes and in our churches. Christians are not protected from sin in others or in themselves. Sin is a feature of the world in which God has placed us and our task is to fight it in ourselves and in all our situations, including our work situation, helped by the power of the Holy Spirit. Our workplace is an important area for us to be playing our part in this exposing and healing task. In doing this we will be communicating the Gospel.

We will be greatly reinforced in this task as we reflect on the life of Jesus and on his work. We will recall that he spent most of his life working as a carpenter making ordinary things that people needed. We will recall the way in which he used the picture of the good shepherd, that is a shepherd who is good at his job with sheep, as the model of Christian service. We will recall how he used the fruitful vine and the rich harvest as pictures of good ministry. But, above all, we will recall every time we participate in Holy Communion what Jesus did as he initiated that central act of Christian worship – he picked up a piece of bread and he took into his hands a cup of wine. He took these most material things, these products of human agriculture and manufacture – not natural products, but products which are the outcome of human inventiveness and human labour – human artifacts – and with these *things* he gave thanks and offered them as his body and his blood.

These are the guidelines that help our work become one of the ways by which we can communicate the good news. Our work itself will matter to us as Christians – not just for what we earn by way of wage or profit – but by the value and usefulness of the goods or services we produce. In order to be able to produce those goods or services we will need the help of our fellow workers, and we will be selling those goods and services to customers and we will be buying materials from others, so the network of our working relationships will almost certainly include, directly or indirectly, fellow workers, customers and suppliers. Our relationships with all those people will reveal and communicate our Christian faith. If we are known to be Christian we will be communicating our Christian faith in our workplace by our attitude to our work itself, to the products of that work and to the relationships in which that work involves us.

We will be helped in that life and work and witness if we refuse to divide our lives into two parts – our working life and the rest – and if we refuse to separate the material from the spiritual. And we will be reinforced in this life and work and witness – in our work and at our workplace – as we recall at every Eucharist the work of thousands of people in many lands which lies behind the provision of the bread and the wine which is to become for us his body and his blood.

The Arts

Leisure, work, contemplation – all are expressed in, sustained by and contribute to "The Arts". Richard Harries writes about their "spiritual dimension" in the context of the ambivalence towards the arts of many Christians today.

For many of the most sophisticated minds of our time, the arts are enormously important. Judging by the relative space given to the arts in our quality papers, they matter more than religion. Though cultural snobbery and financial considerations are present, there is a spiritual dimension to this interest in the arts, which we neglect at our peril. For many people today the arts are a source of inspiration, insight and solace. The vast amount of classical music listened to on CD, cassette and record suggests that many people find through music what in the nineteenth century they might have found through religion.

Despite the enormously rich artistic heritage of Christian civilization, Christians today, as often in the past, are ambivalent about the arts. Sometimes they see them as a threat. More frequently they fail to discern their religious importance. Yet works of art, by their very nature, have a spiritual dimension. From a Christian point of view they reflect and share in the work of the eternal, creative logos. In the beginning there was chaos, the earth was without form and void. Then God created form out of the formless. We look at a leaf or a crystal and are amazed by the miracle of pattern which we discern there. In every aspect of creation, from the subatomic level through to the most sophisticated multicellular structures, we discern form and pattern. Form is also what all works of art have in common. There can be no work of art without form. Forms change and sometimes developments can startle and shock admirers of older forms. But form of some kind there must be and it is this which gives us music rather than a cacophony of sound, a painting rather than a splash of paint, a poem rather than babble.

So the first task of Christians in relation to the arts in this Decade of Evangelism is to affirm, rejoice in and celebrate them. The eternal, creative logos, active through the length and breadth of creation, has allowed us to share in this creativity through both the production of art and its appreciation.

One of the city centre churches in Oxford, St Giles, mounts an exhibition of art almost every week of the year. This is important not simply for the work depicted but as a sign that the richly artistic life of Oxford in music, drama, poetry and paintings is affirmed and celebrated before God.

The Christian appreciation of art goes even deeper than this. For nearly three centuries the iconoclasts tried to banish all specifically Christian art. Icons were destroyed. Then in 787 at the seventh Council of Nicaea the Church affirmed that Christian art was not only allowed, it was essential. Again in 843, the message, celebrated in the Orthodox Church on the Sunday before Lent, is that art is not just an optional extra but crucial to Christian truth. As John of Damascus put it:

> I boldly draw an image of the invisible God, not as invisible, but as having become visible for our sakes by partaking of flesh and blood. I do not draw an image of the immortal Godhead but I paint the image of God who became visible in the flesh.

So it is that icons have a very special place in the Church. There is a sense in which they are the foundation of all the visual arts. So it is that Holy Week, in which Christians walk with Christ, dying and rising again with him through the events of the Triduum, has a special place in relation to all drama. There is a profound sense in which all drama, tragic, epic and comic, has its theological foundation and rationale in the drama of Holy Week.

The Christian Church ought therefore to have a special interest in commissioning works of art of every kind. Although Western Christian art has deviated from the canons of Orthodoxy, nevertheless in its own way it witnesses to the reality of Christ incarnate and risen. We should not accept in a defeated way the notion that the Church's patronage of the arts belongs to the past when it was wealthier and more influential. Walter Hussey showed what could be done at St Matthew's, Northampton, and later at Chichester Cathedral, commissioning the best artists of the time to produce works on Christian themes. More recently, Canon Keith Walker, then vicar of a very ordinary church at the edge of Basingstoke, commissioned a window by Cecil Collins and a sculpture by Elizabeth Princk. Why should we resign ourselves to the tawdry and second-rate when there are superb artists of all kinds who would welcome the challenge of working for the Church?

The Church can wholeheartedly celebrate all genuine works of art as an expression of our human creativity in which is reflected the creativity of the eternal logos. More than this, we believe that the Word has become flesh. The poet Edwin Muir was brought up in the Orkneys under a religion of the Word. It was only when he went to work in Rome that he discovered through public works of art on such themes as the Annunciation, the religion of the Incarnation. In the Orkneys "nothing told me that Christ was born in the flesh and had lived on the earth." But in Rome, "It was publicly shown, as Christ showed himself on the earth. That these images should appear everywhere, reminding everyone of the Incarnation, seemed to me natural and right."

Art used as propaganda, as it was by the Nazis and by the Communists in Russia, is hateful. But no art is neutral. Every work expresses a feel for life, a particular perspective. It is entirely right that now, as in the past, there should be great works that witness to Christian themes. But before that it is no less important that all genuine art should be celebrated before God as a gift of God.

Chapter Seven

EVANGELISM AND OTHER WORLD-VIEWS

The Decade of Evangelism has been one of the factors that has made the Church more aware of the presence and claims of other-faith communities. It has also highlighted the mixture of apprehension, misunderstanding and shallow judgements that Christians of all persuasions have when faced with other religions. Some too easily turn to an unthinking triumphalism, and yet others are lost in hopeless confusion about what to to. Roger Hooker was for many years a missionary in India, and since 1982 has been seconded by CMS to the Diocese of Birmingham, for ministry among people of other faiths. He is able to clear away many fears, uncertainties and hasty judgements as he commends an approach which is both positive and open towards other religions while seeking to be true to his own clear understanding of Christian mission.

Evangelism and Other Faiths

Members of other-faith communities make up about 4.5 per cent of the population of this country. Some of their leaders have expressed anxiety about the Decade of Evangelism. Church leaders have attempted to reassure them by pointing out that the Decade is directed towards lapsed Christians, or at any rate to those indigenous inhabitants of Britain who have been nurtured in a culture whose roots are Christian, but who are in real danger of losing their Christian heritage. Yet in spite of these reassurances real and large anxieties remain. Members of other-faith communities know perfectly well – even if many Christians have forgotten it – that Christianity is inescapably committed to evangelism. They also know that what Christian leaders may say publicly, and what some members of their flocks may actually do are by no means identical. Therefore public reassurances are hardly enough to allay the fears of minority communities that they, and especially their more vulnerable members, may be subjected to unwelcome pressure during the Decade.

Many Christians too are uneasy though for rather different reasons: if we simply ignore people of other faiths are we not implicitly accepting the view that in spite of their differences all religions are equally valid and effective paths to salvation, and that Christianity's traditional claim to have a message for all people everywhere is no longer tenable? Some Christians do indeed hold such a view, but many more, while feeling the force of its persuasiveness, feel they cannot go along with it for it appears to involve abandoning too much of what they believe is central to Christian faith and life. Yet often the only alternative seems to be the very evangelism which, not surprisingly, troubles and angers other-faith communities. It is the conviction of this writer that there is a middle way between these two positions. It is already being quietly and unselfconsciously practised by many Christians in their daily lives but needs spelling out more clearly. Further, far from being a peripheral issue, our theological and practical relationship to other faiths, and to those who live by them, is a fundamental question for Christians in Britain today, for it raises issues which go to the very heart of our own identity as a community of faith. Only if we are on the way to getting this issue right are we going to discover a kind of evangelism which we ourselves can practise with conviction, and which does not threaten other religious groups.

BEGINNING WITH GOD

Let us begin, where the Lambeth Conference of 1988 began, and that is with the Trinity. Christianity is based on certain basic convictions about God, about Christ and about the Holy Spirit. Discussions about our relationship to other faiths often begin with Christology. This is important, yet even more fundamental is the nature of biblical monotheism on which Christology is based. One way of reading that body of literature which Christians describe as the Old Testament is to see it as a struggle for the unity of God. There is only one God who is lord of all life and of all experience. The Hebrew people first experience God in deliverance from Egypt at the Exodus. As they settle in Canaan they have to decide who gives them the "grain, the wine and the oil". Is the provider of these essentials of life the God who has delivered them from Egypt, or is it the Baals of Canaan, the local deities of particular places and tribes? That is the battle fought in the book of Hosea and elsewhere. The Hebrew people faced a very different threat in the shape of foreign invasion from Assyria but again the same essential issue arises, although in a different form. Is Assyria, as it claimed, empowered by the gods of Assyria or is it the instrument of God as worshipped by the Hebrews – "the rod I wield in my anger, the staff in the hand of my wrath" (Isaiah 10.5)? So again the issue at stake is belief in the one God of all people and of all experience. In Jeremiah and Ezekiel a question is whether the writ of God runs outside the land of promise. Does God go with the people into exile? These prophets believe that God does, and so those left behind in the promised land are not specially privileged compared with those who have been taken captive to Babylon. The further implication of this is that God is not, like the Baals, restricted by territorial limits: God is now seen, especially in Isaiah 40–55, as the one God of all the earth and of all peoples – whether or not they acknowledge God.

Read in this way – which is only one among others – we can see that the Scriptures show us how the Hebrew people are constantly having to face new and often painful and threatening experiences. They have to decide whether these experiences can be interpreted within the parameters of their historic faith. Those parameters have to be continually extended, and the people's vision of who God is and of what God can do are constantly enlarged and deepened in the process. We can see that as a paradigm for all Christian faith and life. That paradigm has not simply to be accepted and believed in, but actually relived by every Christian generation. God is an uncompromising imperialist. There can be no "no go areas", for if there are, then God is no longer God but merely another Baal.

GOD AND PARISH RESPONSIBILITY

In the life of the Church of England belief in biblical monotheism is embodied in the parish system. To the vicar and congregation of every parish church is committed responsibility for every person who lives in that parish. What that responsibility consists of and how it should be exercised are large questions and can be answered in different ways. The important issue for every parish church is that it should recognize that the responsibility is there.

This means that a church which turns its back on any group within its parish boundaries and says to itself, "We have no responsibility towards them because they follow another religion", has, whether it recognizes it or not, ceased to believe in biblical monotheism and has opted instead for a form of Baal worship.

This responsibility towards all can be exercised in a proprietary and triumphalist way – to the intense and proper annoyance of our Free Churchs sisters and brothers; but at its best the parish ideal enables Christian congregations to accept responsibility for unobtrusive and long-term service of those who live in their area. Of course no congregation can reach everyone, but if it does not have a significant outreach to at least some of those who do not worship in the parish church then questions have to be asked about its identity and about its mission.

For Christians, biblical monotheism cannot be separated from the person and work of Christ. For us Christ is "the human face of God", God is Christlike and in God there is nothing unChristlike at all. This means that Christ is the focus for the universal and undiscriminating love of the one God which embraces all people without distinction. Christians cannot claim to have a monopoly of such love, either as its recipients or as its imitators. The love and devotion shown by people of other faiths often takes us by surprise and puts us to shame. Indeed, there are not a few cases on record of "nominal' Christians being reconverted to their own faith as a result. It follows that the universal love of God is not an argument which enables Christians to enjoy the security of believing they are superior to others, but is a summons to follow Christ in the way of vulnerable and costly service. Moreover, the love we see in Christ and his story gives us the key to understanding divine omnipotence. This does not mean that God's power is irresistible in the face of human or other efforts to withstand it. It does mean that God's love is undefeatable, no matter what suffering and humiliation it may have to endure, and no matter how much Christians may obscure and deface it.

GOD AND THE UNPREDICTABLE

Turning now to the third person of the Trinity, the Holy Spirit is, among other things, about the unpredictable and unexpected element in God's dealings with humanity. For example, in nearly all stories of how people are brought to faith in Christ there is an element of surprise. Something happens which the Christians involved had neither intended nor foreseen. This can best be described by way of illustration: a teacher of English Literature was one day surprised to meet a former pupil and even more surprised to see that he was wearing a clerical collar. While he had been a pupil at the school he had never taken the slightest interest in religious education classes and never once attended the chapel. So the teacher asked him what had set him on the road to faith. The reply was, "The way you taught Wordsworth." Similarly a high-caste Hindu in India was brought to faith in Christ by reading the genealogy in the first chapter of St Matthew's gospel. This is hardly a chapter which most of us would want to commend to an enquirer, but this was a man steeped in an immemorial family tradition. He realized that a person with a pedigree like this must be someone special, and so he read on.

In each of those stories there is a common pattern of ordinary and unobtrusive Christian faithfulness: the teaching of English Literature and the making available of the Bible. But in each case the key is the element of total unexpectedness: in neither case did those who were faithful intend, or indeed even at the time know, of the effect they were having on the two young men concerned.

In other words it is always the Holy Spirit who converts, not the Church. The Church's task is simply to be faithful, and that embraces the basic activities of everyday life, like going to the shops and meeting people in the street. If we take this seriously it has two consequences. First, we are delivered from the guilty conscience of thinking we have to speak openly about our faith to all and sundry. To do that may indeed·be to deny the Holy Spirit and try to substitute our own efforts for the Spirit's work. People of other faiths are rightly angry at this sort of thing and so should we be. Second, it means that if we are faithful we are inescapably evangelists anyway whether we know it or not, for the unexpected interventions of the Holy Spirit can only happen when Christians are faithfully following in the steps of their master. And we grow in the confident discernment of when it is right to speak and when not.

The Holy Spirit works surprises in other ways as well: the Scriptures and the tradition of the Church have more to give us than we have yet discovered. Different periods of history and different stages of our lives can open up our hearts and minds to many things which we had previously missed. Many years ago, when speaking of the experience of the Russian Orthodox Church under Communist rule, Archbishop Anthony Bloom remarked that while the Church had lost the Christ of the great cathedrals and splendid liturgies, it had found the Christ who was homeless, persecuted and a stranger. No doubt he would have added, if pressed, that the discovery was only possible because the loss had happened first, and that it was not, and could not, have been foreseen before the loss. In different language we can say that he was pointing to the Spirit's constant work of taking us by surprise.

233

GOD AND PEOPLE OF OTHER FAITHS

If then the universal love of God in Christ is for all people everywhere, and if the Spirit of Love is constantly doing the unexpected, how are we to understand our responsibility towards those of other faiths?

Our first task is to acknowledge that they really are people of faith. For example, a Sikh teacher in a Church School once said, with tears in her eyes, "But Guru Nanak is just as real to me in my prayers as you say Jesus is to you." On that basis we can attempt to understand them, knowing that we shall never finally succeed. Such understanding has two dimensions: personal meeting and study. There is no substitute for warm and friendly personal relationships. We all appreciate those who take a genuine interest in us and in our lives, without any ulterior motive, though there is always a fine line to be drawn between genuine interest and discourteous intrusion. It is not always easy to say where the one ends and the other begins. This essential paradox is expressed in the story of the Christ of the Emmaus Road. He drew near to the two disciples who were walking together and asked them why they were sad. In other words he intruded, and in that sense all evangelism is intrusive. Yet when the disciples were about to go into the inn, "he made as if to continue his journey" (Luke 24:28), and only went inside to join them at their express invitation. In other words he refused to intrude and in that sense genuine evangelism is never intrusive. All evangelism and indeed all Christian ministry takes place in the tension between the two terms of that paradox.

Personal meeting which hopefully leads to rich and lasting friendship goes hand in hand with study. There are now plenty of books available which explain the content, history and practice of other faiths. These range from the simplest introductions for primary school children – and these can profitably be read by adults with little time to spare – to major works of scholarship. A few Christians are called to a lifetime of study in this area, while others are properly busy for most of their time with other things. The vital point is that we are so interested in other people that we want to learn more about them. To be genuinely interested in another person or community is to be already halfway to loving them. What matters is not the volume of knowledge we manage to acquire but the attitude of mind and heart which we bring to it.

THE DESIRE TO UNDERSTAND

Human groups have never been good at understanding those whom they regard as different. We have usually turned other people into caricatures and stereotypes, banishing them beyond the frontiers of our mental world, so that we can avoid the need to take them seriously. Now that people of other faiths are often quite literally our next-door neighbours such attitudes can no longer serve us. Instead our task must now be so to understand the life and faith of others that they themselves will own our description. That is how we are called to honour the tenth commandment of the Decalogue. To refuse to "give false evidence against [y]our neighbour" (Exodus 20:16) is, in this context, to refuse to say anything about another faith which those who follow it would deny.

This has more to do with imagination than with knowledge. It means that, as far as we can, we try to put ourselves into the place of those who follow the other faith, and to see the world through their eyes. The world that we look at from this new perspective will include Jesus and his Church. Much of what we then begin to see may be painful and disturbing to our own faith, but it is precisely at this point that we must refuse to draw back. For example, for some Jews the very name of Jesus may be anathema and they may tell us that they want nothing whatever to do with us: all they ask is to be left alone. If that is the case then we must respect their wishes, but that does not take us far enough. We must make ourselves familiar with at least some part of the church's appalling record of anti-Semitism, a record of which the Holocaust was the climax. That record summons us to a depth of penitence which few of us have yet been able to contemplate. If we set out on that journey we may begin to understand why for some Jews a Christian is the last person they want to meet and Jesus the last name they want to hear.

The West has for many centuries had a distorted understanding of Islam for rather different reasons. Fear of being overwhelmed by Islam made it dificult if not impossible for European Christendom to look at it with the imaginative sympathy which I have described. Nor were the necessary tools of scholarship or opportunities for meeting available in the way that they are today.

With Eastern religions the situation is different for we do not have the same record of historic misunderstanding and close theological relationship, but the principle of imaginative sympathy is just as important because the differences of outlook and language are so much greater. The quarrels between Judaism, Islam and Christianity are almost a family affair. Because we share a common background and to a certain extent a common language it is possible to disagree. With Hinduism and Buddhism there is much less of that common background to build on.

Further, there are, of course, different versions of every faith as there are different versions of Christianity – indeed every religion is a coalition between what are often, quite literally warring factions. If we are honest about the past history and present reality of our own Christian dividedness we can reasonably hope that in time others may be similarly honest. Then too there is always a difference between the faith of the scholar or leader and the faith of the ordinary person, who may be less sophisticated and confident but in fact more profound. We shall also notice common threads like the suppression of women, the importance given or not given to ritual purity, the tension between marriage and celibacy, and the place of voluntary poverty. All these themes appear in different religious contexts and illustrate the fact that a shared human nature underlies all our other differences.

To explore another faith in the context of friendship, such reading as we can manage, and above all of imaginative sympathy means that all our discoveries are provisional. Our views are always open to revision as we add to our knowledge and learn to put what we have learnt in wider contexts. Where possible an important element in this is literally learning another language. We can only do this effectively if we are willing to meet those who speak it and put ourselves in a position of weakness over against them, a weakness which is closely related to the vulnerability of love which we discussed earlier. Few things are more humiliating and disturbing than learning to speak a new language, for the learner is in a real sense reduced to the impotence of childhood. Yet few things are more appreciated. To eat the food or to wear the dress of another community costs us nothing. To attempt to learn the language, even if we do not get very far, is to show a real willingness to take trouble and time on their behalf.

UNDERSTANDING AND ACTION

All this comes under the general rubric of understanding. Along with it there are opportunities in contemporary Britain for Christians to work alongside people of other faiths for the good of society. The kind of friendship we have described above, vitally important though it is, is desperately precarious. To work with people is to build friendships into structures of co-operation which no longer depend on the continuing presence of one or two key people. People of different faiths who live side by side in a particular area can form such things as residents' associations which can address local authorities on matters like housing and health. They can form inter-faith groups which often discover a surprising degree of unanimity over such topics as the care of the elderly and the education of children. When people are working together in a common project they can begin to share some of the deepest convictions and questions of their lives. A shared structure provides a context in which trust can be established. Only when trust is there can real meeting begin. Here is the context where evangelism takes place, but it is an evangelism which works in both directions. Christians are now open to learning from those of other faiths about the deepest convictions which undergird their lives and only as they listen can they properly expect that listening to be reciprocated.

What this calls for is not merely a Decade of Evangelism but *lifetimes of incarnation* for which the Decade is only a beginning. Our problem is that either we are impatient, wanting to get to evangelism too quickly and so ignoring the incarnational context in which it must be set if it is to be authentic, or else we are too diffident, not really believing that we have anything worth sharing with others. The understanding, meeting and working together need to be matched by a continuing study and deepening appropriation of our own Christian faith. In the churches we need, as a matter of urgency, to find effective ways of teaching and learning the faith together. Here is another area where people of other faiths often put us to shame. Christians who meet Muslims, for example, are often impressed by the direct and simple way in which comparatively uneducated Muslims are able to tell others what they believe and do.

Where churches are genuinely rooted both in their faith and in their locality much quiet sharing and exchange is already going on across the frontiers between communities; but some churches are little better than religious clubs which have turned their backs on their neighbours about whom they then fantasize in negative ways which only serve to make meeting still more difficult. A healthy realization that we are part of a world Church which comprises many different cultures and many different ways of living the Gospel can go some way to undermining that false way of Christian living and opening the hearts and minds of its prisoners to the true dimensions of the faith they profess.

VALUING *THE OTHER*

All that has been said so far assumes a positive theology of "the other", whether the other be a whole community or simply one of its members. None of us exists as a self-sufficient isolated individual, we need the other person or community in order to discover who we are. If we have a negative view of the other based on ignorance, prejudice, and fear then our own identity is correspondingly diminished and we are reduced either to turning our backs on the other or to shouting slogans across the chasm of unknowing. Conversely if we start from the presupposition that all religions are equally valid routes to the top of the same mountain there is no real motive to meet the other since we are all well able to get to the same place by our own chosen routes. In neither case is it necessary to meet the other at any level beyond the superficial. There is a parallel here in Christian ecumenism. In the past Catholics and Protestants functioned by describing each other's practice in negative terms: Catholic papalism was matched by Protestant anarchy. Catholics exalted the mother of the Lord and so Protestants ignored her, and so on. Sometimes ecumenical enthusiasm can react against that barren history in such a way that now no one really notices what denomination the others belong to. Each of these attitudes is misguided, for neither of them encourages us to take seriously the other who is both enemy and friend, fascinating and menacing at the same time. Real meeting means entering into each other's life and history as far as we are able and seeing ourselves through each other's eyes.

We do not suggest that meeting people of other faiths is simply an extension of Christian ecumenism: that is much too cheap and facile a proposal, but we do suggest that the attitudes which undergird these two enterprises are similar. So we take seriously the otherness of the other, and we recognize that our discoveries are constantly open to correction and enlargement. Further we realize that our understanding of our own faith is always provisional and open to correction and enlargement in the same way "Christ gave his life: it is for Christians to discern the doctrine" in the words of a great Christian scholar. This is but another version of the well-known dictum that God always has more treasures to reveal from God's holy word. This means that there is a vulnerability and open-endedness about all our evangelism which is a perpetual risking of

Christ and therefore of ourselves for Christ's sake. We can dare to take such risks if we believe that beyond them there lies a richer discovery of who Christ is.

If the Decade inspires and enables more of us to set out on this exacting and rewarding pilgrimage it will bear fruit and go on doing so long after the turn of the millenium. And if the Holy Spirit is the source of our life then the nature of that fruitfulness will take us all by surprise.

The Challenge of Secularism

Many in our parishes, mistakenly, believe that they have no need to bother themselves with the question of other-faith communities. Very few make the same mistake about the presence of the secular challenges to our Christian faith which confront us every day. Whether we are those who speak of living in a pagan, post-Christian country, or whether we are more inclined to emphasize the continuing importance of the vestiges of Christian faith within the folk religion of many of our neighbours, none of us can escape the fact that most of our contemporaries give very little thought to the Christian faith — and not much place to God in their daily lives. Often, we find ourselves in a noticeably minority position when we express some specifically Christian viewpoint.

We asked Dan Beeby, the co-ordinator of the project, The Gospel and our Culture, to point up the challenges of secularism in the light of the Churches' task of evangelism.

The words "secular", "secularization" and "secularism", are ambiguous and confusing. "Secular" means "concerning the world" and is not necessarily a challenge, except in the sense that we are challenged to be grateful for the world and to care for it. "Secularization" is "the process whereby societies liberate themselves from religious control and domination". As such it can be either commendable or evil depending on the religion and the nature of the control.

If "secular" and "secularization"' are ambiguous, "secularism" (like most "isms" – race/racism, and nation/nationalism) is almost always a challenge. Genesis 1–3 deals with the place of the secular in God's total plan. Genesis 1 secularizes the whole of creation in the sense that it is radically desacralized. The heavens and the earth are creatures; they are things with no inherent divinity. They are wholly secular but because they are God's creation and subject to him, their secular nature is a cause for celebration and rejoicing. They are "very good". Problems, and the advent of secularism, only appear when one of the creatures, the one made in the image of God, resents his secular nature and, in conjunction with other creatures – trees, fruits, animals, beauty, taste, wisdom – begins to deify his own judgement and make up his own mind about what is good and evil. The great and central problem of human life is when creaturely things are not content with their status; when man, the elevated creature, destined to maintain order among the rest of creation (Genesis 1, 27–8) further exalts himself beyond creaturehood and turns the first "image" of God (himself) into the first idol.

I take the word "secularism" to cover most of what follows from man's first fall, the change from the truly secular into something other; into an ideology which is both thing and god; an idol. Secularism is when the creature declares the Creator redundant. So the challenge we are to consider is not from the truly secular but from the secular standing in the holy place – an "abomination of desolation".

LIFE IN THE ORPHANAGE

One of the features of modernity is the one-parent family – usually a mother and child. This is accompanied by another feature – the feminist argument for the dispensable father. These phenomena in family life are symbolic of what has happened in secularist culture at large. By liberating ourselves from the fetters of religion we have become parentless; we live in an orphaned universe in which a majority have come to assume that God is dead, or if not dead, at least frail and possibly mentally ill. Life without a Father is paradoxical. If we are uncreated then perhaps we are self-engendered and, in consequence, entitled to display the assurance, confidence and arrogance of the self-made man or woman. But then there is the other side. Orphanages are lonely places, and can be poor substitutes for the home we never had, but still miss. To this we must add the haunting memories of two "world wars", the threat of nuclear holocaust, widespread moral breakdown, increasing violence, and much else. There is much cause to be unsure, uncertain, rootless and fearful. We are both cocksure and, at the same time, hollow beings in a wasteland. Waiting – not even for Godot. These two sides of Western life have been described by a Chinese theologian as "technological optimism and literary pessimism."

The features of this orphaned universe which affect the Church are legion because secularism is a totalitarian ideology with strong religious features. It can be dogmatic, prescriptive, limiting and censorious. For instance, it can produce the sociologist who also writes about theology but has to do it under a pseudonym. It accounts for the Christian psychiatrist who, qua psychiatrist, said she would never dream of mentioning her Christian belief to her patients because that would be unprofessional and unethical, but who, at the same time, rejoiced that she could draw on the great resources of her "secular" training for her pastoral work in the church. It came as a great shock to her when she realized that she was living out of two opposing faiths; it was the "liberating" secular faith which provided the dogma and the censorship, and the presumed dogmatic Christianity which provided the real liberation.

Alongside this prescriptive element within secularism there is the apparent opposite – the absolute priority it seems to give to toleration. As everything is inevitably relative without a Father's rule, toleration of all points of view is essential. This can be very good, but also evil. Toleration of everything can include the toleration of all restraint, and the toleration of forces that lead to destruction, even the destruction of toleration itself. This process is also deceptive, in that it confines toleration to the "nursery", for it does not prohibit illusion and fantasizing; often it encourages them. We are, for example, quite free to "imagine" that there is a God who created us and redeemed us in Jesus Christ. We are free to worship this God, even (in some forms of secularism) to commend him to others. What we are less free to do is to insist that this God is real, existent and universal, and that he cannot be confined to nursery imaginings; also that he did in fact create all things, redeem all things, and is Lord of all things – the secular world as well as the religious imagination.

A world where God is confined to private imaginings is a world bereft of all authority except that which we ourselves create. In place of commandments, laws and statutes which have an existence and grounding outside of society, secularism provides us with authorities which are based solely on the authority of human opinion, the will of the majority, or the will to power of the powerful individual. Such a world is open to the dominance of "reason", so-called, which is given the appearance of possessing external reality but which is, in large part, our own creation. A Godless world is open to all manner of relativism because the ground of the absolute has been taken away.

THE CASUALTIES OF SECULARISM

Truth is one of the first casualties of secularism. Destabilized by the loss of an anchor in revelation, and in the God of revelation, truth tends to be at the mercy of intellectual fashion or social necessity. Seeking some norm, it often finds it in the ways of science, which is wholly inadequate. Free of religious restraints, and shorn of inhibiting "authority", the modern intellectual is now completely free to seek for the truth but, because of current secular myths and his own implicit dogmas, he does not really believe that there is an objective truth to be found or a real reality to be apprehended. Consequently, much of her intellectual endeavour is a kind of game which has been likened to philosophical contraception. The search for truth is a carefully sterilized search which makes sure that the truth is never found. The point of the search has to be the search itself; the object of the search must not and cannot be found. It is a kind of academic foxhunt which would cease to have meaning if the fox of truth were sighted and slain. The declared end is not the end at all. The means has now become the end. It is an eternal love-play without the responsibilities of conception and birth (Christopher Derrick: *Escape from Scepticism*).

Freedom, a close relative of truth, also changes its nature and role in a secularist world. Instead of being a creation of truth, the roles are reversed. No longer does truth make us free, rather freedom (very freely defined) becomes the necessary condition for the discovery of truth; and the end result tends to be licence not freedom.

Dogma is another of secularism's main casualties. Partly due to the influence of Descartes, doubt, which was destructive of faith, changed places with dogma, which had been the custodian of redemption. Doubt became the way to knowledge (always partially true, as we see with St Thomas): dogma became a word of abuse. It has become imperative for us to conceal the dogmas which we all have and live by, in case we are condemned for the unforgiveable sin of being dogmatic. The end result of this is that dogmas of every shade and description, because they operate clandestinely, become enormously powerful. Modern secular individuals, as a result, are frequently monumentally self-deceptive. Convinced that they are liberally non-dogmatic, they live complacently in their dogmatic frame, and, assured of their tolerance, they can be appallingly intolerant – especially of those who are aware of their own dogmas because they have chosen and confessed them.

Our orphaned universe hears a great deal about values – about seeking values and creating values. Because we are presumed to be orphans and repudiate all authority external to ourselves, these values are our values (nothing more) with all that implies. But sometimes, the old vocabulary of "good" and "bad", "true" and "false" is still employed, and it is assumed that our words, actions and attitudes are continuous with those of an age where values were external and given: divine data in fact. But a value which I create is by definition my creation; it is indistinguishable from my opinion unless somehow it is rooted in a reality beyond me and all my fellow human beings. "My values", in the sense that I myself make them and opt to value them, is a contradiction in terms. A value is only a value if it addresses me authoritatively from a location beyond and above me.

The Church finds itself witnessing, like Adam and Eve,

in a world that has repudiated divinity and eaten of the fruit of the knowledge of good and evil. This is true both in the public and the private sphere. We have a world without real values and where the pseudo-values change with the fashion. Twenty years ago smoking in public places was acceptable, but "living together" was not. The situation is now reversed. In the scale of moral values, within a fairly brief period, tobacco and fornication appear to have changed places.

THE DEPTH OF THE CHALLENGE

As most acknowledge, the main challenge of secularism is a cultural one. What is not sufficiently acknowledged is the depth of the problem. We often talk glibly of materialism, naturalism, scientific humanism, consumerism and the like, and indeed these are obstacles to mission, but they are second-order obstacles. The real issues lie deeper. They lie in the assumptions and presuppositions of our post-Enlightenment culture, a culture once limited to the West but now already a global phenomenon which I have characterized as the orphan universe. This culture transmitted through our educational system, the media, commerce, literature, etc. builds in us a threshold against Christianity which is so high that only the "culturally eccentric" can possibly cross it. Perhaps this is why Western Christianity is predominantly middle-class. If the grain of the culture denies the Gospel, and loyalty to Christ (as it must) demands that we go against the grain, then this calls for confidence, education and a dissenting spirit; qualities most often found in the middle classes.

One of the ironies of the present situation is the role-reversal between European Christianity and many of the Churches in Europe's nineteenth- and early twentieth-century "mission fields" – in Asia, Africa and the Pacific. The latter now flourish while we decline. This change highlights the nature of the secularist challenge.

Missionaries from strong, confident European Churches went to traditional cultures which were very resistant to the Gospel. Asians, Africans and others had their own revelations, their own gods, goddesses, heavens and hells, demons and angels, their own miracles, priesthoods, shrines and moralities. All these opposed what the missionaries preached but, gradually some conversions took place and an early trickle soon became a flood. Why did converts come? One answer is a simple cultural one. These cultures had revelations opposed to Christ but they did not deny revelation. Their gods were different but they did not deny divinity. Their heavens were different but they did not deny that there was an all-powerful heaven. Their history was not controlled by Christ but it was controlled by forces outside of humankind. The demons were not Satan and the mighty ones were not angels, but the places for Satan and angels were in place. The categories demanded by Christianity were virtually all there. The cultural opposition was very strong but it was "surface" opposition. Deep, deep down the door was ajar and the Gospel entered and flourished, and is still flourishing. But will it continue to flourish as they increasingly adopt Western secularism? There are already signs that our malaise will soon be theirs.

On the surface, Western secularism leaves us free to pick and choose in the religious supermarket, but what about deep down? Are the deep doors anywhere ajar? The world's schools and universities, factories and farms, banks, politics – almost everything public – function without reference to revelation, deity, creation, redemption, miracle, prayer, worship, judgement, confessed absolutes, and eternal life. Where nineteenth-century missionaries filled existing categories with the Gospel of Christ, today's mission within modern secularism faces a world that does not possess the categories necessary to receive the Gospel. Some "liberal" missions try to do without the absent categories; some "conservative" missions assume they are still present. Clearly new ways to do mission are required.

THE GOSPEL AND SECULARISM

For too long we have been content to stand within our culture and, with its assumptions and presuppositions, pass judgement on the Bible and on Christ. We have asked, "What can I still believe?" The challenge now is to stand firmly and confidently on the faith we have confessed, and to question our culture. We need to adopt the biblical view that we are "resident aliens", a diaspora-force called in Christ to live within the counter-culture created by God's word as well as in our own culture. This counter-culture is first called to understand the Gospel it professes to believe, and then, in the light of that Gospel, to understand the cultures all around it. Finally, armed with these two understandings we create more Christian eccentrics who by their counter-culture and diaspora-witness provide a word of judgement and a message of redemption which gradually enables people to recognize the alien counter-culture as the true culture. We are called to culture-mission so that the kingdoms of the world become the Kingdom of our Lord.

The Scriptures appear to have little or no place for atheism or agnosticism. The two Testaments are remarkably black and white on the matter and seem only to envisage two possibilities: the worship of the true God or the worship of idols. Romans 1:21ff seems typical of the whole of Scripture; we either worship the Creator or we worship creatures. The constant in the equation is the worship; the variables are in what is worshipped. Not to worship God does not impart the freedom *not* to worship; it leaves only the possibility that something else becomes the object of worship. "To worship, or not to worship" is not the question. Atheism is only apparent. Our societies are not secular; they frantically worship the idols, ideologies, principalities and powers that inevitably crowd into the God-vacuum we have created. "Where God is excluded all things become goddable".

Are then "atheism", "agnosticism" and even "secularism" misnomers? Or – more brutally – are they cover-ups for idolatry? Is secularism really secular, or is it merely a new form of humanity's oldest ailment – the worship of a humanly-created god? Is the challenge not a secular challenge after all but the challenge of another religion? Are the "knowledge" and the power and the wisdom of secularism also faith-based? Are there "creeds with everything" and do the unjust live by faith as well as the just? Is the distinction between ages of faith and unfaith a deception? Are we all "religious" all the time, the only differences being that some are aware of their faith while others are not, and that some have the true faith while others honour an idol? Recent suggestions from sociologists that secularism does in fact produce overt religiosity, combined with the growth of the New Age Movement and other forms of so-called "spirituality", support the need for new definitions of religion.

THE MISSION TO SECULARISM

So we engage in mission as Christians, not speaking to a secular rationalist culture but to another religion or religions. Our task is not to convince people who believe nothing, but to confront their belief in other gods. Our situation is similar to that of the prophets and the apostles. We recognize that God is Father, Son and Holy Spirit. We accept that he has revealed himself in Scripture and is present in the world which he created and in his Church through which he witnesses. We present this as fact, not as personal longing, private opinion, legend, or myth. Anything resembling myth is because the Gospel is the myth that happened; the happening that other myths may feel after, and not a myth among other myths!

Consciously, humbly, but with assurance, we stand upon these dogmas and engage in a missionary encounter with the prevailing public doctrine of our culture. Our conviction is that only Christ as Lord has claim upon the allegiance of all culture, and that if we are not rooted in these dogmas we shall be unconsciously standing on the dogmas that are every-where present in the culture – dogmas of an apostate faith. We must apologize, not for arrogance in what we now do, but that for too long we have arrogantly judged the revelation in Christ according to the hidden creeds of the idols we have made and which, in turn, have mismade us.

As the culture is ubiquitous, so mission must be ubiquitous. There cannot be any no-go areas. From being the quirky pastime of the few who address the limited area of life normally considered available for conversion, mission must become the glorious effort of the whole Church facing the whole world. The task has been called "Heineken Mission" because it is mission that reaches the parts that other missions do not reach. As the apostasy in the West was slow and almost unnoticed, so the new dimension of mission must work within a timespan more of centuries than decades. It might take decades to train those who will gradually lead the Church out of the ghetto and point out the real battlefields.

And this mission has to begin in the West, a part of the world not unacquainted with mission. Indeed its own missionary effort has been magnificent, sacrificial and, in many ways, remarkably successful. But it has usually been mission elsewhere, and our missiology has benefited almost everywhere, except the birthplace of Western culture. We exported the Gospel and left the West bereft. Now this mission must begin with the West's acceptance that it is, almost, the most resistant of all mission fields. The mission must begin in the West but must spread to the "new West", *i.e.* the rest of the world that has taken our culture and made it theirs. The acids of modernity which have eaten into old Christendom, and almost eaten it away, are already at work in the younger Churches, which are more and more set in the midst of modernity. Old and new, East and West, North and South, the whole universal Church, must accept the global task of mission to modernity.

A New Vision for Mission

The task of mission that confronts us will lead to many specific missions. These, in brief, are some of them:

1. A mission to theology: the "best" theology, Western theology, is deficient because it has had little place for missiology and has not been nourished by mission.

2. A mission to biblical studies, too long dominated by alien creeds.

3. A mission to ministerial formation that the Church may learn its missionary nature.

4. A mission to the missions, hindered by false divisions into overseas and home; driven often by guilt rather

than forgiveness; at present caught up in an identity crisis and busied with many things, some of them the right things.

5. A mission to academic disciplines: too long they have been walled gardens starved by isolation. The mission is to declare them part of the great estate and to tell them the Gardener's name.

6. The new mission will be to economics as well as to economists, to biology and medicine as well as biologists and doctors – to the essence of the discipline as to its practioners.

7. There must be great missions to language: the great languages are now often the missionary media of paganism. How do we use words like "nature", "reason", "academic", "professions". What meaning do we give to "religion", "pluralism", even to "God"?

8. Dare we think of missions to institutions, to educational theory, to the media, to the arts? How are we to think of the new Europe now emerging? Is it to be understood solely in "market" terms or even in political terms? Can Europe exist apart from the Christian faith which was so much part of its creation and preservation?

9. The new missions should attempt to reclaim the "high ground" of academe (and its textbooks) but they should operate at all levels. They must be pastoral, practical, classless and in every class, artistic, educational, industrial, commercial, family – above all they must be lay missions.

10. The new missions will need new communities to embody the new concepts. They may give rise to a wholly new type of missionary order.

The Gospel and New Age

Whether or not many of us have been used to thinking of secularism specifically as a religion, we have all been made aware of the religious challenge of the New Age Movement. Most of us, however, have an extremely vague idea of what New Age is all about. We are grateful to Philip Seddon from the Department of Biblical Studies at the Selly Oak Colleges for providing us with this introduction to the reality and challenge of New Age religion.

At the heart of the New Age is a vision of interconnectedness.[1] This is distinct from the Christian vision of all things co-inhering in Christ, and in reaction to the analytical and objectifying procedures of modern Western thought. The New Age principle is a "rebirth of images" – specifically of the Great Chain of Being. This is a continuum and amalgam of tradition from Pythagoras' philosophy and Lucretius' materialism, through Gnosticism's emanations and neo-Platonic spirituality to the Ranters' social radicalism[2] and Darwin's nineteenth-century physical–evolutionary world-views, right up to current discussions on the relationship of matter and spirit. All is bound together in One. This is the New Age's "Holistic World-view", contrasted with previous "fragmentationalist" ones[3] and buttressed (often meretriciously) by the *imprimatur* of triumphalist modern science.[4]

1. D Lorimer, *Whole in One*, subtitled *The Near-Death Experience and the Ethic of Interconnectedness*, Arkana, 1990; G. F. Orenstein, *The Reflowering of the Goddess*, Pergamon, 1990, pp. 15, 17.

2. N. Cohn, *The Pursuit of the Millennium*, Paladin, 1970, p. 293.

3. S. Greig, G. Pike, D. Selby, *Greenprints For Changing Schools*, W.W.F. and Kogan Page, 1989, pp. 16–17.

4. B. Appleyard, *Understanding the Present. Science and the Soul of Modern Man*, Pan, 1992.

From this centre derive concerns for integration, wholeness, harmony, balance and a "reconciliation of opposites".
Examples abound: whole-brain theory, worship of the
Goddess alongside worship of (the supposedly male
Christian) God, planetary healing, yin and yang polarities,
the quest for androgyny, the welcoming of irrationality as
well as rationality. Such a wide spectrum of approach
and concern does not militate, as some argue, against
any comprehensive overview of apparently disparate
phenomena; rather, it illustrates precisely the New Age's
range of claims, and the eclectic and pragmatic base on
which it builds its synthesis.

Evolutionary *dogma*, for instance, has become an essential
(not merely an incidental) undergirding of its own
millenarian vision of a new – spiritual – humanity. The
New Age is not simply concerned with the multiplication
of altered states of consciousness. The key word, rather, is
transformation, and the goal is a universal change, or
paradigm shift, in human consciousness to the point of
ultimate identification with all life. This is precisely
pantheism (though the term is rarely used): the discovery
that all life is divine. "This transformation is manifest in a
new sense of personal divinity" (William Bloom). It is an
enlightenment, an awakening from ignorance in order to
transcend all dualisms. It is "illumination without
repentance" – explaining how it is possible for believers of
any faith, or none, to enter the New Age. "Belief" is
relatively unimportant and constricting. "Experience" is so
self-authenticatingly liberating as to destroy the need for
any creeds or boundaries. "Spirituality" dissolves religion.

This presenting principle of interconnectedness is at the
heart of this ancient world-view, revitalized for the cultural
and spiritual context in which the age of Pisces will be
replaced by that of the age of Aquarius. Nothing short of a

"universal Pentecost" or "Luciferic initiation" is anticipated. In consequence, any forms of dualism are, by
definition, to be resisted as the remaining vestiges of that
"Old Age" which hinder the breakthrough into the new.
The great sin is "the sin of separateness" (Alice Bailey), the
sin of distinguishing in any way – e.g. between humanity
and creation, between one religion or another. Hence the
importance of the – purely horizontal – theme of reconciliation: reconciliation between human beings and the rest of
creation, between good and evil, between the principles of
Christ and Lucifer, and ultimately between any subject and
object.

THE UNDERLYING CHALLENGE

However, it is extremely important to realize that within
this presenting principle of interconnectedness, the New
Age proper is undergirded and motivated by the esoteric,
psychic, occult ("hidden", "secret") traditions of all
religions and nations. (Not all "New Agers" are either
aware of, or adherents of, this inner commitment.) Of
course, in its optimistic vision of a transformed world, any
religious insight can lend assistance, including amenable
themes and figures from Christian tradition such as Celtic
spirituality, Francis of Assisi, and Eckhart. But in its
essentially negative approach towards orthodox Jewish and
Christian faith, the revival of neo-paganism, magic and
shamanism, along with the high profile given to aboriginal
religions, and the evangelistic outreach of "folk" practices,
forms by far the most significant part of this process of
"recapturing ancient wisdom" (a modern version of the
myth of the "noble savage"), unfettered by the dogmas and
supposed exclusivities of Christian tradition. The ultimate
goal of the New Age, sometimes expressed, sometimes

not, is the end of the Judaeo-Christian tradition: either its elimination or its incorporation into the New Age. The explosion of the repressed spirit brings with it the re-demonization of the world.

So it is not surprising that Christian and Jewish faith, in particular, with their fundamental insistence on the distinction between God and creation, are the object of frequent paternalism, scorn and vitriol[1] in New Age writing. Some authors view humanity as the cancer, others Jewish and Christian faith. Some see Christian faith as a 2,000-year detour; others see the new environmentalism as "well advanced towards replacing" Judaeo-Christianity.[2] Eastern faiths, with their greater reluctance to make distinctions and their greater concern for the All and the One, are comparably lauded,[3] especially in contemporary environmental debate. (Eastern Orthodoxy's vision of *theiosis* – divinization through Christ and the Spirit – is, despite the language, far removed from similar New Age concepts, or any dissolution of subject-object relationships.)

1. M. Brearley, "Matthew Fox: Creation and Spirituality for the Aquarian Age" in *Christian Jewish Relations*, Vol. 22, No. 2, 1989, pp. 37–49; and "Matthew Fox and the Cosmic Christ" in *Anvil*, Vol. 9, No. 1, 1992, pp. 39–54.
2. D. Nicholson-Lord, "Cities and Spirituality", in *Resurgence* 145, March/April 1991, p. 26. cf. T. Higton, "The Environment as Religion" in M. Cole et al., *What is the New Age?* Hodder & Stoughton, 1990, pp. 78–95.
3. E. Lucas, "Scientific Truth and New Age Thinking", in *Science and Christian Belief*, Vol. 4 (1), April 1992, pp. 13–25.

THOUGHTFUL CHRISTIAN DISCERNMENT

At the same time, in an age of remythologizing and of gullible cynicism (Philip Walters), it is important to recognize the impetus that has been given to spiritual questions by New Age thinking – precisely in such areas as economy, ecology and science. George Steiner and Eugenio Trias are among those who see that the end of the twentieth century will put religious questions at the forefront, in reaction against spiritual apathy, the failure of the gospel of secularism, technology's pie-in-the-sky promises to meet all human needs, and the anaemia of a rationalist Christianity which has sold out to the spirit of a previous age.

Christian discernment in response to the New Age will accordingly need to be spearheaded by the qualities of love and truthfulness: by practitioners motivated by the humility of a compassionate heart and a listening ear; and by intellectuals fired by the Holy Spirit to wrestle with complex challenges. Similar and at times identical language is used with quite different meanings and resonances. Helped by media propaganda, the New Age has blazed trails of thought and practice which privatizing Christians have avoided. At the same time, the note of menace and threat discernible in a range of New Age literature must not be ignored. The task of reclamation is not simple, but equally there is no need for fear in engaging with distorted and attenuated beliefs, or with misrepresentation of Christian beliefs. The following seem to be some of the areas where dialogue and criticism are required.

● The focus on inter-*relationship* must be recognized as a major contribution to current worldwide issues, and as a major critique of inherited individualism. Genesis 1–11 can be read fruitfully along these lines, and the theme of human beings as "priests of creation" further explored. Ironically, at the same time, because interconnectedness is a principle and not located in the Person of God, unsubtle ideological consequences are frequently drawn.

- Fundamental *human* questions of existence, meaning and identity, of the relationship of the past, present and future, of place and destiny in a universe of unbelievable proportions, underlie current fascination with astrology, astral travel, sacred sites, the paranormal, etc. However, a discovery of a God whose love is faithful and self-sacrificing, rather than any deterministic abstraction, provides an objective base for personal and corporate identity.

- A rich Trinitarian vision of *God* enables a proper balance between transcendence over creation and immanence in creation, on which is built the awesome doctrine of the incarnation and the outpouring of the Spirit; without such distinctions, self-delusions proliferate.

- A cultural context which chooses models of flux, process, growth and development for its self-understanding finds a singular historic event of revelation in *Jesus Christ* awkward, if not offensive; Jesus as *a* Christ it can accept, not Jesus as *the* Christ. But Christian faith does not minimize universal perceptions of the presence and work of God. Conversely, however, a cyclical view of "death and resurrection" cannot give itself any ultimate or focused goal apart from the central interpretative gift of Jesus' death and resurrection.

- We need a more balanced grasp of the *Holy Spirit* as the One who is not only at work in believers, drawing the whole creation to the Father through the Son (New

Testament), but is also the Universal Creator Spirit at work in all and in all things, in beauty and ugliness, in secular and sacred, natural and supernatural (Old Testament).

RESPONDING TO THE CHALLENGE

At the same time, Christians must not be afraid to "expose the works of darkness" which are an inevitable consequence of the New Age's militant anti-dualism. Its strong streak of nature-mysticism itself militates against confronting the depths of human wilfulness, obstinacy and depravity,[1] and Anselm's saying applies: "You have not yet considered the weight of sin". There is a spirit of destruction and dissolution which aims ritually to effect decisive spiritual breaks from the supposed negativities of the Christian past; which encourages a spouse to break with a partner if they have "the wrong karma" or are not progressing sufficiently along the required spiritual path; or which invokes the power of spirits, entities, gods and goddesses, or ascended occult Spiritual Masters as part of the process of transforming consciousness. The breaking of existing (negative) ties is seen as essential to releasing the power of the new, true (positive) self.

But there is also a spirit of quest and longing, a desire for the healing of a hurt world, and a summons to a new asceticism. Christian witness through the ages has been

---

1. Popular usage of the word "depravity" is not that intended by Calvin, and current scholarship has to some extent been rehabilitating the proper technical use; but it is deeply ironical that a century in which theology has rejected virtually wholesale any use of the word at all should be perhaps the one above all others which has produced the most massive and horrific evidence to support the truth of either meaning.

concerned both to refute the false and learn from the unfamiliarly true. The temptation today is to choose one or the other: to deny that there is any particular illusion, or presence, or work of evil in the New Age; or to deny that there are serious worldwide issues with which Christian faith must grapple at the end of the twentieth century. Popular writing tends to heighten the demonic element, forgetting that even here it is unwise to point out the splinter in the other's eye when there may be a plank in one's own. Establishment theological assessments tend to be strongly idealist, editing out disturbing elements in the picture, and forgetting that we do not wrestle against flesh and blood, but against spiritual powers in high places.

Intellectual honesty requires a response as total as the vision presented. Christian integrity invites a passionate discipleship of Jesus Christ combined with ever-deepening intercession for the world for which Christ died, and a patient but acute refusal to identify sin with the sinner or the sinned-against.

Further Reading

A. New Age Presentations

William Bloom, *The New Age. An Anthology of Essential Writings,* Century, 1991

Matthew Fox, *The Coming of the Cosmic Christ*, Harper and Row, 1988

Peter Spink, *A Christian in the New Age*, DLT, 1991

B. Christian Responses (in England)

Wesley Carr, *Manifold Wisdom. Christians in the New Age*, SPCK, 1991

Lawrence Osborn, *Angels of Light? The Challenge of New Age Spirituality*, DLT, 1992

Michael Perry, *Gods Within*, SPCK, 1992

Philip Seddon, *The New Age – An Assessment*, Grove Booklets, 2nd ed., 1992

Chapter Eight

GROWING POINTS

This chapter's table of contents, together with its position in the book, may suggest to the reader that it is a kind of "catch-all" into which we have gathered whatever could not be fitted elsewhere! On the contrary, its contents are here by design, commissioned as pointers to some of what we see as likely Growing Points, some of them quite sharply controversial in the Church of England, for Christian reflection and action as the Decade progresses.

The Church and the Media

There is, for a start, the matter of attitudes in the Church to the media, on which Patrick Forbes writes with feeling.

"The trouble with you lot," said the local newspaper editor, glaring at the assembled clergy, "the trouble with you lot is that we only hear from you when you want us to help you with publicity for a restoration appeal. You ask for posters, for articles, for publicity, for balloons. We're happy to oblige, we're in the good news business too. Then after the event, we don't hear from you until five years later when you've found there's not quite enough money and you need some more publicity for another appeal. Haven't you had anything to say to us in between times?"

He was cross, and he was making a serious point.

Christians, particularly Anglicans, seem unable to grasp that the media are part of God's world, that they are the means of telling others about God and His love for them in Jesus Christ. Certainly many many clergy seem to have waking nightmares about the media. Headlines like: *"Vicar wouldn't baptize my child," sobs mother – Bishop to Probe* bedevil our imagination.

Just suppose, for a mad moment, that the Church exists to worship God and to tell God's good news to others, whatever happened to our involvement in the media? I spent years going to meetings in one diocese explaining the opportunities afforded by local radio. It was a sobering exercise. "We don't listen to local radio," they said. I hadn't made myself clear. I wasn't talking about opportunities for them to talk to themselves or to fellow church members using local radio. They could do that in church on Sunday mornings. I had been talking about reaching out to the thousands and thousands who aren't in church week by week. They wanted to know why our religious magazine programme was on when they were in church on a Sunday morning. "We're trying to reach a non-churchgoing audience," I answered. Shocked silence. "And you want *our* money for *them*?" That was precisely why I wanted their donations of a fiver or a tenner to help keep the programme on the air. My nine years in local radio religious broadcasting taught me a number of important lessons. There are hordes of good Christians with good news to tell, and the God-given ability to tell their stories on radio. Many of them don't believe that anyone would be interested in what they have to say, and so need encouragement to dare to say it. Few of them believe that what they are about is good news, and fewer still believe that they are at all capable of speaking up for God and the Gospel. They need convincing. "Surely, you want to talk to the vicar," they'd say. No, I wanted to hear from *them*. I could have filled the programme with bishops, clergy and returning missionaries. But the effect of only using professionals would be to convince the listener that faith, and prayer, and theology could only be handled by experts. And if that is true, then the Church is lost and the Gospel will fall.

Once we've overcome our anxieties and rediscovered the gifts of communication that God has given us, there's another challenge: the words and phrases we use. Much church talk is in code or jargon. A non-churchgoing listener will not understand my "giving my life to the Lord". Other words must be found to convey our meaning, words they will understand and be comfortable with. Some clergy have been taught to write theological essays at college, and firmly believe that they can write essays and read them as sermons or Thoughts for the Day. It won't do! A corrective is to stand in a bus queue or sit in a launderette and just listen. You won't hear too much theological jargon there. No trace of an ontological hermeneutic on the 7.32 to Kings Cross. No eschatological theory on the 38 bus.

So why inflict this code, this jargon, on potential believers? We must use the language of the marketplace if we're hoping to interest or attract those who are there. Comedians, who depend totally on their relationship with their listeners, spend time listening to current conversation. An American liturgy editor told me, "they have to know what flies," by which she meant they had to know the buzz-words, the slang, the catch phrases of the moment in order to be sure they were reaching their audience. There have never been so many opportunities for Christians to engage with local and community radio. One current estimate suggests that 30 million people listen to local radio every week. Hard-nosed radio station managers are admitting that good religious broadcasting will not only build but hold a significant audience.

Religious programmes are, however, only a small proportion of the output. There are phone-ins, news and current affairs programmes, chat shows, advice and help lines. Where are the Christians, where is the Gospel in these areas? One of the difficulties to be faced, as hinted earlier, is the attitude of churchgoers to the media in general, and to those involved in them in particular. Christians involved in local radio can find they are marginalized by the churches, underfunded, unsupported, and often misunderstood. They are "playing" at broadcasting while the "real" work is being done by the parish clergy. They are fringe workers, boundary riders, essential to the work of the centre yet operating on the edge. And the edge is where work has to be done too. It is pre-evangelism, changing attitudes, banishing ignorance and prejudice, telling stories, sowing seeds, floating ideas. Evangelism is the work of the local church. The media, print and broadcast, will never be a substitute for that local face-to-face encounter. But for good growth, the ground must be prepared.

I began with a sort of horror story. It still haunts me, the sight and sound of a media man of good will who couldn't understand why the bearers of good news weren't making better use of his medium, reaching more people week by week than they'd ever preach to in a lifetime's ministry. I've dwelt on local broadcasting for that is where I have spent much time and sweat. But the same questions need to be asked about our relationships with all the media, network radio and television, national newspapers, regional television, local radio, local newspapers, community radio, cable, and community newspapers. Have we the imagination, the vision to see how these media could carry the Gospel? Have we the will to invest time and money in training and personnel? And, crucially, will we support those already working in the media for God and his good news, Jesus Christ? I wonder.

Town or City-wide Evangelism

Some of the same questions, concerning the preparedness of the Churches to grasp the opportunities presented by the immense richness and variety of any contemporary urban area and by their own location throughout its life, are explored by David Hawkins as he writes about City-wide Evangelism out of the experience of the Leeds Festival '92.

THE IMPERATIVE

It is not surprising that city-wide evangelism has a bad press following the recent scandals of US tele-evangelists. Added to that we live in an age which cherishes pluralism and the privacy of each person's conscience. Jimmy Durante sharply expressed the collective subconscious: "Why doesn't everybody leave everybody else the hell alone?"

Having said that, mass communication is a fact of life and always has been. Advertisers and pressure groups vie for the biggest impact on the hoardings and media channels. Jesus communicated with crowds wherever he found them. The apostles addressed the general public in the market-place and the Acropolis as well as in the temple courts. The difference was that Jesus and the apostles communicated with integrity and accuracy and never resorted to subliminal sales techniques.

The fundamental fact which we must grasp and hold to is that the public proclamation is to do with an understanding of the very Gospel itself. Jesus preached the Kingdom of

God as "public truth". He and the apostles communicated in societies as pluralistic as ours and expected people of every religion, philosophy, race, class and age to respond. Lesslie Newbigin puts it this way: "A serious commitment to evangelism . . . means a radical questioning of the reigning assumptions of public life. It is to affirm the Gospel not only as an invitation to a private and personal decision but as public truth which ought to be acknowledged as true for the whole of the life of society." The Christian Gospel is not a body of religious opinion presented alongside other opinions for the consumption of those interested in such things. It is an announcement about the state of the world and so its public communication, way beyond the orbit of churches, is integral to the message itself. Marshall McLuhan's oft quoted slogan is disturbingly true: "The Medium is the Message".

In order to preserve the integrity of the Gospel we must certainly avoid manipulation but we must also avoid privatization. The Gospel of Jesus is unreligious. That is why it confused and upset the religious people of his day. Yet we choose to keep the communication of this message within the religious sector. City- and town-wide evangelism is imperative lest Christianity becomes a minor religious sect. United public evangelism is also good for the Christian community. All churches need goals to work towards which are beyond the immediate bounds of the parish or congregation. However committed churches may be to the ideal of continuous evangelism and church growth, human nature requires the motivation of goals to strive for. Working together with churches in a deanery or city means that churches which have a vision for evangelism can encourage those which do not.

The reflections that follow come from the experience of the executive committee of a city-wide evangelism project in Leeds: Festival '92.

THE OPPORTUNITIES

The opportunities for city- and town-wide evangelism are greater than ever if we are prepared to take them. In no previous decade have all the main-line denominations announced that mission and evangelism are to be at the top of the agenda. The designation 'The Decade of Evangelism' across our denominations must surely be interpreted as God's *kairos* to work evangelistically and ecumenically like never before.

For this reason the aims of the Leeds Festival were expressed as follows:

1. To bring people to faith in Jesus Christ and discipleship within the Church.
2. To demonstrate how Christians of diverse backgrounds can unite in the primary task of evangelism in this decade.

Once there has been a corporate ownership of a mission project by church leaders, ministers and lay people the potential of mounting evangelistic events and programmes of social action becomes an exciting possibility. "None of us have got it together but together we have got it" quotes the evangelist J. John in his training programme for missions. Resources from one church can be reinforced or complemented by those of another. All too often churches work in isolation and there is little appreciation of each other's contribution to evangelism.

Mission has always been the most fruitful incentive

for ecumenism as well as being the theological one. Ecumenism and mission are irresistibly linked in the prayer of Jesus in John 17: "My prayer is that all of them may be one . . . so that the world may believe that you have sent me." Bishop Michael Marshall expresses this conviction most succinctly, "Evangelism is inevitably ecumenical."

There are no short cuts in reaching that unity or corporate ownership in inter-church projects. In Leeds the consultation stage took a year and the planning and preparation a further two and a half years. The consulting and planning only came together because of long established councils of churches, ecumenical councils, fraternals, chapters and less formal networks. If Christians do not like each other they will not work together.

If mission is to break out of the religious sector, good media coverage of Christian opinion and activity is essential. Town or city Festivals can provide the necessary "buzz" to convince editors that Christian news is newsworthy. An excellent example was last year's *Everyman* programme featuring "Nightstop", the Leeds landlady scheme for homeless young people. This shining example of Christians putting their faith into action proved a good conversation starter.

THE OBSTACLES

Because of the breadth of theological and social outlook in any group of churches the task of achieving corporate ownership of an evangelistic project is considerable.

There is a justifiable dissatisfaction and even disdain for the somewhat bland recipe of town and city missions down the years. The style has often been compulsive and aggressive, as Bishop Peter Ball eloquently illustrates! "I see, over and over again, evangelism being done like a pheasant shoot. First you get the beaters to worry the birds, usually while they are enjoying themselves quite happily; then when you have frightened them into the air – bang! – you shoot them down, followed by a few friendly dogs who have various names like counsellors or sharers, to pick them up and bring them into the bag!"

Too often evangelistic campaigns have excited the twenty per cent of keen members of a select number of evangelical churches and have been boycotted by the majority of Christians. If the Decade of Evangelism is to be owned by the whole Church, with all its denominations and traditions, we must find new recipes that will unite and not divide. We need recipes that will recognize the diverse ways in which people feel comfortable about expressing and sharing their faith. Recipes that will enlist the eighty per cent of faithful "passivists" as well as the twenty per cent of activists. We must live down the stereotypes which have caused the majority of church members to give evangelistic ventures a wide berth. In search of such recipes we embarked on a lengthy period of consultation and preparation through ecumenical Lent groups and regional teaching centres. We used five emphases that have come to be known as "The Five Ps". they came from the training material of our missioner, J. John, and in turn were largely borrowed from David Barrett's work on mission strategy. For the Leeds Festival we interpreted them as follows:

PRAYER The Festival will encourage churches of all traditions to deepen their spirituality and intercede together for the life of the area.

PRESENCE The Festival will affirm and further the many ways in which Christians in and around Leeds are involved in social issues.

PROCLAMATION The major Christian denominations have designated the 1990s as the Decade of Evangelism. Festival '92 will be a focal point early in the Decade for the proclamation of the Gospel. It will stimulate us to use the remainder of the Decade more effectively.

PERSUASION The Christian faith is a subject for debate, discussion and dialogue. The Festival will provide opportunities to do this through a variety of local and central events.

POWER The 1980s saw a renewed emphasis in Britain of the healing power of God in the life of individuals, churches and society. Festival '92 will teach and celebrate this power.

Exploring these emphases enabled a larger than usual range of church members to be committed, with integrity, to the business of evangelism. The social activists who had been disparaging of city missions in the past became involved in emphasizing Christian "Presence" as part of proclaiming the Gospel. Valuable work in helping such groups to respect the complementary role of the evangelist was done by Roy McLoughry. Roy is a lecturer in social theology and is critical of the pietistic individualism of much evangelism, and yet believes passionately in personal salvation and the role of the evangelist in bringing people to faith. John Stott described social action and evangelism as the two blades of a pair of scissors; they need to be firmly riveted together in order to sharpen the other and cut effectively. In Festival '92 we arranged conferences and theatre productions to highlight social issues and help promote Christian initiatives. Those involved in the long hard slog of work with the homeless or unemployed sometimes feel superior or are made to feel inferior by large evangelistic events.

Those whose inclinations lie in spirituality, intercession or the healing ministry are finding these emphases to be integral to the dynamic of evangelism. Father Ian Petit of Ampleforth Abbey, and broadcaster Margaret Cundiff in their different ways made great contributions in encouraging people who would never have touched evangelism with a barge pole but who got involved by praying for people.

Persuasion is an area in which the Church is weak and yet it has been an important feature of the Church's proclamation ever since St Paul debated on Mars Hill. The Leeds Festival arranged seminars, debates and interfaith dialogue events with the help of the university in order to appeal to people's minds. It is in this area that the liberal tradition has an important contribution. Ethical and political issues are increasing in complexity in an age when technology is accelerating faster than our capacity to think theologically. People are less prepared than ever to be fobbed off with easy answers. We arranged a Day Conference featuring debate between Roy McLoughry and the Bishop of Newark, New Jersey, John Spong, on the subject of Sexuality.

In any town or city mission careful attention must be given to good communication with communities of other faiths. In Leeds, through discussions between the Festival Executive and the Interfaith Council, Concord, we arrived at a Statement of Intent for conduct during the Festival. This process of discussion was an important journey in helping to replace misconception by trust. Our experience was that the locally drafted statement has gained greater favour than official ones drafted from outside. The process of drafting was of more significance than the final form of words. It is our conviction that interfaith worship is an inappropriate activity and breeds unnecessary confusion and hostility. However interfaith dialogue is an essential and respectful part of mission in our pluralistic society and should be seen to be going on in any town or city mission. We planned dialogue events for several localities in Leeds as well as a round-the-table dialogue for seven faith communities in the Civic Hall.

A danger of the broad approach is that it may involve more people but at the same time lose its cutting edge. It was the determination of the Leeds Executive that this should not happen. From the beginning it was emphasized that regional and central presentations of the Gospel must form the focus of the Festival using the distinctive gifts of the invited missioners.

A standard obstacle to city or town missions is that the amount of effort required to mount such projects falls on already overstretched resources and overloaded diaries. For this reason the strategy we aimed at was to use, wherever possible, existing structures and slots in church calendars rather than creating new ones. The basic administrative network we chose was the Councils of Churches, in the belief that these would undergo some renewal through the experience of the Festival and would as a result be the more effective in the future. For example instead of communicating through a special "Festival Newspaper" we used an existing Leeds Christian Newspaper and by so doing enlarged its significance and distribution. We are convinced that if existing organizations and infrastructure are used to forward the aims of such projects there is a greater chance of those structures being strengthened and the impetus of the Mission continuing into church life.

SIX MONTHS ON...

As this book goes to print a year has elapsed since the main focus of Festival '92. It is difficult to evaluate the effect of the Festival with any accuracy because of its decentralized and comprehensive nature. What is evident, however, is that the *à la carte* vision of local events caught on with greater energy and enthusiasm than anyone could have foreseen resulting in over a hundred events and projects.

As a result the centrally planned presentations of Christianity in the Town Hall suffered, not in quality but in numerical support. Clearly much energy was consumed carrying off local initiatives which could not be called on for the central programme. A separation of a few months between the local and central thrusts might have helped.

Timetabling the Youth Festival in February worked well and much credit must go to the Oasis Trust for their professionalism and high standards of communication and methodology. Six thousand teenagers encountered Oasis in schools and one thousand six hundred attended hi-tech evangelistic presentations. Two hundred young people made responses of faith.

Generally the quality of events was felt to be high. This is important for witness opportunities today. The general public, as well as having less Christian background, is becoming more sophisticated and discriminating by the year. Christian entertainment acceptable five years ago does not draw audiences today.

CROSSOVER EVENTS

What we have learned from Festival '92 is that we must become increasingly practised in arranging well planned *Crossover Events*. At such events people with and without

Christian commitment will be attracted to attend on an equal footing and everyone will be entertained, informed and challenged. British people are becoming increasingly secularized and it is harder to invite friends and colleagues to Gospel presentations. This creates a sense of guilt and failure which degenerates into apathy. Crossover events need to be occasions where either the subject or the personality performing or speaking creates a *draw*. We need to minimize the off-putting dynamic of Christians *dragging* their friends to events where they are going to be evangelized. Crossover events weave Christian perspective and testimony naturally into the course of the presentation whether in the context of a pub supper, a suburban coffee morning, a concert, a seminar on medical ethics or a debate on the environment.

Black Anglicans and the English Captivity of the Gospel

Particularly in the decades following the Second World War, thousands of people from the New Commonwealth came to this country. Many of them, and especially many from the Caribbean, were not only Christians but Anglicans; but very few of them, and still fewer of their British-born descendants, have found a home as members of the Church of England. Dr John Sentamu is Chairman of the General Synod's Committee on Black Anglican Concerns.

The Elizabethan ideal of making the Church of England a spiritual home for all Englishmen, independent of both Rome and Geneva (hence State Establishment), inevitably meant the inclusion or comprehension of a wide variety of religious practice. There was never a stage when the

Church of England saw itself as a sect – it regarded itself as a Broad-Catholic Church because of its comprehensiveness. But how far has this Broad-Catholicism of the English Church, that included Protestant and Liberal features, led to the English captivity of the Gospel? A captivity almost perpetuated by the development of three post-Reformation movements (Evangelicalism, Anglo-Catholicism and Liberalism) into self-conscious traditions![1] These three movements were developments of attitudes which have a long pre-Reformation history; all three developed from the three principles of systematic theology, namely, Scripture, tradition, and reason, but without sufficient regard to each other. This has resulted in a one-sidedness that could not help towards reconciliation in a Church that prides herself in her comprehensiveness. How can the Church of England recover its Elizabethan ideal? How can the Church demonstrate in this Decade of Evangelism, especially to many British-born young black people in this country, that the Church of England can still be their spiritual home – yes, a home for all British people and not just for the English?

The first growing point which might help the kernel of the Gospel to break out of the hard soil of English captivity is an awakening to the fact that Anglicanism is not just the Sees of Canterbury and York. "The blessed company of all the faithful people" as described by the Book of Common

1. All these three movements are a sharpening of ideas which one can find in the Reformation Age and in much earlier periods. See, for example, "The Church as Eucharistic Communion in Medieval Theology" by G. H. Tavard in *Continuity and Discontinuity in Church History*, Eds. F. Forrester Church and Trinity George (*Studies in the History of Christian Thought,* Vol. XIX), E. J. Leiden, 1979; *The Anglicanism of William Laud*, by E. C. E. Bourne, SPCK, London, 1947, especially pp. 50–74, 183–203.

Prayer is today a worldwide Anglican Communion; and in its overseas composition none of its ecclesiastical institutions has an "established" status. As a worldwide Communion, it must surely take on the varied cultural characteristics of its setting-in-life. In the British context today, a context which is both multi-ethnic and multi-cultural, what is the characteristic Anglican doctrine of salvation? How far do the images, symbols and language of Anglicanism fit into the contemporary British context? The Church in Britain today must seek to express what is universal in the Gospel. We are not calling here for a universal truth, but rather a rediscovery of the particularity of the incarnation which gives the Christian revelation its universal significance. For the Gospel implies the acknowledgement too of the particularity of humankind. Too often the English Church appears to be preoccupied with strengthening the Christian faith in the Christian community and its proclamation in such a way that it is not easily understood by those outside it.

Does her language, which is so bound up with Anglican liturgy and worship particularly in its Englishness, strengthen the British Anglican community which is capable of giving it cash value, but also render it totally vacuous so that it makes no sense to those outside the Anglican community let alone those of another culture? The Church must adequately answer the question, "Who is Jesus and what does he mean for those who put their trust in him?"

But the answer to such a crucial question will not be adequate if we do not face up to the question of secularization: namely, that we embrace the world as a human world. How do we face up to the challenge of living in joy and pain when traditional ways of referring to God seem doubtful? In a society in which people's views of freedom run beyond hitherto accepted ethical guidelines, how can the Christian make reasonable and sensible decisions today?

The second growing point in liberating the Gospel from its English captivity in Britain today is for the Church of England to ask herself the questions, "How truly has she lived up to God's vision of wholeness, freedom, order and peace?", "Does she visibly show what heaven will be like?" and "Has she managed to keep in balance the tension between the claims of earth and the eternal claims of Heaven?" Any "business as usual" mentality, especially in our over-zealous commitment to the old methods of doing theology and what constitutes good worship and witness, must die. The Church can neither afford to treat race and justice questions as peripheral to the good news of creation and redemption, nor adopt a defensive and knee-jerk response to them. Such attitudes have left the Church of England deprived and impoverished.

The Church of England needs to wake up to the fact that many black Anglicans in England carry in their souls the suffering of rejection at the hands of their Mother Church, the Church of England. The Report of the Committee for Black Anglican Concerns "Seeds of Hope"[1] recommends and encourages the Church of England to think theologically about racial justice issues and to place them on a higher level of priority with respect to the Church's mission.

The Church cannot effectively tackle the brutalizing

1. "Seed of Hope": Report of a Survey on Instruments for Combating Racism in the Dioceses of the Church of England by the Committee on Black Anglican Concerns, The General Synod of the Church of England, GS977 (1991).

force of racism[1] in the wider society if it is not prepared to tackle racism within its own systems and institutions from its roots. A three-fold theological framework, namely, the Nature of God, the Nature of Humanity and the Nature of the Church should be her guiding truth. This will be a Church that is gifted with the greatest gift of Pentecost: the gift of hearing. Many of us have the answer before we hear the question. We have the solution before we hear the problem. We know the situation before we are told it. If I understand the hurts of the black ethnic minority in England aright, the deepest hurt of all is the inability of the white ethnic majority to reverse roles – that is, to become the listener instead of always doing the speaking and deciding what is good for the black person. But surely, when God's Word became flesh he sacramentalized all human history. The Gospel is not a structure of metaphysical thought, but a whole way of life. To become fully human and to help others to the birth of their full humanity means bringing God's incarnation to fruition. And we can only do this if we are prepared to let the other person show us how to enter into their shoes and to experience what it feels like. So how will this gift of hearing given at Pentecost be ours today?

The third growing point that will help in liberating the Gospel from English captivity and help us to receive the gift of hearing is by taking on board certain aspects of the Gospel which have been neglected by the Church for

---

1. *Ibid.* "Racism" is defined in the report as "the theory, prejudice and practice of disadvantaging or advantaging someone solely on the grounds of their colour, culture and ethnic origin", p. viii. Chapter five of the report makes recommendations on how the Church of England can effectively tackle the brutalizing force of racism within its own systems and its institutions and in the wider society.

centuries because of what one may call a Western pervading theology of a Master-Slave, a Colonial-Colonized view of salvation. While not neglecting the seriousness of sin, Britain today needs a theology that offers us life, culture and human potential instead of running them down or fearing them.

Many Christians today seem to be so sin-soaked! The good news of Jesus clearly shows us a God who trusts and values us far more than we value ourselves. If we take a gloomy view of man as weak, inadequate, irresponsible and empty then our theories, the practice of discrimination and psychological attitudes towards those of a different colour, culture and ethnic background tend to be manifestly racist. In such a context, people are preoccupied with the problem of finding God in their failure instead of facing up to a more serious question of responding to a God who trusts and loves them in their strength and success.

This calls for a fresh look at Scripture, the Church and its mission, and ministry as an ALL-MEMBER MINISTRY, as an aid to recovering the "joy, simplicity and compassion of the Gospel". This demands a holistic approach to revelation. For example, Scripture is often interpreted through the spectacles of the doctrine of salvation which tends to emphasize the part played by a gracious and almighty God and the sinfulness and helplessness of man. Unwittingly this leads to a self-understanding of a people whose estimation of themselves is low and lacking the needful gifts to take responsible decisions commensurate with their knowledge and power. What is required is to approach Scripture, worship and culture through a bi-focal creation-redemption lens. This approach will reveal Jesus not simply as the one who saves us from sin, but also as the Last Adam who fulfils the vocation of the First Adam.

So to confess Jesus as Lord means believing that he is true

God whom to serve is perfect freedom but also true Man in whose humanity we now share. As the Westminster Catechism put it: "Man's chief end is to glorify God and to enjoy him for ever." This means that we redress the balance by seeing people as valued, powerful and free – as people who feel good about themselves, capable of exercising and accepting responsibility for themselves and their fellows. Seeing people not just as sinners in need of saving, but also as potential saints.

A theology, a liturgy and an institution that makes us see ourselves only as slaves in "Egypt" waiting for a Moses to lead us out or as a pilgrim people at the foot of "Mount Sinai" learning how to obey is inadequate. We need a theology, a liturgy and an institutional community of faith that expresses the truth that "all men and women of every race and ethnic group belong to the one human race, are all made in the image of God and that each is of unique worth in his sight". We are fellow-citizens because we are fellow-saints. As St Paul put it in Colossians 3:11, Christ has broken down all the barriers of race, culture, masculine domination and social class. Christ is the end of all barriers for he is all in all.

This is nothing short of the Church in our time going back to is beginnings. For the Church at Pentecost began with a multi-ethnic and multi-cultural congregation (and so it shall be at the end of time when "the splendour and wealth of the nations shall be brought into the city" (Revelation 21:26). This in itself was a return to the original creation when God in creating human beings said, "It is better to be God with human beings around." This view of humanity clearly shows us that the individual as an isolated person is always an abstraction. Human beings are a family. And it is in this context we must all learn to say, "I am because I participate." Effective worship and witness demands of us to stop seeing ourselves in individualistic, congregational or parochial terms: rather we must understand ourselves in covenantal and institutional terms.

Although it is important, and biologically correct, to affirm that "under the skin" we are all the same, it is none the less important also to insist that what makes us human beings is more than biology. Our humanity begins there, but it is made, shaped and formed by our involvement with one another and the world around us – that is our culture. In today's world the danger is that there is still assumed to be only one model for a fully developed human being: "Western Rich Man". Our cultural identity and difference must be balanced with a clear understanding of a shared humanity and membership of one world.

What the Decade of Evangelism must do in proclaiming the Gospel to God's people in his Britain is to make it possible for all to learn to serve, worship and witness to the God and Father of our Lord Jesus Christ, completely freed from racist ideas, prejudice and discrimination. This requires a people who are eager to talk about God just as easily as they talk about British weather. A community that allows the praises, witness and ministry of all those on the margins of the community to be heard, known and experienced. We will not know joy in the future coming of the Kingdom until we are prepared to grieve about the present order: "Blessed are you who weep now, for you shall laugh" (Luke 6:21); "Blessed are those who mourn, for they shall be comforted" (Matthew 5:4). What will God do when he "wipes away all tears" (Revelation 21:4), in the New Heaven and the New Earth, to all those who have never wept? Surely, there is grief work to be done in the present so that the future may come. Maybe those who have not cared enough to grieve for the present situation and with those who know pain and suffering, lack the power and freedom to give it expression

and will not know joy! Is Jesus saying to us, "This is the
door and way to true joy?" Grieving about ourselves and
our nation; and somehow discovering God's own grieving
now who too will rejoice when what he is grieving about is
fully liberated from mortality (Romans 8:18–30).

And perhaps the last growing point in liberating the
Gospel from its English captivity is by allowing ourselves
to step into the shoes of others and checking with them
whether the shoes fit. How does a white Anglican respond
to the grieving of many black people as expressed by the
peom of Margaret Burroughs?: "What Shall I Tell My
Children who are Black?"[1]

> They are faced with abhorrence of everything that is
>   black.
> The night is black and so is the bogeyman.
> Villains are black with black hearts.
> A black cows gives no milk. A black hen lays no eggs.
> Bad news comes bordered in black, mourning clothes are
>   black,
> Storm clouds, black, black is evil
> And evil is black and devils' food is black . . .
> What shall I tell my dear ones raised in a white world?
> A place where white has been made to represent
> All that is good and pure and fine and decent,
> Where clouds are white and dolls, and heaven
> Surely is a white, white place with angels
> Robed in white, and cotton candy and ice-cream . . .
> And angels' food is white . . . all, all . . . white.'

It may be that one of the gifts black Anglicans can offer
to the Church in England is the gift of never taking

1. M. Burroughs, *What Shall I Tell My Children who are Black?*,
Chicago, M.A.A.H. Press, (1968) p. 8.

ourselves too seriously, by focusing on the freedom offered in the Gospel in terms of freedom for openness, oneness, newness, truth; as well as the freedom to be truly human, ecumenical and evangelical.

Grieving also means that we learn to laugh with each other. A good example for me was a letter on the notice board at the reception desk of the Namibian Council of Churches in Windhoek, on January 23rd 1990 which read as follows:

Dear Boss,
When I am born, I am black.
When I grow up, I am black.
When I am ignorant, I am black.
When I go out in the sun, I am black.
When I am cold, I am black.
When I am embarrassed, I am black.
When I am ill, I am black.
When I am jaundiced, I am black.
When I die, I am black.
BUT YOU!
When you are born, you are pink.
When you grow up, you are white.
When you are ignorant, you are green.
When you go out in the sun, you are brown.
When you are cold, you are blue.
When you are embarrassed, you are red.
When you are jaundiced, you are yellow.
When you are ill, you are off-colour.
When you die, you are purple.
And you have the nerve to call ME COLOURED.
Your loving garden boy, Sam.

Learning from Other Parts of the World (1)

There is much, too, that the Church of England can receive from the experience, witness and suffering of the Church elsewhere in the world. First Dr Chris Wright, then Bishop Michael Nazir-Ali, reflect on what there may be for us to note and to learn.

It would probably come as a shock to many in Anglican churches in England on a Sunday to be told that there are more Christians worshipping in Anglican churches in Nigeria than in the Anglican churches of the whole of the UK and North America put together. It can be an equally great shock for Anglicans from overseas to experience an average English congregation for the first time. An ordained Anglican African student at our college commented, on the church he had been assigned to for his practical ministry, that in his country it would be regarded as fit for closure in a matter of weeks! The reality of the worldwide Anglican communion is not often grasped or even imagined among British churches, even if they may have become aware that the Decade of Evangelism, with all the ferment it is causing, was originally suggested and adopted at the Lambeth Conference of 1988 on the initiative of African bishops. My concern is simply to highlight a few areas where we in Britain would do well to be better informed about, and more open to insights and inspiration from, our fellow Anglicans in other parts of the world.

A VISION FOR GROWTH

The churches of the Two-Thirds World are where the life and growth of the worldwide Christian faith are to be found. The centre of gravity of Christianity has shifted from the west and north to the south and east. The Anglican

Communion also reflects this. In some places the most remarkable growth of the Church has happened in Anglican contexts. Singapore has a multitude of Christian denominations, of course, but the Anglican diocese there has played a major part over the last two decades in the phenomenal increase in the numbers of those turning to the Christian faith. In 1950, Christians were 3 per cent of the population of Singapore. The 1990 census revealed that the figure was then 18 per cent and growing. Among the young and educated the percentage is even higher – 30 per cent at the National University. The charismatic renewal, a phenomenon much wider than the Anglican Church of course, played a major part in this; but there has also been clear and effective strategy to achieve and sustain such growth, which we shall turn to below.

The diocese of Mount Kenya East was in recent years the fastest growing diocese in the Anglican Communion, so much so that it has been divided in two. Much of the growth there was among nomadic and scattered rural communities, utterly different from the high-rise urban density of Singapore. In Nigeria, the growth of the Church, both actual and potential, was marked by the establishing of eight new missionary dioceses with their bishops in 1989. In Santiago, Chile, an Anglican Church is geared for continuous growth and making a remarkable impact among the richest and most influential segment of the community there. One thing, then, that we in Britain could learn from the Anglican churches abroad is a fresh enthusiasm for the life and growth of the Church.

STRATEGIES FOR GROWTH

Growth does not happen by sitting around waiting for it. The examples I have mentioned have in common that somebody had a method and strategy for achieving what began as a vision. In Singapore, James Wong, of the Chapel of the Resurrection, set about establishing churches in each high-rise housing block, with the vision of starting 200, such mini-congregations. Within a very short time after conversion, new Christians are taught four essential aspects of discipleship before going on to other forms of training: how to study the Bible for themselves, how to pray, how to tithe and give systematically, how to share their faith with others. This simple initial teaching sets the new Christian on the road towards personal maturity and sets the church on the road towards self-supporting and self-propagating growth.

In Santiago, Alf Cooper, a missionary with the South American Missionary Society, describes the evangelistic life of his church like this:

> We have a church structured for mission rather than maintenance. Evangelism happens continuously . . . We have used different methods. We have discarded evangelism that does not win people or add them to the church. We have adopted the continuous, every member, sparkle and testimony, dinner-party, answered-prayer lifestyle evangelism that not only works, but keeps on bringing people in all the year round, whether we are holding special evangelistic efforts or not.

As in Singapore, this is accompanied by systematic teaching and training of all church members, using an alternating programme of theological education by extension courses and practical experience of hands-on ministry of some kind.

In Nigeria, the Anglican Church has revived a very ancient concept – the missionary bishop. In the early centuries of the conversion of Europe from pre-Christian paganism, sometimes a man would be appointed bishop over an area where there were as yet no Christians. His job was to evangelize and plant the Church there, and effectively grow his own diocese. One of the greatest such missionary bishops was Wynfrith of Crediton, later known as Boniface (c.680–754), "apostle of Germany". The present Archbishop of Nigeria, Joseph Abiodun Adetiloye, had the vision of multiplying the Anglican Dioceses in his country since 1973 and finally accomplished it in 1989. The purpose was not greater administrative efficiency, but greater evangelistic effectiveness. Bishops would not just patronize or supervise, they themselves would actually evangelize in what were called "missionary dioceses". Bishop Emmanuel Gbonigi of Akure diocese organized fresh programmes for training both clergy and laity in evangelism, leading by personal example as a keen evangelist himself. He quotes one participant as saying:

Prior to this time of training, none of us would want to share our faith with others because some pastors would feel envious and may even accuse us of wanting to take their job. However, things are different now. The fact that the Bishop is behind this training gives us boldness . . .

SHARING THE NEWS

How can we become more aware of such exciting developments among Anglican churches overseas? One way is by ensuring that parish churches have significant and living links with the Anglican missionary agencies. This needs, however, to be much more than a routine sending of some proportion of the PCC's budget off to one society, or divided up into pitifully small sums to several of them. This concept of "missionary support", if unaccompanied by other things, has two detrimental effects. First, it does not result in learning. The congregation is not fed and informed and challenged by new knowledge. Second, it perpetuates the paternalism that "we" are the giving churches and "they" are the grateful receivers. The congregation never learns what partnership and mutuality mean in mission, let alone being made aware that it is now the churches of the Two-Thirds World that are giving and sending far more in mission than we in Britain. All the Anglican overseas missionary societies, BCMS Crosslinks, CMJ, CMS, MAM, SAMS, USPG, have grown out of that kind of paternalism and have a great desire to facilitate true partnership between churches and dioceses here and those abroad. They see their role as no longer merely a matter of "sending missionaries from the West to the rest", but as one of facilitating and serving the Church in its mission – here and overseas. But it is up to churches to make proper and imaginative use of their resources by intelligent liaison with their Education departments, and not by an unplanned "Send us a missionary for our Missionary Sunday" from time to time.

Another way is by direct links between churches and dioceses in Britain and those abroad. Quite a number of dioceses have had exercises of "Partnership in Mission", with invited guests from an overseas diocese coming to live here, to observe, participate and offer constructive criticism. These can be useful, provided attitudes and expectations are carefully prepared in advance, so that we are willing to be vulnerable and to listen with integrity and maturity. My limited experience of one such diocesan exercise in my curate days was that people's response to the visitors was either one of a slightly patronizing, polite dismissal ("It's so nice to have you here!"), or one of paralyzed guilt and frustration ("Our church is so dead compared with theirs; we could be like theirs if only our leaders weren't so stiff and stuffy . . .!"). The first reaction had no room for the idea that we might have something to learn from churches that have outstripped us in life and growth. But the second was unaware of cultural and contextual issues that rule out a naïve hope that African church life might be transplanted undiluted to Kent.

Exchange visits of both clergy and lay people have perhaps been more fruitful, since there is no substitute for actually going and living in another culture and among other Christians if one is really to learn from abroad and also to see one's own church culture more objectively. The reports I read of such a group exchange between the churches in the Derby region (wider than Anglican alone) and the Delhi diocese of the Church of North India were impressive in showing how much people's ideas, attitudes and understanding had been moved forward. Even individual churches could arrange such visits, e.g. through sabbatical leave for their staff, with the expertise and help of mission agencies. The benefit can be great, provided, again, that the church is open to genuine learning that extends beyond the dreaded missionary slide-show when the vicar comes back. And if it is a genuine exchange, where a pastor or evangelist from overseas comes to live and work among us, he or she must be allowed to minister with integrity and respect and not always be treated with the assumption that they must have come to learn, or as a student.

An exercise in such partnership took place in the world of theological education and training for ministry when the British Council of Churches in 1987 invited five theological educators from the non-western world to visit, observe and comment on a number of training establishments in Britain, including some Anglican colleges. Their report, *Partners in Practice*, exposed serious gaps in the curricula of these colleges and in the awareness of the global Church and its mission among both staff and students. Things are changing, though still very slowly. Several Colleges now have Lecturers in Mission who have served for many years in other parts of the world.

SHARING THE COST

Not, for once, talking about money! British Anglicans need to be far more conscious of the fact that their fellow Anglicans in some countries overseas face serious opposition and conflict and pay a heavy cost for their faith. We can become so comfortable and parochial, and so used to the "niceness" of Anglicanism, that we scarcely imagine the struggle in some parts of the world. We can also become so concerned (and rightly so) for good relations with our neighbours of other faiths in this country that we say and do things which fellow Anglicans in other countries find astonishing and distressing, since they live under much more hostile and threatening conditions, religiously and politically. I have participated in international conferences with Anglican theologians and pastors, including quite senior leaders and bishops, and been buffeted with the frustrated disappointment and anger at what sometimes goes on in Britain in relation to other faiths, and especially Islam. Episcopal statements, acts of multi-faith worship, etc., are widely reported overseas and can be used to taunt minority Christians. I am not saying that overseas Anglicans are always right in their response; but I am appealing that we in Britain at least recognize their existence and exercise sensitivity and a greater global awareness of the impact of what is said and done here. Bishop Emmanuel Gbonigi of Nigeria, where there is serious political and social conflict between Christians and Muslims, has this to say:

> Nigerian Christians, along with Pakistani Christians, look to British Christians for help against the discrimination shown towards them by Muslims. They are surprised when British Christians who argue for religious pluralism seem to respond with apathy. It seems as if religious freedom is important in the United Kingdom, but not elsewhere. The view seems to be that such freedom would be against the religious views of the country in question. Such a view is racism. Nigerian Anglicans would favour a statement by Anglicans worldwide supporting Christians under pressure in Nigeria, Pakistan and elsewhere and calling for a guarantee of their religious freedoms in the same way that freedoms for other religious groups are guaranteed and enjoyed by religious minorities in the West.

I believe this to be important because it may not be very long before we may need to look to these very same Christian sisters and brothers abroad for help in learning how to survive and continue to witness to our faith in the midst of hostile political conditions. The freedoms of our Western secular democracies may be more fragile than we think. It is not inconceivable that legal prohibitions on evangelism among communities of other faiths could be imposed in the name of racial harmony. That was the response of the Singapore government with its "Religious Harmony Bill" of 1990. How then would we respond if faced with such legal obstruction to Christian witness? "Learning from other parts of the world" might then become more than merely an exercise in politeness.

Learning from Other Parts of the World (2)

Michael Nazir-Ali, a Pakistani Bishop who is now General Secretary of the Church Missionary Society, takes up a particular theme to contribute to our "Learning from Other Parts of the World".

THE QUESTION OF LOCALITY

The parochial system highlights the presence of the Church in local communities. At the time of the Reformation, it was thought important to emphasize the relation of the Church to the nation. For long, both local communities and the nation were relatively homogeneous and it was possible to relate the cultural and the communal, the geographical and the social to the Church in a somewhat simple way. In a multi-cultural, plural society this becomes more and more difficult to do. It should not be imagined that Britain is now plural only in the sense that there are significant ethnic minorities present here. An adequate understanding of contemporary British society must include a proper view of the different subcultures which exist in the indigenous community as well as the presence of ethnic minority cultures. The notion of a subculture can enable us to discern community among people of a particular band of professions, a specific style of life, interest in particular forms of art or music and even adherence to certain kinds of spirituality. People today live according to a whole variety of world-views and this plurality of ideologies needs also to be taken seriously. A question that needs to be posed in its sharpest form is whether the Church continues to be incarnate in antiquated ways. Should the principle of locality lead to the incarnation of the Church in the different subcultures of contemporary Britain?

There are indeed signs that some at least are taking the subcultures seriously. The Restorationist "House-Churches" are seeking to express their style of worship, if not their organization, in terms that are easily accessible to popular cultures. Church historians have commented on the consonance of the emphasis on experience in some kinds of contemporary spirituality with the high value given to experience in the modern world.[1] "Cult" congregations, even within mainline denominations, are seeking to relate faith to lifestyle. In such an atmosphere, it is not enough to reiterate the primacy of traditional structures, whether these are parochial, diocesan or national.

It is not only in Britain that the parochial system is under pressure. In Latin America it is under pressure in a largely Roman Catholic context. The shortage of clergy has often meant that the parish priest is a remote figure and the parochial structures are seen as distant. This sense of "distance" has led small groups of Christians, frequently in poor areas, to organize themselves into worshipping and witnessing communities, largely independent of the parish

---

1. D. W. Bebbington, *Evangelicalism in Modern Britain*, Unwin, London, 1989, pp. 229ff.

priest and the far away parish organization. The emergence of those ecclesial communities is a new way of expressing incarnational presence in very needy settings.[1]

In his address to the Lambeth Conference 1988, Bishop David Gitari spoke of the need to adapt structures to pastoral and evangelistic need. In his diocese they have discovered that parochial and even "mission station" structures are quite unsuitable for reaching the largely nomadic peoples of Northern Kenya. They have had to develop ways and means of ministry and mission which are themselves nomadic! Pastors and evangelists now adopt the nomadic way of life of the people they serve. This is the only way of being incarnational in such contexts.[2]

In the highly urbanized societies of Japan, Korea, Singapore and Hong Kong, on the other hand, the prohibitive price of land has often forced the Churches to rent apartments for use as places of worship. Necessity has, however, led to opportunity; a visible Christian presence is established in an apartment block and this provides numerous occasions for witness and service. Fr Omaichi is a young Japanese priest working in the northern diocese of Hokkaido. He has charge of a small "apartment church" in the city of Sapporo. He lives, with his family, in another apartment next door to the church and is also the caretaker for the whole block! This latter role brings him into contact with every resident in the block and creates opportunities for sensitive witness.

1. Leonardo Boff, *Ecclesio-Genesis: The Base Communities Reinvent the Church*, Collins, London, 1986. See also *Transformation*, July–Sept. 1986, Vol. 3, No. 3.

2. David Gitari, "Evangelization and Culture: Primary Evangelism in Northern Kenya" in V. Samuel and A. Hauser (Eds.), *Proclaiming Christ in Christ's Way*, Regnum, Oxford, 1989, pp. 101ff. See also the Video *To Canterbury with a Camel*, CMS, 1990.

In England, the parish church remains important as a focus for Christian presence and witness within a definite locality. The "House-Church" movement has, however, demonstrated that there are other ways of expressing such a presence and witness at the different levels of community life. Indeed, the emergence and proliferation of "house-groups" within the mainline churches themselves has shown how it is possible, and even desirable, for Christians to come together in a whole number of non-traditional ways. On the whole, however, such "house-groups" have had an orientation towards fellowship, worship and Bible-study rather than witness and service. If, during the course of this Decade, they could be inspired by the example of the basic communities to organize themselves for witness and service in their immediate vicinity, as well as to the wider community, this would be a signal advance. Under the leadership of Canon Peter Price, now General Secretary of USPG, the insights gained from the basic communities were being brought to bear on parochial situations in the diocese of Southwark. This is an admirable illustration of how the world mission context impinges on local mission. It is to be hoped that this work will not only continue in the diocese but will spread to other parts of the country.[1]

Christian Witness in the Hospital

In different ways, both Dr Christopher Wright and Bishop Michael Nazir-Ali emphasize the Church's responsibility to note where people actually are and to structure itself accordingly for evangelism. One way in which the Church of England has done

1. Peter Price, *The Church as the Kingdom*, Marshalls, Basingstoke, 1987.

this over centuries, though often with little understanding from the church in the parishes, is through the ministry of chaplains in institutions. An earlier chapter included some consideration of Christian work in schools, colleges and universities; as David Stoter writes here of the chaplain's ministry in a modern hospital, he also points by implication to some of the opportunities and demands that face Christians who, whether in the statutory or the voluntary sector, serve stressed or needy people in the context of other fast-changing institutions.

An examination of the Church's role in a modern hospital will show that despite the changes brought about by an increasingly secularized society, the emergence of a multi-faith/multi-cultural society, and the development of medical science, a new and arguably more profound understanding and partnership is emerging. This partnership creates many opportunities to share the "good news" of the Gospel in situations of deep challenge and to people in real need. It likewise gives opportunity to share in and influence the decision-taking process of the institution and thus to help shape its practice of care.

MINISTRY TO PATIENTS

The patient is the focal point of ministry as well as for medical/nursing care. To be a patient is in itself a challenge as, with rare exceptions, to enter hospital is at best a regrettable necessity. For some the outcome will be routine treatment leading to a complete cure; for some there will be a lengthy treatment leading to a full or partial recovery; for some the challenge of long-term chronic illness; for some disfigurement or disablement; for some death. The need to face change (for some, radical change) presents a challenge which may cause devastation, despair, helplessness and hopelessness; but which may also enable real growth and integration, and some reassessment of attitude, lifestyle, relationships and belief.

To be regularly given the opportunity to minister to patients at their moment of need can only happen if there is a true partnership established in which the chaplain/minister is accepted as part of the team. This will only be so if trust and respect is established. In a modern hospital high levels of professionalism are practised and expected, not least from chaplains and ministers. All members of the team are expected to know their role and each other's; also to know and accept the parameters of practice. There is no place for hard sell, confrontational evangelism: proselytizing is not acceptable. Furthermore all staff are expected to value and respect the beliefs and values of each patient and their families and to facilitate the practice of that faith though this may conflict with their own beliefs.

Does this mean that evangelism cannot take place? By no means! But it does mean that this ministry must be very sensitively practised within the framework of ministry which gives choice and indeed control of the agenda for the relationship to the patient.

Crisis moments for patients, which sometimes equate with significant medical points, i.e. diagnosis, an operation, change in condition and at other times relate more to the internal thinking, understanding or feelings, frequently offer opportunities for effective ministry. There are moments when fear (of what is happening or of what it is anticipated may happen) creates vulnerability, helplessness and a feeling of isolation. Jesus experienced such moments as he faced the prospect of death. He went into Gethsemane taking his closest friends with him and "began to be distressed and agitated" and said to them: "I am deeply grieved even to death; remain here and keep awake." He threw himself to the ground praying that he be spared death on the cross: "Remove this cup from me." As we read in Luke's version as his anguish increased great drops of sweat fell from him – the humanity of Jesus is starkly revealed in this manifestation of fear – he is strengthened in his anguish and enabled to say "not what I want, but what you want" (Mark 14:36). This process of anguished pleading and acceptance is repeated three times. The acceptance is finalized at that moment when the crowd arrive to arrest him and he yields himself up to them. It is arguable that the strength of Jesus silent before his accusers and forgiving to those nailing him to the cross came from the power received through the expression of naked honesty in Gethsemane. On the cross itself the human experience of pain, anguish and isolation is evident in the cry "My God my God, why have you forsaken me?" (Mark 15:34). At the end of his suffering he places himself into his father's love: "Father, into your hands I commend my spirit" (Luke 23:46).

This pattern of suffering and need is mirrored over and over in the suffering of patients and their families. The minister who is ready to accept the patient with the vulnerability of unconditional love and to share the pain and the questions may be taken into the privileged territory of the patient's innermost feelings and thoughts. Here may be revealed feelings of helplessness, hopelessness, anger, fear, guilt and despair – feelings and thoughts often kept hidden for fear of the pain they may cause to loved ones and the fear of being seen as weak or cowardly by friends and the professional carers. In this place of stark reality there is no place either for pity or for easy answers or indeed answers at all – to give answers at this point belittles the experience of the patient. Here the minister sits alongside, listening, sharing the pain and tears, holding in love and often in silence (Oh that we could truly grasp the power of creative silence [see John 8:3–11]) or with its use of few words. To accompany and help facilitate the exploration of the feelings, the pain and the questions may well bring the first glimmer of hope into the picture – a hope born out of the experience of being heard in the depths and of having the unacceptable accepted. Here is rich ground for reappraisal of life, meaning, faith, relationships and the discovery of new aspects of truth. Here the Gospel is lived and shared through pastoral care; any confrontation takes place inside the patient and may then be explored at her/his request – here there is no avoidance of the Gospel message but rather the courage to have one's own faith questioned, explored and attacked and to experience the anger being directed at oneself or directly at God. The wise minister finds that exploration of pain, with the encouragement to express anger, is creative as this leads into a relationship (with both minister and God) which is based on real honesty at all levels and the discovery that the truth does indeed set free.

This ministry not only needs to be offered without pre-condition but also evaluated without a sense of failure if the patient is only able to accept the help at a human level and unable or unwilling to embrace the deeper message of the Gospel. Here we need to look at the way in which God the Father, and his gift to the world, Jesus, minister. There is a seeming profligacy in the love of God poured out on the good, the indifferent and the bad, e.g. ten lepers have their need of healing met but only one is made whole to return and give thanks to God. The care given may also have a profound effect on the patient's family, friends, other patients and members of staff.

RELATIVES

Although we have looked at some length at the patient we must never lose sight that the patient is part of a family. The family both individually and also as a unit is profoundly affected by illness, disability, disablement, dying and death. Many of the feelings already explored above are experienced by relatives and friends with the added burden (also experienced by some patients towards their relatives) of believing there is a need to hide all feelings from the patient and to allow no such opportunity to the patient. This may well lead to the removal of true communication and the imposition of a "safe" agenda distanced from the true needs. Here the minister needs to be aware of the underlying fears and encourage them to be shared. To enable each member of the family to communicate with one another and with the patient allows the power of family love to be effectively shared. The enabling of honest communication not only allows patient and family to speak but also to support by holding and crying together (something which may well have been experienced in the past over lesser challenges). This is not only important at the time but if the patient dies it leaves behind a healthy legacy, the legacy of love shared through the suffering and sadness.

Children need a special mention here. Too often children experiencing illness or who have a close relative or friend ill or who suffer a death in the family find themselves kept at a distance, not only physically but also by being denied access to information or, in the case of death, opportunity to participate in the funeral. The minister may need to help families to see that children are perceptive and so have picked up information which they are denied the opportunity to explore and digest with support and understanding. To minister to the family and ignore the children is to miss an opportunity of helping the children to grow in understanding by exploring their thoughts and feelings in a safe environment and denies the adults (as well as the children) the therapy of holding in love.

STAFF

There are unique opportunities for ministry to staff in a modern hospital. A high percentage of staff, especially medical students, doctors, nurses and paramedic staff, are young (the largest group being 18–28). Chaplains, and increasingly their teams, work with such staff caring for patients and relatives. The staff are faced day in and day out with situations which confront each one with their own mortality, and raise fundamental questions of belief and culture, ethics and morality. There are, too, the demands for greater professionalism as modern technology and the increasing range and power of drugs leave no room for error, and the calls for greater cost effectiveness; as well as all the normal pressures and challenges of life, further complicated for many by shift work and unreasonably long hours. The chaplain has opportunity to give support and understanding, and if accepted as a colleague the opportunity to help individuals and groups of staff to explore their feelings and beliefs and to respond to their pain as well. Opportunities are there to minister to staff through involvement in teaching both within the various schools (medical, nursing, physio, etc) and also in the wards.

MINISTRY TO THE HOSPITAL AS AN INSTITUTION

The developing partnership with the institution and its consequent opportunities for ministry is based on two important factors:

(i) the growing recognition and increasing expertise of chaplains,

and

(ii) the developing awareness of the institution (through its managers) of the need to use all available expertise to provide the highest standards of care.

The chaplain may well have the opportunity to influence practices within the hospital; the change, for instance, to a more humane way of caring for families who experience stillbirth or miscarriage and to more sensitive funeral arrangements for the same has been greatly influenced by a number of chaplains.

Participation in committees and specific interest groups, e.g. bereavement, multi-faith provision, ethical committees, gives opportunities to be involved with the "politics" of the service and the development of policy and practice. Here at the frontiers of knowledge and research and at a time of immense change both in the organization and funding of the Health Service and in society and its expectations, the Gospel message which values each person is able to be heard and to influence.

A modern hospital is rich ground for the seed of the Gospel to be sown. To be alongside patients and families at these challenging moments which have so much potential for growth and to be part of the fabric of the institution should be greatly valued. Ecumenical co-operation both between chaplains inside the hospital and linked to churches in the community can provide an efficient and effective ministry to all sections of society with sensitivity and without confrontation.

Healing and Evangelism

We follow that study, and end this chapter, with a more general consideration of healing and evangelism. It is Carl Garner's conviction, as it is ours, that healing is an essential element in the church's ministry, as it was in that of Jesus. Yet many Christians today find this aspect of Jesus' ministry, and then of Christian practice today, a source of anxiety rather than an encouragement. The Church still needs a good deal of persuading that healing and evangelism are, for followers of Jesus, necessary companions.

Jesus "proclaimed the Gospel and healed the sick". So close is the relationship between the two in his ministry that it might at first appear that both activities are of equal weight or value. This is not in fact the case, although they are so intricately connected that the distinction is not always easily apparent. Since it has always been reckoned that the ministry of Jesus has some significance for the Church as a model for its own ministry, exploring this interconnection may be illuminating.

Firstly it needs observing, though it may seem obvious, that the healings of Jesus happen through Jesus. He is the agent of this activity. God's presence and grace is focused on him. He is not simply announcing some general principle of prayer so that if only people had got the formula right, this could have happened anywhere. On the contrary, the Kingdom of Heaven is breaking through in Jesus, irrupting into a world that is not only naturally intractable but also gripped by other forces. It is so hard a struggle, so fierce a battle, that the beachhead is not assured until death itself is defeated on the cross.

The "focusing" of God's presence in Jesus is also very tangible. Jesus touches people, anoints them with spittle, lays his hands on them, puts his fingers in their ears, speaks personally to them. Towards the beginning of his ministry the synoptics record that great crowds assembled after his healing of Peter's mother-in-law. St Luke's version runs: ". . . and he laid hands on them all" (Luke 4:40).

It could work the other way round as well – people could touch Jesus and experience healing flowing into them, "all who had disease pressed upon him to touch him" (Mark 3:10). One such person crept up behind him, saying to herself, "If I but touch his garments, I shall be made whole" (Mark 5:28). She did so, and her haemorrhaging ceased. Jesus, however, "knew that power had gone out of him". When she revealed herself, Jesus tells her that her "faith has made her whole (lit. saved)".

It is probable that a distinction is being made between the mere physical healing, and the wholeness that comes from faith in Jesus. The distinction is more obvious in the story of the ten lepers. All ten are healed and told to go and show themselves to the priests to confirm the healing. One of them turns back to thank Jesus, who says to him, "Arise and go your way: your faith has made you whole (lit. saved you)" (Luke 17:19). For him something greater has happened.

Healing may therefore be the doorway to "saving" faith, where what has started as little more than a glimmer of hope for an individual is transformed into a real faith in, and following of, Jesus. They have not only had a healing, they experience God. It is a "pastoral evangelism". Healing also establishes a context for the Gospel to be proclaimed and heard and explained. Crowds came because of what they had been told by others: "a great multitude hearing what great things he did, came to him" (Matthew 3:7–12).

The effectiveness of his healing ministry in drawing people to him could also cause difficulties. The balance could be threatened, and the needs and demands of people take over from his own need for solitude with God, and the strategic needs of the proclamation of the Gospel. He goes away to find somewhere to pray, and still they discover him. He has to disappoint people by asserting the need for the Gospel to be proclaimed in other places (Luke 4:42–3). He tells "Legion" to go and tell his friends what had happened to him, so all the Decapolis knew (Mark 5:20); but he is inconvenienced when a leper speaks too freely of his healing despite being asked not to, with the result that he cannot enter into certain towns (Mark 4:43).

The subsidiary and correlative nature of Jesus' healing ministry is also demonstrated in the case of the paralytic, where Jesus knows the heart of his problem, and speaks forgiveness to his guilt. His physical healing comes later and points back to the fundamental inner healing that has already taken place. The "sign" element in Jesus' healings is evident in this instance, though it may be more complex in nature than simply pointing towards the truth of the Gospel. The healing of the man born blind becomes a parable of the blindness and sickness of those who opposed Jesus: while at the same time Jesus is at pains to assert that his blindness is not due to sin, rather it presents an opportunity for God's power to be shown (John 9:3). A healing has the capacity of creating crisis; it can cause awareness of the reality of God: I shall remember how the immediate improvement, during prayer, of a lady suffering from senile dementia, seemed to lead to people becoming more aware of God, and more ready to change their ways.

(She recognized her husband for the first time in well over a year, and became tractable and pleasant instead of violent and abusive, though she was still confused.) A healing may also cause a different sort of crisis: it can give rise to anger and resistance – instead of being glad that someone has been helped, people can become indignant and critical. It is as if they feel exposed. In some cases today it seems that it makes God too close and unpredictable for people who have learnt to live with a comfortable distance between them and God, and with a doctrine of prayer which explains why nothing ever happens. When it does it is very threatening – and may be perceived almost as a personal insult! Jesus had the same experience: "they were filled with fury" (Luke 6:11).

The wider ramifications in specific healings, also brings up the issue of what may seem like random particularity. People were also "filled with murderous rage" when Jesus referred in the synagogue at Nazareth to Elijah and Elisha only helping and healing strangers (Luke 4:25f). The implications were not lost on his hearers. When he went to the Pool of Bethesda, a place like a hospital, he focuses, so far as we can detect, on one individual only. This presents a different picture from that which might be gained by paying attention only to those passages which speak of great multitudes coming to him, and of him healing "many" or "all". This has already been modified, however, by the fact that the need to proclaim the Gospel was paramount, and led him to move on to other villages. It must also be modified by recognition that even Jesus' power to heal was at times limited by the corporate atmosphere of incredulity and unbelief – as in his birthplace, Nazareth: "He could do no great work there . . . he only laid his hands on a few sick people and healed them. He was greatly surprised, because the people did not have faith" (Mark 6:5–6). When healings did occur, most of them seem to have been immediate – but not all. It is easy to miss the fact that the lepers were cleansed "on the way", and that when Jesus laid hands on one particular blind man, his vision was not immediately restored, instead he saw people as if they were trees, and Jesus had to do it again before he saw properly. It may be that at times "power flowed from him and healed them all", but many of the healings that occurred clearly involved personal interchange and specific insights into the spiritual condition of the persons concerned. The paralytic has already been quoted, but there is also "Do you want to be healed . . .", and "it is not right to take the children's bread . . .", and "You won't believe unless you see miracles" as well as "Sin no more less worse befall you". There are then complex factors to do with the nature of creation, human receptivity, freewill, belief and unbelief, levels of good and evil, as well as the incarnational embodiment of God's presence in Jesus. All this is subject too to the overriding purpose of evangelism – of drawing all people to know God's love in Christ. It involves Jesus himself being utterly guided by the Spirit, and aware of when "the power of the Lord was with him to heal" (Luke 5:17). A dynamic "incarnational" framework for understanding the subtlety of what is involved in Jesus' ministry is essential if we are to avoid seeing his healing ministry (and that of his Church), as unacceptably random. After all the ultimate cost, the measure of the difficulty of God's grace reaching us, is the cross.

THE APOSTOLIC MODEL

There is no doubt that healing played a key role in Jesus' own evangelism: but was it intended to be continued as a ministry within the Church? All the evidence is that it was. The resurrection of Jesus from death meant that the experience of grace was universally available wherever it was proclaimed and the conditions of repentance and faith were met. Of itself, however, the message was not one which would carry conviction beyond an immediate fringe unless assisted by the same sort of spiritual presence and power which had attended the mortal ministry of Jesus. It was precisely the promise of such power that was involved in the gift of the Spirit at Pentecost; this explains the combination of commands in Luke's gospel: "this message must be proclaimed . . . you shall be my witnesses . . . but wait until you are endued with the power from on high". The teaching in the New Testament about the role of the Spirit leaves little room for doubting that the essential elements of evangelism as found in the ministry of the Lord himself were to continue within the Church. "When the Spirit comes . . ." is the underlying governing concept behind "Whatever you ask in my name shall be done for you . . ." and "Whoever believes in me shall do the works I do" (John 14:12f). "You shall do greater things than these" may mean superlative miracles as such. What it cannot mean is "You shall not do anything like this". And "these things" were seen specifically to include healings, though within a frame of reference that saw all such manifestations of the Spirit's presence as signs of, confirmations of, and avenues to the Gospel.

The longer ending annexed to Mark's gospel indicates the general understanding of the Church of New Testament times: "Go into all the world and preach the Gospel to the whole creation . . . and these signs shall accompany those who believe: in my name they will cast out demons, they will speak in new tongues . . . they will lay hands on the sick and they will recover . . . and they went forth everywhere, while the Lord worked with them and confirmed the message by the signs that attended it". The same understanding is evident in Hebrews: "This salvation . . . was declared at first by the Lord, and it was attested to us by those who heard him, while God also bore witness by signs and wonders and various miracles and by gifts of the Holy Spirit distributed according to his own will" (Hebrews 2:3–4).

The Acts of the Apostles presents us with germane examples of how evangelism took place within the early Church. The healing of the lame man at the temple gate by Peter using the Lord's name gave Peter an opportunity to speak of Jesus. Peter and John were then arrested. On their release, the Church actually prayed that the Lord would not only continue to make them bold, but that he would perform healings and other "signs and wonders": "Now, Lord . . . grant your servants to speak your word with all boldness, while you stretch out your hand to heal, and signs and wonders are performed through the name of your holy servant Jesus" (Acts 4:29–30). It is clear that the commission that the Apostles had received to preach and heal was not abrogated by the coming of the Spirit, but fully activated. Their ministry was a model too for the Church at large in its evangelism. Thus Philip, a deacon, evangelizes a town in Samaria, and "the multitudes with one accord gave heed to what was said by Philip, when they *heard* him, and saw the signs which he did: for unclean spirits came out of many who were possessed . . . and many who were paralysed or lame were healed. So there was much joy in that city." The same model of evangelism was followed by perhaps the greatest of evangelists, that Apostle of "untimely birth", St Paul. In his Epistle to the Romans, Paul describes his evangelistic ministry in the following words: "I will not venture to speak of anything except what Christ has wrought through me to win obedience from the Gentiles by word and deed: by the power of signs and wonders, by the Power of the Holy Spirit, so as that from

Jerusalem to Illyricum I have fully preached the Gospel of Christ" (Romans 15:18–19). Acts gives some particular instances. At Iconium Paul and Barnabas "remained for a long time, speaking boldly for the Lord, who bore witness to the word of his grace, granting signs and wonders to be done by their hands" (Acts 14:3). On the island of Malta, Publius, the chief man of the island, "lay sick with fever and dysentery. Paul visited him and prayed, and putting his hands on him healed him. And when this had taken place the rest of the people on the island who had diseases also came and were cured" (Acts 28:8–9).

DESPITE OBJECTION

The evidence seems conclusive that the ministry of healing was believed to be a continuing part of the Church's ministry, and that it was seen as significant not merely in pastoral terms, but as a key in evangelism. Why then is there still resistance? Why should the Lambeth Conference in 1988 have to commend it so strongly? Two main streams of objection can perhaps be identified: the "Reformationist" and the "Rationalist".

The "Reformationist" argument is a form of "dispensationalism". The particular gifts and manifestations of the Spirit (like healing) recorded in the New Testament are viewed as being only for the time of the New Testament, in order to establish the Church. This breathtaking diminution of the value of the Scriptures which nowhere imply such a thing, is only excusable against a historic concern to shake free of some of the imbalances and superstitions of the Middle Ages. One also suspects that it was convenient as a justification for the absence of such signs in the new Protestant churches of the Reformation, with their need to rebuff the support given to Roman Catholic claims by the healings and visions and spiritual gifts evident in the lives of contemporary saints. Whatever the dogma, healings crept in however! The Holy Spirit could not be debarred when people tried to be faithful to Scripture. Thus John Wesley recorded many of the phenomena which some now imagine to be new (such as people falling down during prayer, and trembling and crying), and speaks of the healings that occurred in his ministry. He asserts that it "is only our lack of faith" which prevents the gifts of the Spirit being manifested in the same fulness in our days as in those of the Apostles. From the perspective of history and of contemporary experience, the "Reformationist" argument has no leg to stand on, and it is found to be subverting the very authority of Scripture which those who hold it are so keen to exalt.

The "Rationalist" objection is more powerful, and one suspects also lies behind the real objection of some who publicly take a dispensationalist stance. Put baldly it is that "miracles" do not happen, or that there is no proof of them every happening. When faced with people who say that they have been "healed through prayer", the response is that the complaint was psychosomatic in the first place, or that it was a type of illness where spontaneous remissions occur either regularly or occasionally, so that there can be nothing unusual or miraculous or spiritual about it. "Miracles", it is suggested, have to be something that could not have happened any other way, they have to be instantaneous, without any means being employed and without any explanation: to be "against nature". The definition employed is really the problem, and creates a fundamentalism of attitude that inhibits any real investigation into what is actually going on! Typically, the patient testifying to a healing is not listened to! The universe envisaged is a mechanistic one, with God on the outside, if he exists at all. The understanding of "medical" healing may be equally mechanical, ignoring the fact that drugs and surgery can only assist the biological capacity for healing within the human organism. Yet it is well known how support and care, and a person's own will and motivation, may help or hinder healing. The psychosomatic is always a factor even when it is not evidently a cause. And if the psychological, then the spiritual, if the universe is not "closed". It was an inadequate definition that led to almost no "miracles" being recorded at Lourdes for several years – not the absence of satisfied pilgrims! (cf Fr R. Laurentin "Viva Christo Rey!", appendix C.)

So today, as in all the Christian centuries, there are many people ready to describe the healing they experienced when they received the laying on of hands. In many instances this involves remarkable remissions, improvements, or recoveries. Such healings did not happen without a context or "without means": the context was one of faith and the means included prayer and contact, sacramental sign, and often involved a tangible awareness of the working of God. It is, strictly, quite unscientific to ignore all this simply because it is inconvenient to a system of thought!

An Avenue of Evangelism

What emerges upon investigation gives an important clue to the type of universe in which we live. The experiences of "heat" or "electricity" which are commonly described are normally indicators of something occurring both at a physical and a spiritual level and improvements may be quite measurable at times. Even apparently odd thrashings of limbs or champing of jaws occurring during the time of ministry, though strange and sometimes disturbing to bystanders, may be part of a process of physiotherapy;

remarkable not because the basic processes are unknown, but because of the rapidity with which they are taking place, and the absence of any visible agent manipulating the occurrence.

A similar acceleration of healing processes is also observed at times when the healing is taking place on the emotional or psychological level. A phenomenon that sometimes occurs in healing services is that of people falling to the ground and remaining in some sort of semi-conscious state for a period of time. A consultant psychologist investigating what was occurring (on behalf of the St Alban's Group for the Ministry of Healing) said that what appeared to be happening in many cases was that the unpleasant experiences hidden in the subconscious were coming to the surface either as actual memories, or in symbolic form, and were being dissipated. The improvement in some people was dramatic. It was like an accelerated hypnotherapy, but without anyone specifically inducing it, or guiding it.

The concepts of *acceleration* and *focus* are important for an understanding of the Christian healing ministry, slotting in as they do with some of the fundamental categories relating to the incarnation which make sense of the ministry of Jesus. It helps understanding in many areas. There is no denial in orthodox Christianity of the important role of normal medical and psychiatric care. On the contrary the Christian Church throughout its history has supported hospitals and encouraged nursing. Prayer and the laying on of hands is not some alternative to medical means of healing as if those who are "real Christians" receive prayer, while the rest go to the doctor. The Church inherited the holistic notions of contemporary Judaism, as evinced in the book Ecclesiasticus with its call both to pray and to "honour the doctor with the honour which is his due". Paul, who was used by God to bring amazing healings, tells Timothy to "take a little wine for his . . . frequent ailments" (1 Timothy 5:25); he has to leave Trophimus "sick in Melitus" (2 Timothy 4:20); and he reminds the Galatians that it "was because of a bodily ailment" that he first preached the Gospel to them. The ministry of healing is essentially a ministry of prayer, and the prayer covers not only the sick specifically, but all those who are concerned with and care for the sick person. For not only are the sick enjoined to call for the "elders of the church to pray over them, anointing them with oil", but all of us are to pray for each other "that we may be healed" (James 5:14f). As the doctor who was present at an anointing that played a crucial role in the development of my own ministry said to me, "I felt that prayer, and I need it. I often have to make difficult decisions and perform delicate operations . . .". Prayer itself can have an essentially sacramental dimension, where it becomes the very medium of God's grace moving among us. Two extremes need to be avoided: on the one hand any denigration of normal medical care and treatment; on the other any closing of the door to the extraordinary things that God may do through prayer and obedience. An expectation that of right a Christian should be miraculously healed and should never need a doctor is a pernicious error that can lead to terrible guilt – especially if linked with teachings on "faith" which make it a blind assertion of healing even when the symptoms are otherwise. It also closes the door to something of paramount importance: wherever there is a modicum of faith, God's grace or presence is experienced. In looking for instant cure some have missed the beginnings of both a "temporal" and greater healing.

There are many factors involved in what precisely happens when prayer is offered over someone. The faith and motivation of those ministering is significant. So too is the faith of the community (as we saw was the case with our Lord at Nazareth), the degree of openness to the Holy Spirit, and the setting in which the prayer is offered. Then there is the personal element itself. The person seeking ministry may be dishonest, may hold back information, may be "testing", may be unwilling to grow in faith or let go bitterness. Why some are "healed" when they seek ministry and others are not may seem evident in some cases yet almost impossible to discern in others. Leaving aside the fact that all of us are mortal and our bodies naturally run down, within a "free" and complex universe there are so many things that need to come together for the Lord to be "present and heal". Jesus' own teaching on prayer implies that for some healing is "hard" and calls for sustained prayer, coupled with fasting. This was certainly the case with someone with whom my wife and I were having supper who complained of numbness in his legs, which rapidly became a paralysis that moved right up his body. By the time the ambulance came, he could only move his eyelids. A continuous 48-hour vigil of prayer and fasting by a number of people came to an end in the early hours of the third day with the sense that something had happened. It had. The man concerned had experienced a vision and got up out of his hospital bed. He was back home within three weeks. The rapidity of recovery was quite out of the ordinary for Guillaume Barre syndrome – and led to an invitation to speak to a group of medical staff.

Any discussion of the subtle dynamics involved in the Christian healing ministry must also include a reference not only to the activity of the Holy Spirit in general, but also to the specific ministry gifts. St Paul's tabulation of these gifts includes not only "gifts of healing", but others like the "word of wisdom" and the "word of knowledge" which fall into a more prophetic category, and may be of great assistance in the ministry of healing. Such gifts are keys of the Kingdom, unlocking people's hearts to the grace of God, revealing their innermost secrets so that they "fall down and say truly God is in your midst" – and are helped, and healed, and "saved". These gifts help the Church meet the individual not so much with "healing" as some impersonal activity, but with the Healer himself, Jesus, "by whose stripes we are healed". They are of great value in evangelism, and are available, within the providence of God, to any Christian, and not just focused on the clergy or the leaders of the Church. Of course they need monitoring just as much as they need fostering: but they are vital to a Church seeking to rediscover evangelism, and finding the place of healing, not only as a pastoral ministry, but as the evangelistic avenue the Lord intended it to be. It must at least mean that services of healing become more than occasions where a set formulary is used – but rather an opportunity for personal interchange in the Lord, the proclamation of his Gospel, the exercise of the Spirit's gifts, and the involvement of lay people. It must mean too the taking of opportunities beyond the confines of church buildings. Then, like Paul, we may be able to speak of an effective evangelism, of "fully proclaiming the Gospel of Christ".

Chapter Nine

IN SEASON
AND OUT OF SEASON?

The Archbishop of York

This book is predominantly, and rightly, concerned to bring home the point that evangelism lies at the heart of Christian commitment. That said, however, it is important to remember that the evangelistic command cannot always be obeyed, nor are circumstances always appropriate for explicit evangelistic witness. This chapter, therefore, is for the hesitant evangelist, who senses that evangelism is a necessity, yet shrinks from the image of directness and forcefulness usually conjured up by the word. I also have in mind the puzzled evangelist who wonders why the world finds it so hard to listen.

Liberation from an unwelcome image of evangelism came for me many years ago through reading Edmund Gosse's *Father and Son*. This is a classic study of what it was like to be brought up in a strongly evangelical household in the heyday of Victorian England. Gosse's father was a distinguished naturalist, the dominant figure in a small evangelistic sect, and author of the much-ridiculed theory that God created the world in six actual days complete with all the evidences of a lengthy past, later described as the theory that God put the fossils in the rocks to tempt geologists into unbelief.

I remember encountering the book at a time when, as a young evangelical undergraduate, I was myself aware of being under strong evangelistic pressures. I warmed to the young Edmund's gentle irony, and especially to the passage in which he spelt out his anxieties about his father's evangelistic expectations:

> He was accustomed to urge upon me the necessity of "speaking for Jesus in season and out of season", and he so worked upon my feelings that I would start forth like St Teresa, wild for the Moors and martyrdom. But any actual contact with persons marvellously cooled my zeal, and I should hardly ever have "spoken" at all if it had not been for that unfortunate phrase "out of season". It really seemed as if one must talk of nothing else, since if an occasion was not in season it was out of season; there was no alternative, no close time for souls.
>
> My father was very generous. He used to magnify any little effort that I made, with stammering tongue, to sanctify a visit; and people, I now see, were accustomed to give me a friendly lead in this direction, so that they might please him by reporting that I had "testified" in the Lord's service. The whole thing, however, was artificial, and was part of my father's restless inability to let well alone.

"Artificial" was the word which rang most bells with me. Edmund's experience chimed in exactly with the feeling of unreality at carefully contrived undergraduate coffee parties where the conversation was gradually worked round to spiritual matters and the opportunity to "testify". The imperative to evangelism seemed to cut across normal human relationships. As a committed evangelist one always seemed to be trying to sell something. It became an embarrassment, an imposition, an exercise in well-intentioned sleight of hand. And so, as for Edmund, the feelings of unease led to the gradual questioning of the value of such evangelistic zeal.

I start here because I am sure I am not alone in having suffered the embarrassment of artificiality. In fact I suspect that fears about being caught up in this kind of scenario are a major inhibiting factor when ordinary church people are urged to witness to their faith, to gossip about Jesus, or to tell the story of the Gospel. In most polite English circles religion is not a normal topic of conversation unless one is talking to clergy. To introduce it, therefore, out of context is to put up the barriers against effective communication; and to press its message home is to become typecast and to run the risk of ostracism.

Such social embarrassments, however, should be a trivial consideration in comparison with the danger of becoming false to the people whom one is trying to evangelize, false to oneself, and so false to the very thing one is trying to do. "Do you love us because you want to convert us, or do you want to convert us because you love us?" asked an Indian student. Burdensome evangelism lacks the essential qualities of love, respect and integrity, which alone can save it from becoming impertinent and intrusive. They are not qualities which can be generated by being told about the need to have them. The roots of honest evangelism lie much deeper than in the mere acknowledgement that the task has been laid upon us. Accepted grudgingly as an obligation it is bound to fail.

Falsity to oneself takes many forms. There are plenty of bad reasons for shrinking from explicit evangelism. Shame, cowardice, laziness, fears about one's own ignorance or the depth of one's own commitment, the desire for a quiet life, all contribute to religious hesitancy. The fear of hypocrisy gets nearer to the wariness about artificiality I am trying to describe. Nearer still is the widespread perception that in a matter so deep and personal as religious faith a certain reticence, a delicacy of touch, is needed if the essential thing itself is to be respected. The Oxford Movement made much of the notion of "reserve in communicating religious knowledge" as one of the implications of God's transcendence and holiness. Reticence has close connections with reverence. To blunder into religious discourse, therefore, out of a sense of obligation, may be to do violence to the heart of the message itself as well as to one's own sensitivities towards it.

Human nature being what it is, this more profound and genuine reason for being cautious may even be used as a cloak for the bad reasons, referrred to earlier, for chickening out from evangelism. But this is only a further illustration of the wide variety of ways of being false to oneself.

The late Bishop John Tinsley was fond of quoting Emily Dickinson's lines

> Tell all the truth but tell it slant –
> Success in Circuit lies
> Too bright for our infirm Delight
> The Truth's superb surprise
> As Lightning to the Children eased
> With explanation kind
> The Truth must dazzle gradually
> Or every man be blind . . .

"Tell it slant" was the message he reiterated again and again. Truth does not lie on the surface of things. It is not like a parcel which merely has to be delivered to the right address. Jesus did not wear his divinity on his sleeve, and much of his teaching was through parables open to many levels of interpretation. At the centre of Christian faith is the belief that truth was incarnate amid all the relativities and ambivalences of history, and therefore has to be perceived and received through signs, glimpses, personal discernment and involvement. It must "dazzle gradually", as Browning well knew when he wrote

Pure faith indeed – you know not what you ask!
Naked belief in God the Omnipotent
Omniscient, Omnipresent, sears too much
The sense of conscious creatures to be borne.
It were the seeing him no flesh shall dare.
Some think Creation's meant to show him forth:
I say, it's meant to hide him all it can . . .

To "tell it slant", as Jesus did, is not just a precept about the communication of the Gospel, but an indication of the content of the Gospel itself, a form of knowing in which our own creative engagement plays an essential role. In Tinsley's own words: "Christianity has constantly been threatened by moves to replace the personal, reticent, self-forgetting style of revelation by an assertive, overpowering, indisputable authoritarianism." If Tinsley was right, then the reticence of the hesitant evangelist may be saying more about the nature of the Gospel than a message designed to conscript its hearers into acceptance.

Herbert Kelly, the founder of SSM, could be accused by nobody of lacking evangelistic zeal. In his autobiographical fragments he mused, "Men ask, Why cannot we do again by Wesley's methods what Wesley did? – and others, Why can we not do again by Newman's methods what Newman did? I answer, Nothing is ever done again."

Kelly was not here writing just about methods. The precise circumstances of Wesley's and Newman's ministries are not repeatable, so obviously methods must change. He is making the more profound point, close to Tinsley's, that the precise contents of their preaching and teaching are not repeatable either, and this is not just because the contexts are different. In our encounter with God we do not travel the same road twice, because every encounter is a discovery. We may, indeed we must, tell "the old, old story", but there is an essential and continuing newness about the way the old story is conveyed and received. It is not a parcel delivered repeatedly at the door. It is "a well of water springing up unto eternal life", and it is in this sense that, in Kelly's phrase, "nothing is ever done again".

This is not, alas, the impression left by some forms of Christian proclamation. Robert Browning gently mocked the uncouth preacher in the little chapel where he had sheltered on a blustery Christmas Eve:

> After how many modes, this Christmas Eve
> Does the self-same weary thing take place?
> The same endeavour to make you believe,
> And with much the same effect, no more:
> Each method abundantly convincing,
> As I say, to those convinced before,
> But scarce to be swallowed without wincing
> By the not-as-yet convinced . . .

Yet for all its uncouthness and repetitiousness, he was able to come back to this dreadful sermon after his journey round the rest of the Christian world, to find in it the freshness of a new meeting with the One whom he no longer called Him, but Thee.

I have drawn on various literary sources to make the point that hesitant evangelists may have good reasons for their hesitancy. At its best it is a reluctance to intrude on what God must himself do if blind eyes are to be opened. It is a rejection of manipulation, of dishonesty in relationships. It rests on the conviction that in the encounter with God a new thing happens, and that it is to be approached in awe and humility. And so it values indirectness, the allowance of space for creative illumination. Roger Hooker's essay in chapter seven makes the same point when he writes about the encounter with other faiths. God surprises us. "It is always the Holy Spirit who converts, not the Church."

Nevertheless it is still possible to fool oneself about the reasons for one's reluctance. Karl Barth caricatured the Church as a snail "that carries its little house on its back and is so well off in it, that only now and then it sticks out its feelers, and then thinks that the 'claim of publicity' has been satisfied". Not an unfair description of many parishes. But we also need to remember that it was Jesus who likened the Kingdom of Heaven to treasure buried in a field, the implication being that there is no escape from the hard work of digging it up.

A theological undergirding for the approach suggested here was provided by Ian Ramsey's theory of divine disclosures. This never developed into the comprehensive philosophical work he was always promising himself he would write, and his ideas are now frequently ignored. Nevertheless his basic pattern of thinking remains profoundly true to experience, and the fact that his presentation of it always remained fragmentary is consistent with the nature of the pattern itself. We know God, he said, only by his own self-disclosure. He is not a mere item in some great philosophical system, nor is he a mere presence who might be noticed and described as one might notice and describe a mountain. Knowing God is more like the experience of seeing the point of something, or finding a new dimension of depth in some demand made on our lives.

Religious language, according to Ramsey, makes use of ordinary models and images, many of them drawn from our knowledge of good, wise and holy people, and "qualifies" them to the point at which the image breaks – or as Ramsey was never tired of saying "the penny drops", and a new dimension of reality is disclosed. This experience of disclosure entails both discernment and commitment.

To know God is to see in a new way, but it is also to act in a new way. In fact it is a knowledge which changes us.

As a comprehensive way of understanding the Christian faith this approach has its limitations. It belonged to a particular phase in Christian apologetics when the main philosophical attack was coming from those who asserted that religious language was meaningless. That phase has passed. The enduring value of Ramsey's thought, as I see it, lies in his description of what actually happens in the process of believing, and this is why it remains relevant to evangelism. It is notable that Ramsey was probably more respected by those with whom he worked in the fields of science and ethics than by professional philosophers and theologians. By drawing on secular experience, and the moral dilemmas of those in the forefront of change, and by showing how these too could become the basis for religious disclosure, he renewed the confidence of many that Christianity had something to say to their condition.

A sensitive and honest evangelist, twenty years after his death, can learn from his example. Sometimes we can talk best about God by not talking about him directly. The task may be to clear away misunderstandings; to show that there is space within our ordinary apprehensions of the world for unsuspected depths to be revealed; to dig down into moral issues in a way which exposes their roots in beliefs about the nature and meaning of ourselves and our world; and then to let the penny drop by itself.

I think it is fair to say that much of my own ministry has been of this kind. A bishop has endless opportunities to meet and to address large numbers of not particularly religious people who want somehow to be recognized and affirmed in what they are doing. Such occasions can be opportunities for a bland distribution of blessings. They can also provide scope for sympathetic entry into some fraction of the experience of the people involved, in a way which both illuminates it religiously and also provides some criteria for examining it critically. This reflection on other people's experience, coupled with the attempt to push the boat out a bit further into deeper waters, is as I see it precisely the kind of preliminary exploration of models and images which Ramsey saw as the setting for disclosure. It is a kind of evangelism which sticks very close to where people are, and points without shouting. It rarely produces dramatic results. But I believe it helps to keep open channels of communication in an age when the sense of God is increasingly in danger of being narrowed down to a small area of private consciousness.

I had a recent good example of its effectiveness in a conference set up to help geneticists, particularly those working at the frontiers of genetic manipulation in human patients, to think about the wider and deeper implications of their work. Two main religious themes emerged directly out of the scientific studies. One centred on the self-understanding of human beings and the extent to which knowledge of their genetic structure touches their essence as persons. The other raised large questions about how far the natural world is, or should be, manipulable, and where one draws the line between scientific creativity and arrogant self-assertiveness. Both questions are ultimately unanswerable, but asking them draws attention to the wider spiritual context in which practical medical decisions have to be made.

This may seem a fairly sophisticated example, but the same principles apply in much simpler and more homely contexts. Anyone who prepares a couple for marriage and tries to draw out some of the deeper implications of committing oneself to another person in love, is in fact using an everyday experience as a way into what he hopes will be a deeper disclosure. And this is evangelism. A neighbour who helps a friend to look more honestly at her own motives may be opening up a new and deeper dimension in that person's life. And this is evangelism too. A faithful churchgoer, who may be much too shy to speak openly about her faith, may unconsciously act for many people outside the Church as a symbol of reliability and integrity, even as a vicarious reminder of what they themselves might in their better moments wish to be. Such a person might never think of herself as having an evangelistic ministry. But she has.

There is a place and a role, therefore, for the hesitant evangelist, and the problems which bother such people may have something to say to those whose evangelistic style is more direct and explicit.

For instance, there are bothersome questions about motives. If the evangelistic task is not to be taken on merely as a burden or a command, and if there is a consciousness of the danger of imposing oneself on others in a way which smacks of falsity, why do it at all? The Jewish community survives quite happily without any hint of wanting to proselytize. Many Jews look somewhat wryly on their calling to be a chosen people, and see it as a responsibility to be shouldered rather than a privilege to be shared. They are content to think that God may have other plans for other people.

Christianity by contrast is inherently universalist. The underlying reasons have to do with the finality of God's action in Christ. If Christ really is, as Christians claim, God's final answer to the human predicament, then there is no human situation to which he is not relevant; the possibilities of divine disclosure lie everywhere. This claim to finality in turn depends on the experience of grace. If God has himself done all that is needed to draw human beings into relationship with himself, then his action must be complete and final, needing only our response for its effectiveness. This, as I understand it, is the deep structure of Christian thought which gives Christianity its universal vision, and undergirds the evangelistic imperative. Christ must be universally proclaimed because what God has done in Christ is of universal significance.

It makes sense, therefore, for Christians to believe that Christ can authentically be found in every human life, because by grace he is there before we ourselves have made any move towards him. Whether he can authentically be named in every human life is a different question altogether. The answer depends on the possibility of recognizing him and responding to him in a way which is true to experience, and in circumstances which may for personal or cultural reasons be inauspicious. Attitudes and experiences which Christians might claim as needing Christian interpretation, could in appropriate circumstances be spelt out in quite other terms, terms which are more authentic for those actually involved in them. The desire of the Christian evangelist to name Christ, therefore, has to be tempered by sensitivity towards people's own self-understanding.

Take a simple piece of charitable work in a local community, performed by people with no particular Christian allegiance. A Christian interpreter of this activity may well find in it clear evidence of the hand of Christ; for where love is, God is. He may long for those who unwittingly express what he sees as the love of God, to recognize it for what it is, and thus to enter into a fuller appreciation of the resources of love available. But what he must not do surely is, on the one hand to reject the work as not being "distinctively Christian", or on the other hand to try to appropriate it by putting a Christian label on it. The hesitant evangelist will welcome and affirm it, and seek to explore its deeper implications, hoping and praying that the penny will drop, but at the same time respecting the integrity of those for whom he prays.

Such an approach studiously avoids manipulation. Nevertheless, even the best-intentioned evangelism may find it hard not to contain a manipulative element. In its more subtle forms it can creep in through the feedback between faith and success.

Faith is more than a personal matter. Even the most individualistic faith depends to some extent on social supports. In general the stronger the surrounding ambience of faith, the easier it is to believe. This is not universally true, as we shall see later, but as in most other areas of life, religious success tends to feed on success. A full church attracts converts. An empty one discourages them. Public criticism or ridicule of the Christian faith intensifies the struggle of the individual believer. The many agonized letters I receive from correspondents when the Church has a bad press testify to the insecurity which rumours of failure provoke. By contrast "successful" evangelists sometimes exude an unnatural, and in the long run off-putting, air of confidence. Indeed the Church Growth movement is essentially a set of techniques for generating success, and commends itself by demonstrating statistically that they work. Success and new confidence and further success go hand in hand.

There may, in other words, be an unrecognized element of self-serving in some evangelistic efforts. To win converts can be an excellent way to strengthen one's own faith. At first this may simply be a by-product; then an aim; and finally a necessity. The reverse process can be observed in clergy who gradually lose confidence in themselves, and ultimately in God, as their congregations dwindle.

It is in this tricky area where affirmation by the faith of others becomes increasingly important that the dangers of manipulation are most apparent. It is here also, perhaps, that the sensitivities developed by the hesitant evangelist are most needed.

There is a more radical approach to the problems of success adopted by those for whom the equation "success feeds on success" only raises their hackles. What, they ask, has Christianity to do with success anyway? Certainly not with the success which can be measured by church attendance figures. It was Kierkegaard who posed the most radical question of all. "How is it possible to be a Christian in Christendom?" Isn't the Christian always the outsider, a sign of contradiction, part of the minority standing with God against the world? "Woe to you", said Jesus, "when all men speak well of you." In the unregenerate days of the Soviet Union there were many Christian believers who deliberately courted persecution, convinced that only a persecuted Christian could be authentic.

Evangelism is such circumstances is a call to stand out from the comfortable majority. The difficulty is that it thereby automatically sets limits on itself. To ignore the majority is to fail in Christian vision. To convert them would be to destroy the distinctiveness of the Christian minority's vocation. Maybe it is possible to envisage a kind of infinite regress with a small band of highly committed believers always separating themselves from mere followers. Indeed some Christian sects have behaved like this, the ill-fated Sandemanians for example, who required total agreement among their members, and in consequence fragmented themselves into oblivion. Their sad story reinforces the point that an evangelistic policy which sets up too formidable boundaries around the converted is likely to suffer fatal internal contradictions, as well as running the danger of ministering to a perverse kind of elitism.

This phenomenon was well known in the early Church. Kenneth Kirk in *The Vision of God* gives this description of some fourth- and fifth-century "athletes for Christ":

the younger Macarius maintained a record of one
hundred (prayers) a day for more than sixty years. Paul, a
hermit of the Sketic desert, improvised the first known
rosary by carrying with him three hundred pebbles, with
which to reckon the three hundred prayers which were
his daily toll; but lost heart when news reached him of a
neighbouring virgin who accomplished seven hundred a
day, in spite of fasting five days in the week.

These spiritual athletes were in their own peculiar way
courting success. No doubt they thanked God that they
were "not as other men". The consciousness that one is
special, and the issuing of a call to one's followers to be
special, can in fact minister just as much to self-serving
tendencies as the call to follow an easier path with the
crowd. Nor is this entirely irrelevant to the increasingly
popular distinction between "real Christians" and the rest,
useful though the distinction can sometimes be. The
difficulty about specialness is that there are too many
dangerous elements in our human nature onto which such
perceptions can latch, and there are too many tempting
appeals which can be made by subtly reinforcing human
pride, even pride in one's faithfulness.

The uncomfortable truth is that the question of motives
in evangelism remains full of pitfalls, whether the call is to
the many or to the few. The self-questioning and hesitant
evangelist may have an essential role to play in providing a
corrective.

A related question needs to be asked on the topic of
evangelistic certainty. It is a familiar piece of wisdom that if
one is trying to sell something one needs to know exactly
what it is, and why the customer needs precisely that and
not something else. Certainty is a prerequisite of salesman-
ship, and there are many voices which lambast the

Churches, and the Church of England in particular, for not having got our act together as salesmen, and for dissipating our energies in criticizing our own product.

Suppose, however, that one is not in the business of selling finished products, but of fashioning new lives, then the demand for certainty looks less convincing. Or to change the metaphor, are we tourists through life, visiting only well-known landmarks? Or are we explorers, setting off into the unknown? Whichever we are, some fairly reliable maps are obviously desirable. But our expectations about how far these may take us will be radically different.

At stake here is what we believe Christianity essentially to be. All evangelists would want to stress that at the heart of it there is a personal relationship with Christ. But some would want to express the character and meaning of this relationship in much more precisely defined terms than others. There are points on which perhaps all can agree. No matter how personal our relationship with Christ, it must be with the Christ revealed in Scripture, and not with the Christ of our imaginations. Nor can such a relationship be merely individual. Like it or not, the knowledge of Christ has to be mediated through the witness of the Church, and relationship with him inevitably entails relationship with other believers. Even the most adventurous explorer does not and cannot travel alone, or as if no one had set out on this quest before.

Nevertheless it is striking that when Jesus himself called disciples, it was done with almost everything left unsaid. "Follow me . . . preach the Kingdom." They left all and followed him, not knowing where they were going, with only the vaguest idea of what the Kingdom might be, and under an authority which was never defined – indeed the definition of authority was deliberately refused.

This call to adventure was not by itself enough to sustain

the life of a growing Church, and much of the rest of the New Testament can be read as an attempt to spell out its implications. But to allow it to be subsumed within a carefully articulated "plan of salvation" is to my mind to lose an openness and a freedom which are distinctive of Christian faith, and which have given it its distinctive power. A faith based on an open-ended personal relationship can transcend its own time and its own cultural setting to a degree which is impossible for a faith rooted in a set of ideas, or formulae, or rules.

Certainty, in other words, may be of different kinds. There can be the certainty of a well-worked-out system, with an answer to every question, or there can be the kind of confidence which grows within a relationship, and which is content to leave many questions unanswered. Hesitant evangelists, as I have tried to describe them, find themselves more at home with trust than with certainty.

Once again Ian Ramsey may be able to help us. In his book *On Being Sure in Religion* he drew a distinction between religious certainty and theological tentativeness, using F. D. Maurice's distrust of theological systems as his starting point. Theological tentativeness is not the same as vagueness, nor is it to undervalue the public doctrinal inheritance of Christianity as it has developed over the centuries. It is to recognize that this development always belongs within a context, and that as the context changes theologians constantly have more work to do in enlarging their understanding of that which lies at the centre of faith.

In the last chapter of the book Ramsey relates Maurice's thought to Newman's "Essay on the Development of Christian Doctrine", making the point that they were much closer than usually supposed. The chapter is entitled "Subscription to Articles", and represents Ramsey's first thoughts on the work he was later to do on revising the

Declaration of Assent. The present Declaration of Assent, in use since 1974, acknowledges precisely that relation of theology both to its past development and to its present context, which safeguards and encourages the adventurous character of Christian faith as I have tried to describe it. It is a faith "uniquely revealed . . . and set forth . . . which faith the Church is called upon to proclaim afresh in each generation". We affirm our "loyalty to this inheritance of faith as [our] inspiration and guidance under God in bringing the grace and truth of Christ to this generation . . ." There is a proper note of confidence in all this. But it is a confidence which has to explore and express its own meaning with a proper tentativeness. A Christian may say, "I know whom I have believed" and long to share that belief, while being hesitant to impose it just as it is on someone else.

The word "impose" gives the clue to what goes wrong when evangelistic enthusiasm over-reaches itself. St Teresa described how the enthusiasm generated by newly discovered spiritual reality could swamp those targeted by it:

> There is another temptation which is very common – namely to desire that everyone should be extremely spiritual when one is beginning to find what tranquillity, and what profit, spirituality brings. It is not wrong to desire this but it may not be right to try to bring it about unless we do so with such discretion and dissimulation that we give no impression of wanting to teach others.

The circumstances of which she writes belong to the sixteenth century, but the temptations remain the same. We can read her words as a warning, not against sharing faith and enthusiasm, but against heavy-handedness, against didacticism, against emotional manipulation, against the kind of artificiality described at the start of this chapter.

An invitation to hesitant evangelism, which knows when to speak and when to keep silent, may not seem the most inspiring way of ending a book whose main purpose is to recall the church to a deeper evangelistic commitment. Let me stress, therefore, that hesitance is not the same as half-heartedness. I have tried to show that it grows out of an awareness of the greatness of the task. In the end no claims to have the right techniques, or the right words in which to express our certainties or our enthusiasms, or the right answers to difficult questions, can compensate for insensitivity towards the mystery of God's grace.

Some words in a poem by Yeats seem apposite both for evangelists and for those who are evangelized. He has described how he would like to offer his companion a cloth to walk on made of the very heavens, and embroidered with the stars. But he is too poor. So instead he writes, "I have spread my dreams under your feet; tread softly because you tread on my dreams".